28 TH FEB. 1975

T0370105

RACER" Willie

Ride Free

A MEMOIR

Forefront
BOOKS

Published by Forefront Books.
Distributed by Simon & Schuster.

Library of Congress Control Number: 2023905257

Print ISBN: 978-1-63763-086-0
E-book ISBN: 978-1-63763-087-7

Creative Direction by Willie G. Davidson
Cover Design by Bruce Gore, Gore Studio, Inc.
Interior Design by Bill Kersey, KerseyGraphics

DEDICATION

*I dedicate this book to my beautiful wife, Nancy; and
our three children, Michael, Bill, and Karen; and to our
granddaughter, Cara. Thank you for supporting me through
both challenging and great times on this incredible journey.
Memories of our fun and adventures will last forever!*

———————

*This book is also dedicated to all
Harley-Davidson enthusiasts, dealers, and employees.
Thank you for your passion and commitment. The ride
has been truly amazing. To our future customers,
enjoy all of your adventures with our great brand.
Thank you!
Enjoy!*

CONTENTS

FOREWORD

I started my career as a motorcycle designer and clay modeler at Harley-Davidson in 1974. My boss then was Willie G. Davidson. Little did I know that this was to be the beginning of an adventure and journey that would endure over thirty years of design partnership, encompassing the lows and highs of America's greatest motorcycle company.

We both take great pride in the Motor Company's success story and the significance of our professional relationship for more than three decades. To put it simply, we are two guys who love all things Harley-Davidson—riding motorcycles and the process of designing them. I have always had the utmost respect for Willie G's sensitivity as a designer. His skills as a draftsman and sketch artist have provided him with the most important tools a designer can have. The natural capacities to communicate, create, and visualize conceptual ideas will forever be the keystone of effective, emotional design. This aptitude is made commercially powerful through his understanding of the Harley-Davidson brand and customers. To our riders he is an icon and was the creator of the signature style that constitutes "Harley-ness." As a fellow "brother of the wind," he gets it!

Willie G is less well known as an accomplished watercolor artist. This passion and hobby have served as a creative outlet and release, the need for which always seems present in the balancing of artistic individuals. I am honored to have several of his paintings in my home, given as gifts for my twenty-fifth and thirtieth anniversaries with the Motor Company. The foundation of these paintings is still the need and necessity to sketch—a designer's occupational hazard. Pen and paper in the hands of this man have affected design projects from furniture to street rods and all things custom culture in between.

The focus of this book, then, is a look into the life and mind of a prolific, creative industrial designer and fine artist. The stories of Harley-Davidson's challenges and triumphs are told through his eyes and experiences.

The sketches and doodles at the beginning of each chapter go beyond the musings of a design executive at a large corporation; they reveal an admiration and need for humor—something I have always valued in the fast-paced, straightlaced world of business. Many readers will understand the challenge of maintaining focus at marathon corporate meetings. Pencil, paper, and a creative mind can be a powerful prescription for mental release and reflection when needed most. Willie G is an advanced man of medicine in this regard. Potions include flames, skulls, Harley-Davidson Bar & Shield trademarks, bolts with nuts, wheels, flags, extended rake choppers, and the symbolic American eagle. The levity of these sketches enriched my life at work and beyond. Thanks, Willie G.

Contained in these pages is a behind-the-scenes look at the man responsible for elevating the visuals of the Harley-Davidson motorcycle to an art form. He is first and foremost a motorcyclist who was able to combine his vocation, avocation, and family into a single entity. He remains a creative force who, to this day, understands the value of design that stands the test of time.

— Louie Netz

CHAPTER 1

BIG DREAMS, HUMBLE BEGINNINGS

*I*was born with gasoline in my veins and a crayon in each hand. That's what I tell people. Motorcycling and art have been driving passions in my life. I'm not sure where the art part came from, but it's been there my whole life. The motorcycling part runs in the family: my grandfather was one of four founders of the Harley-Davidson Motor Company, and his son—my father—was president of the company from 1942 to 1973. So my work, leading the design of our beautiful motorcycles for half a century, is an unbroken thread leading back to the company's birth in the early 1900s. It's a powerful, important legacy; one that I'm proud to have helped carry into the twenty-first century.

This path I've followed started when my grandfather's brother Arthur and his friend Bill Harley decided they were going to motorize a bicycle. They were neighbors back in the 1890s. Close friends and avid bicyclists, both of them. They didn't set out to start a big company when they first motorized a bicycle in 1902. They certainly didn't dream that motorcycles bearing their names would become globally recognized symbols of American power and freedom. They were just young guys thinking, *We gotta go down the road on two wheels!* That was their frame of mind.

In the same way, back when I was a teenager, I never dreamed that someday hundreds of thousands of passionate Harley enthusiasts would look at me as the personification of this proud brand, the public face of an American icon. I didn't even plan to work for my father's company when I went off to college. I loved motorcycles, but I wanted to be an artist, maybe a designer. But that's getting ahead of the story—first I want to tell you about those pioneers who started all of this.

One thing to recognize is that they were young: Bill and Arthur were both twenty-two when they sold their first motorcycle. Kids went to work at a young age back then. Bill Harley started working at a local bicycle company when he was fifteen, and not long after that Arthur went to work at his grandparents' farm. They were both hard workers, and by 1902 Bill had a job as a draftsman at Barth Manufacturing, a Milwaukee company that made lift jacks and elevators. He suggested that Arthur come work there to learn pattern making. They shared a dream of motorizing a bicycle, making a self-powered two-wheeler that would speed up hills and power through mud. Luckily, they were in the right place at the right time to realize that vision.

The world was changing so fast back then, particularly in the areas of invention and technology. We tamed electricity and made it useful, just as we had done with steam. Then the gasoline engine came in, the radio, the telephone—dozens of new devices were invented in just a few decades. Milwaukee was keeping pace, changing just as quickly. Our city made its name from milling grain, tanning hides, meatpacking, and brewing beer. By 1900 the city had earned a new reputation for making iron and shaping it into machinery. Milwaukee had so many shops, mills, and foundries that it took the nickname "Machine Shop of the World." And being situated on Lake Michigan, we had big ships as well as the railroad to take all these products to market.

It was an inspiring time to be a young inventor with a mind to build a new type of vehicle, and Bill and Arthur were surrounded by everything they needed to make it happen—everything but money, which was in short supply. Arthur's older brothers Walter and William were working in the big railroad machine shops. Friends and colleagues worked in surrounding mills and factories. All over the country tinkerers and innovators were experimenting with gasoline engines, hoping to replace the horse and buggy with a self-powered vehicle. Henry Ford was about to launch his motor company in Detroit, the Wright Brothers were planning to take flight at Kitty Hawk, and back home in the Milwaukee area a number of enterprising locals already had a head start on Bill and Arthur. But those two young men were determined. They put their heads down and got to work, spending evenings and weekends toiling on their evolving designs.

Motorized vehicles had begun to appear on the roads of big cities early in the twentieth century, but they weren't something you'd see every day in Milwaukee. Rich folks in the big Eastern cities were riding in fancy electric cars. Regular folks took the electric streetcars, walked, or relied on the old dependable horse. Bill and Arthur took their particular inspiration from a show they attended one night in a local theater, a risqué performance featuring a shapely woman in tights who rode a nickel-plated bicycle powered by a small gas engine. That sight was enough to ignite their dreams of whizzing down the road without pedaling.

If they'd had more money, or been a little less enterprising, they might have sent away for a gas engine from one of the new companies selling kits for motorizing bicycles. But they were determined to invent their own. Once they started making progress, Arthur began telling his brother Walter about the project. He must have made it sound exciting because Walter came to visit hoping to ride their new motorbike and was disappointed to find that it only existed on Arthur's drawing board. Bill and Arthur enlisted his help, along with that of a neighbor who had a small machine shop, and before long they had a working prototype.

Soon Walter quit his job in Kansas City, where he'd been working as a machinist for the Missouri-Kansas-Texas Railroad. He then found a job in Milwaukee in the big yard of the Milwaukee Road where older brother William worked. That huge complex, where locomotives and train cars were built and maintained, was just three miles from the Davidson home, so both brothers were able to lend a hand improving on that first prototype.

The original foursome knew what they wanted: a motorcycle powerful enough to climb a steep hill without a pedal assist. That would require a bigger engine than the first one Bill Harley had designed in 1901. And they had to redo the frame, making it strong enough to carry that big power plant. We don't know exactly how they arrived at their solution; they weren't keeping notes or records, they were just trying to get that bike done. Unimaginable to them was that we would be wondering how they did it 120 years later.

Those first couple of years, working mostly in the Davidson basement, they made progress through resourcefulness and pure effort. Valuable evenings were spent working in the basement of a neighbor, Henry Melk, because he had a lathe. To make a go of it they needed a real workshop. As I understand the story, our great-grandmother got tired of those guys banging around and spilling oil in her house, so my great-grandfather built them a place to work in back of the family house. That ten-by-fifteen-foot wooden shed in the backyard was the birthplace of the Harley-Davidson Motor Company. That's where they built their first production motorcycle, the first one they sold, in 1903.

That first sale set things in motion, and the amazing thing to me is that they got that motorcycle so right. Those first Harley-Davidson cycles not only worked like a charm but they had a real beauty about them. The wheels, the tires, the forward angle, the beautiful curve of the front downtube, the way it follows the front wheel then wraps around the engine and swings up under the seat—it adds to the way the pieces fit together. To me as an artist, all those things just look *right*. A lot of devices back then *didn't* look right, but ours had nice proportions. Sculpturally, the simplicity of that first Harley is very handsome.

After that first success, the fledgling company sold several more motorcycles in 1904, and they gave themselves a little more room to work by building an addition onto the shed. They signed up a dealer in Chicago, C. H. Lang, who'd built a successful business manufacturing and selling piano-tuning tools. Lang was an important person in the early years of our business. With his help they sold eight motorcycles in 1905, and sales jumped to fifty in 1906. *Fifty* motorcycles out of that shed in the backyard!

Just think about whom they were selling to. Those early riders probably rode horseback prior to purchasing a motorcycle, and the switch had to be scary but exciting. Rather than saddle up their horse, they could just pedal this thing, get the motor running, and take off. It may seem odd to compare a motorcycle to a horse today, but that's where they were back then. They didn't have gas stations yet; you bought gas in canisters at the general store or maybe a fuel depot outside of town. But gas wasn't much harder to find than a bale of hay for your horse.

Another thing: it was accepted that anyone could ride a horse, at least outside the big cities, so it followed that anyone could ride a motorcycle. Men. Women. Young people. A motorcycle wasn't more intimidating than a horse once you got used to the idea of a gas-powered vehicle. You did have to go through a little bit of effort to get it running because the early ones didn't have a transmission, just a direct drive, with a leather belt to drive the rear wheel. You'd pedal it like a bicycle to get it going. Some would start on the rear stand—lift the rear wheel off the ground; pedal; pull the lever that tightens the belt, which in turn got the interior parts of the engine moving to start it running; then get off the bike; push it and lift the rear stand up; and off you go. It sounds like a chore today, but it wasn't any easier to start an automobile of that time: you had to hand-crank the engine, which took some real strength. Gas-powered auto sales didn't really take off until the electric start became available in the mid-1910s. Once that happened anyone could start a car; that made a big difference. However you traveled back then, unless you were in a train, you were out in the open. Whether on a motorcycle, in a car, on a horse, or in an early airplane—everything was open cockpit. You could get the whole family on your motorcycle with a sidecar, so it was as practical as an automobile. And lots more fun!

One significant challenge was to convince the prospective motorcycle buyer that these newfangled machines were as *dependable* as a horse, because in those early days all these vehicles were handmade, and even at best they sometimes had problems, whether mechanical, tires, or something else. So one of the things the founders did was to compete in endurance runs, which of course they did naturally because it was exciting and fun. But now they became focused on proving the reliability of a Harley-Davidson motorcycle. In an endurance run riders had to travel a set distance in a set amount of time; you'd score points for hitting checkpoints on time and lose points if you missed one because of some issue with your bike. Walter, in particular, had some great wins in those first years. Riding his motorcycle in what became known as reliability runs, he was proving to the world that the Harley-Davidson was durable even in its early state. That was really important. Thank God those guys were real enthusiasts because look at what they accomplished. They proved the motorcycle's durability, reliability, length of life—essentially how the thing worked. They were locked into that, they really were. The magic of our brand, the loyalty of our riders, all started with those four guys.

By 1906 the company had outgrown the shed and moved into a real purpose-built factory. It was a wooden, two-story building just a couple of blocks away, modest, but a real step up, and sales tripled that year to 150 motorcycles. In 1907, my grandfather William A. Davidson left his job at the Milwaukee Road to join his brothers full time as works manager, directing the manufacturing operation. He'd been the tool-room foreman in that big railroad shop, and his knowledge of machinery and manufacturing processes was critical as demand for our motorcycles increased. Just as important, he had the personality and temperament to get the most out of every employee; the company now had more than two dozen, as the workforce was growing along with the sales.

The founders took another big step in 1907: they incorporated, formed a board, and issued stock to board members and employees. Their little cottage industry was now a full-fledged operation, and sales tripled again in 1908 to 450 motorcycles. Keeping up that rapid growth, the factory expanded in 1909 into the first section of the brick factory that still stands today, and sales passed the one thousand mark. They were really on their way.

Also important from a legacy standpoint, that year Harley-Davidson made its first two-cylinder V-Twin, the ancestor of the Big Twins that played such a significant role in shaping our reputation. As it turned out, that first one wasn't quite ready for public use; they had to pull it back and make some changes to the design. They got it right a little more than a year later, and it helped move them down the path to incredible growth through the next decade.

The four founders had talent, and so did the people they brought in as the company grew. They were machinists, mechanics, designers; few of them had any formal training, but they built a nucleus of people who were able to turn the company into a powerhouse. The founders took formal titles, but it was always an equal partnership, everybody chipping in and doing whatever it took to move the business forward. Walter became president; he was a tireless leader, carried himself well, and handled the finances. Bill Harley was chief engineer, and with the technology evolving so quickly in that period, he did an amazing job keeping Harley-Davidson at the forefront of innovation. My grandfather

William A. was a constant presence in the factory, keeping everyone working at full capacity and everything running smoothly as the factory and workforce grew ... and just kept growing.

Arthur Davidson was our sales manager, and he was a forward-thinking type of guy. To sell a product like ours, you have to relate to your customers. He started publications—*The Harley-Davidson Dealer* and *The Harley-Davidson Enthusiast*—and various bulletins, getting the word out and keeping in contact with our loyal riders and dedicated dealers. Arthur rode our trusty motorcycles around the country recruiting dealers, growing that all-important network, and then developing programs to teach new dealers sales techniques, advertising, marketing—everything they needed to know to run a good, honest business. They were doing many of the things back then that we're still doing. In today's world we use different words, but the ideas are the same: customers first; do it with good dealers and good service; train 'em, teach 'em how to ride, and stick with 'em after they buy the bike. That's the essence of the business.

There wasn't a blueprint for what those guys were doing, but they somehow made the right decisions. Sales kept doubling and tripling, and they kept building and bringing on more people to meet the growing demand. By 1913, ten years after they sold that first bike, sales approached 13,000. They had nearly 1,300 employees and the factory had expanded to almost 300,000 square feet, with addition after addition, and constant construction even as sales were skyrocketing. From that ten-by-fifteen-foot shed—150 square feet—to 300,000 square feet of factory floor in ten years! And they weren't done; they kept on building right through the decade.

Building and maintaining the dealer network was a major driver of growth in those first decades, but the founders got creative in other ways to maintain the momentum. The focus at first was on building bikes for personal transportation, then they began expanding into other areas, adding different dimensions. They made their first sale to a police department in 1908, and police sales have been a part of our company strategy ever since. PDs figured out that motorcycles were great for traffic control and chasing speeders, and seeing all those mounted officers riding Harley-Davidsons was good for the company's image. Our motorcycles were used by fire departments, too, but big fire trucks eventually took over that work.

Another thing they did in this time frame was adapt vehicles for commercial use, particularly delivery, everything from the US Mail to dry cleaning. They made a delivery vehicle called a Forecar in 1913, with a big forward box between two wheels up front. Then they took the sidecar chassis and modified it for all sorts of delivery uses; that became particularly successful once the Postal Service started using them. This was the nonsporting side of the company; they were trying all types of things to keep selling more motorcycles and get more people in the saddle.

We sold our first motorcycles to the military in 1916, and Harley-Davidson motorcycles played a role during World War I. Once the United States entered that war and our bikes started going into combat overseas, we developed a program to teach soldiers to service military motorcycles. We started that here in Milwaukee, then expanded to some of the major military bases. When the war finally ended, the company kept it going, shifting the focus to teaching mechanics and technicians from our dealerships. The founders knew they had to take care of the customer, give them confidence, so you've got to have service at the top and trained mechanics who can take care of whatever problems might come up.

The guy who ran the Service Department and the Service School was Joe Ryan. When it comes to service and dedication, Joe was a pillar in the company's history. He ran service from 1919 all the way into the 1960s. Over the years Harley-Davidson developed a reputation for employees sticking around for long careers. The company is . . . a love affair. Yes, it's a job, but there's also an emotional enjoyment in being involved with our products and people and riders. Joe was there through all those years, making sure service was well taken care of. He had to keep them running!

Joe was a character; everybody knew him and liked him. When I was growing up and my dad was president, he would bring me to the factory on weekends. He would have something to do in his office and would allow me to walk around, within reason. I knew where Joe's desk was, so I'd walk down to say hello, knowing he practically lived at the factory. Sometimes I'd find him sound asleep at his desk. But you could count on him being there. What a guy.

By the end of that decade—the 1910s—Harley-Davidson was the largest motorcycle company in the world. We'd added another hundred thousand square feet of factory, had over 1,800 employees, and sold nearly 27,000 motorcycles. And we were already a global company. Arthur had set up our first export branch in London in 1914; by 1920 we had dealers in sixty-seven countries. It's hard to picture what it took to ship motorcycles around the world at that time. The bikes were built in Milwaukee, packed into crates, and carted right onto the train—that big new factory on Juneau Avenue backed right up to the train tracks. Or they were loaded onto horse-drawn wagons, taken down to the port on Lake Michigan, and placed on steamers bound for ports all over the world.

It must have felt like Harley-Davidson was on top of the world. But the world was changing. Our sales dipped from that peak year in 1920 and dropped off through the decade. It was getting easier to get around, and people had lots more options. Automobiles were becoming more and more popular and cheaper. The government was building a nationwide highway system. Gas stations were going up along the new roads as well as hotels and restaurants. Airplanes were flying longer distances. The motorcycle industry struggled to keep up.

The founders kept innovating, introducing new models—bigger, faster, better looking. But the market was tough, and people's tastes were changing. It was in that time frame, the 1920s, that we started to see a relationship between design and popularity, that what these things *look* like could be a significant sales tool. It wasn't enough to be practical and reliable; consumers wanted style, something that looked striking and grabbed attention.

A motorcycle has a natural mechanical beauty. Harley's engineering people realized that. They just had to find new ways to enhance it. We didn't have an industrial design department back then; it was done by engineers. But they were people who could relate to these beautiful forms, and when they decided to completely redesign our flagship JD model for 1925, they came up with a design that fit with the times.

The earlier bikes had a lot of rectangular and square shapes. The 1925 JD introduced new streamlined shapes, and our marketing talked about that, comparing it to an airplane. The centerpiece was our first teardrop fuel tank. That was a big step forward. Ask Harley enthusiasts to name an iconic piece, something that says Harley-Davidson to them, and that teardrop-shaped tank is what a lot of them will say. Through all these years we've maintained the teardrop. We've massaged it a bit, but that streamlined form became a trademark of our visuals.

The new design accentuated the way the tank framed the engine. It changed the profile: how the engine, the battery, the whole lower end fills that frame between the front downtube and the forward section of the rear fender. Looking at the side view of that motorcycle, all those key components fill that negative space in a very handsome way. Form follows function, and the 1925 streamline model shows that very well.

As good as that bike was, it faced serious headwinds: Ford had kept building Model Ts, making them a little cheaper every year. About the time that bike hit the market, the cost of our motorcycle and the cost of a Model T became comparable. That caused a shift in the market, because now you could buy a four-wheel vehicle that was fully enclosed for the same money as our top-of-the-line motorcycle. Those cars weren't open-cockpit anymore: you had a full body with doors and windows that kept you out of the rain, so maybe a motorcycle was no longer the most practical way to tote your family around. That's when the leaders of the company realized that motorcycling was becoming a sport-hyphen-hobby.

Being enthusiastic riders and competitors, the founders discovered that motorcycling was actually *more* than transportation, and that's been true all these years. That's why we're still successful, because we're riders and we know the sport. We follow and support the sport, whether it's racing or road-riding or other competitive events. It started then, with the four founders. Those guys were not just engineers and business executives; they were serious sport-rider enthusiasts. That was so important, and it helped them see a different kind of future for our industry.

CHAPTER 2

THE WRECKING CREW

*G*oing down the street on two wheels—there's nothing like it. It's exhilarating; you know that, even if you've only experienced it on a bicycle. You lean to turn, you're in the wind, you're one-on-one with nature. And when you put a motor on a bicycle, you extend that fun level. You add that power to those two wheels and you just soar. You want more.

I've always felt that if there were only two motorcycles on the face of the earth, at some point they would race each other. Competition seems to be in our DNA. As far back as you can go in history, people were racing one another—on foot, on horses, on whatever they used to get around. Bicycle racing was growing in popularity when Bill Harley and Arthur Davidson were boys, and it had evolved into a huge sport by the time they built their first motor. Once people started racing motorcycles, those crowds just got bigger and bigger. Motorcyclists racing on tracks built for bicycle races could achieve speeds bicyclists only dreamed of.

Small companies building motorcycles were sprouting up all over the country in the early twentieth century. There were already two companies in Milwaukee by the time our founders sold their first motorcycle. Those early manufacturers quickly realized that winning a big race delivered natural publicity—usually followed by sales—and they started sponsoring racers and race teams.

There were all sorts of competitive events. Climbing a hill was a natural way to prove the superiority of a motorized vehicle, and both automobile and motorcycle companies organized hillclimbs to show off their products. The two would often compete, and the motorcycles would usually win. Once promoters started building big racetracks, a day at the races often featured both automobile and motorcycle races, but cars and bikes rarely raced each other on the tracks.

Bill Harley and the Davidson brothers competed in hillclimbs as well as endurance runs, but they stayed off the racetracks. The speeds that motorcycles could reach on a bicycle track or horse track were dangerous, and the founders were focused on proving that motorcycles were *not* dangerous. They were pushing the motorcycle as family transportation, and for their little company to grow they had to convince all those people going to town in a horse and buggy to consider trading up to a motorcycle. News stories in local papers told of horses being spooked by automobiles' loud exhaust noises and people having to jump out of the way of a speeding car, unaccustomed to things going that fast on their little dirt roads. Watching a pack of loud racers try to hang on through a tight turn wasn't going to help mom decide to trade in the horse.

The founders' strategy for getting everyday people to accept motorcycles involved telling their customers to be good neighbors and courteous riders; to play their part in helping win people over to the new way of getting around. Go out and have fun but find the right place to do it. Motorcycles were quickly developing a reputation for being loud, so they started calling their motorcycle "The Silent Gray Fellow." *Gray* because that was the color they switched to after the first few years of painting them black. *Silent* because they were engineered to be quiet, with good mufflers to dampen the sound of the engine.

But like most gas-powered vehicles of the time, they had something called an exhaust cutout. The muffler cuts the noise, but it puts pressure on the engine that reduces the horsepower a little bit, so there's a lever you can pull that opens the exhaust up before it gets to the muffler. That adds some power back in, but it's loud. The idea is that when you're out on some road in the middle of nowhere, you can open it up. But in town you keep it closed.

The last thing the founders wanted was for potential customers to find motorcycles annoying. Hence, The Silent Gray Fellow. They also wanted to assure people that motorcycles were safe. It can look scary to see somebody go by fast on two wheels, but there's a magic to the physics of the motorcycle—it wants to stay upright. Once you get going those wheels are like gyroscopes; they want to keep you up. You get a person on a motorcycle, and they can feel that. Look at early Harley-Davidson advertising and you'll see well-dressed people enjoying civilized pleasures, engaging in outdoor pursuits, taking mom and the kids for a spin in the sidecar. There was a clear message: motorcycles are both fun and reliable: good, economical family transportation. Try one out and you'll see!

During that same period, beginning in 1909 or 1910, promoters started building racing-board tracks. They called them motordromes: banked circular or oval tracks made of two-by-fours laid end to end. They took the bicycle velodrome idea and adapted it for high-speed racing, running both automobiles and motorcycles on the tracks. The upper portions of the track were banked anywhere from twenty to forty-five degrees, making it possible to maintain a high rate of speed lap after lap.

The speed and intensity of the competition drew big crowds. The promise of "thrills and spills" was a reliable draw, and board track racing provided plenty of both. It was the spills that kept Harley-Davidson's founders from embracing track racing in the first years of the sport; their singular focus on convincing the general public that motorcycles were good family transportation led them to disapprove of a sport in which even the spectators might be exposed to potentially lethal crashes. The racers accepted, even embraced the danger; danger made for exciting viewing but was more likely to evoke fear in a potential customer, and fear isn't an emotion likely to sell someone on a motorcycle.

As the popularity of board track racing exploded, tracks were built in major cities around the country. There was a big one in Chicago, and one built in Milwaukee operated for a few years. The oval speedways had grandstands along long straightaways like a modern racetrack, but in those days there were also lots of short, steeply banked circular tracks modeled on bicycle velodromes. Viewing stands in those circular tracks sat just above the track, with only a railing separating spectators from the speeding racers. Many early circular tracks were relatively short, a quarter or a third of a mile, and they were referred to as "saucer tracks" because the upper portion of the track was so steeply banked, like the side of a saucer or a cereal bowl. Racing around those steep saucer tracks was like riding on a wall, with racers carried high up the side, pinned to the track by the centrifugal force created at their incredible speeds. Thrill-seeking spectators ringed the track railing, looking down as the tight pack of racers sped by just a few feet below their perch.

Motorcycle technology improved rapidly as board track racing grew in popularity, which led to ever-greater speeds on those wooden tracks. When everything went well, spectators were treated to a fantastic show. If something went wrong, things could go bad very quickly. Blow a tire or have some catastrophic engine problem on one of those bowl tracks and you drop right off that wall while your speeding competitors try to avoid crashing into you, triggering a horrible pileup. Or even worse, one of the racers trying to avoid you flips up into the rail, sending spectators flying.

The spectacle of those speeding motorcycles and the potential for dangerous mishaps kept drawing larger and larger crowds, so more cities built tracks to get in on the action. Though racing along wooden tracks was inherently risky, the larger, more gently banked speedways regularly hosted races without incident. As the rapidly evolving motorcycles got faster and faster, the smaller saucer tracks posed increasing danger for both riders and spectators.

In 1912 a particularly deadly crash at a saucer track in New Jersey generated sensational front-page headlines in major newspapers around the country. Arthur Davidson's fear that track racing would lead to bad press that could undermine broader acceptance of motorcycles was confirmed. What's more, Arthur personally knew Eddie Hasha, the racer who crashed that day; they had worked together in Eddie's home state of Texas to set up a Harley dealership in Dallas. Arthur responded with a heartfelt editorial in *The Harley-Davidson Dealer* emphasizing Harley's focus on selling motorcycles exclusively for pleasure and business and reaffirming the company's opposition to the reckless sport of board track racing. In the national uproar that followed the horrible event at that New Jersey track, racing on shorter bowl tracks was banned, and a series of safety measures was instituted to guard against the reoccurrence of such tragedies at larger board tracks. The crowds returned to the tracks, and though tragic accidents could not be completely avoided, track racing became safer, particularly for the paying customers.

While the board tracks generated the most media attention, the same racing teams and riders regularly competed in road races, following long courses laid out along country roads in places such as Dodge City, Kansas, and Savannah, Georgia. Those races also drew crowds of racing fans, with spectators scattered along the course and seated in temporary grandstands. Racers traveling the country might race on the boards one weekend and on country roads the next. Though Harley-Davidson had no factory-sponsored team, privateers riding our stock motorcycles regularly placed high in the standings in road races. Recognizing the importance of publicity, we often promoted those victories while noting that the factory didn't officially sponsor any racers.

With new safety regulations in place, board track construction accelerated. Huge oval tracks as much as two miles long that could host major automobile races as well as motorcycles were built in a dozen big cities. The grandstands at those tracks held more fans than the big baseball stadiums of the day, demonstrating the popularity of the speed contests. By 1915, when a number of those new tracks opened, there was a new competitor on the boards: a Harley-Davidson factory team.

Just a year after Arthur's emotional editorial in *The Harley-Davidson Dealer*, the tide had turned. Harley-Davidson's sales had been growing rapidly and the company was adding manufacturing capacity, but the founders became increasingly concerned as they watched the factory-sponsored racing efforts of their competitors capture headlines week after week. All that free advertising translated to sales: "Win on Sunday, sell on Monday" was a common saying among vehicle manufacturers of the time. Realizing they needed to jump into the competitive ring, the company hired a racing engineer, Bill Ottoway, to design limited-production racing machines. The program was kept quiet, so the motor-cycling world was shocked when a group of riders showed up with the new Harley race bikes to compete in the big Dodge City 300-mile race on July 4, 1914. Those first Harley racers were competitive, but it took a few months to work out the kinks and assemble the right group of riders. Later that year, the Harley factory team took third place at the Savannah 300, and they started winning races in 1915. That summer of 1915, the Harley team returned to Dodge City for the 300 and won big, just missing sweeping the field when one competitor slipped into third place. That was the real beginning of what came to be known as The Harley-Davidson Wrecking Crew.

That great group of racers regularly won big races, both on road courses and on the boards. In 1916 the factory team cleaned up at one major competition after another. Then, in 1917, the US entered World War I and racing was suspended. Otto Walker, one of our star racers, joined the military and served in Europe. He returned with a captured German aviator's helmet, and when racing started up again in 1919 he wore that helmet whenever he raced. It had a distinctive look— you could always recognize Otto Walker. And he was usually out front, setting the pace, breaking records. It was really in those postwar years that the team earned the name The Wrecking Crew. They'd come in first and second, first-second-third, and sometimes sweep the top four or five places. We had competition from Indian and Excelsior, but that Harley team was really something.

And the bikes! Those early racers were special: very limited production, meticulously engineered. The first ones they called "stripped stock" because many of the stock components—the oil tank, the transmission, the brakes—were stripped from the bike, along with things such as lighting and license plates. They had a minimal rear fender and no front fender—modifications designed to save weight. The frame was a little shorter because you had no transmission. All of it combined to make those bikes lighter, faster, and visually beautiful. They were exciting to watch in action but just as beautiful to look at.

Stripped down to the basics, a motorcycle is an engine and two wheels. With a racing motorcycle, that's really what it is: the most basic statement of a motorcycle, and I think the prettiest. They aren't encumbered with the practical necessities of road riding, so those big-diameter wheels become a major statement, and the frame is dropped in between the wheels with the V of the engine filling the frame. It's just a beautiful proportion, and then the tank kind of finishes it off.

But they were a trick to ride. First of all, with no transmission, the racers needed a push to get going. At the start of the race they'd often be pulled by another motorcycle, then everyone would do a lap or two to get up to speed before they'd wave the flag to begin the race. With just one gear, they'd be geared specifically for the type of race, with different size gas tanks for different lengths. And they had no brakes, which of course reduced weight, but really that was for safety, so a rider couldn't suddenly slow way down in front of another when riding so close together.

If you look at pictures of racers at the end of a race, looking exhausted but triumphant, you'll notice that their faces are covered with dirt and oil except for the area around their eyes that was protected by their goggles. Like other motorcycles of the time, those race bikes had what we call a total-loss oil system: the oil runs through the engine, then out through a crankcase vent, onto the motorcycle chain, with some spraying up on the rider and the rest onto the track. That oil would become embedded in the wood track, which made it even more dangerous. And you'll see a little pump on the side of the fuel tank; the rider could feel when that engine was starting to get tight, and he'd give it a pump that would feed oil to the motor. So he's flying down this oily, splintery board track at a hundred miles an hour, riding in a tight pack on a motorcycle with no brakes, one hand on the handlebars and one pumping a little oil into the engine. Like the X-Games today, that was the extreme sports of the early 1920s. They were real daredevils but also highly skilled.

We had some stars on that Wrecking Crew: Ray Weishaar, "Red" Parkhurst, "Shrimp" Burns, Otto Walker. Household names, at least among race fans. Otto was the first motorcycle racer to average a 100-mile-per-hour lap time. That means he was hitting 120, 130 on the straightaway of one of those big ovals. Just try to imagine that. After the war he would race a motorcycle known fondly as an "eight-valve," which was four valves per cylinder pushing big volumes of fuel and air into the cylinders. That technology is common in today's automobiles, but I'm talking the 1910s. That monster of an engine was the culmination of all the experimentation and development those racing engineers did.

Those Harley-Davidson eight-valve racers were *very* successful; they easily topped 100 miles per hour. We kept making them into the late 1920s, but just one at a time. We don't know for sure how many were made, but it was a small number. They sold for what was at that time a very high price because they were made for race people, not the public. It's one of my favorite vintage bikes, and I was lucky enough to find one years ago.

I'm passionate about all this history, and when our Harley-Davidson Museum was in the planning stages, I made it a priority to acquire examples of those early racers for display. The company has a fantastic collection of motorcycles; they started saving them right off the production line almost from the beginning. It's an amazing collection, truly unique, but they didn't save racers until we got into my era with the company. They saved standard production motorcycles but never put a single racer into the collection in those early decades. So I went on a personal quest to find and acquire some of those great race bikes for the company collection and my personal display. They're such an important part of our history.

As unique as those board track days were in our history, they didn't last long. If you subtract the racing shutdown during World War I, it was really not much more than a decade. Those huge wooden tracks were extremely difficult to maintain and expensive to repair, and by the mid-1920s things were starting to fall apart. Literally fall apart—with broken boards and holes in the tracks, making racing on them even more dangerous. I'm lucky enough to have met one of the original heroes of the board track era, Jim Davis. He was an amazing guy, a really nice man. He told me of one time when he crashed, he went sliding down the boards, and when he came back into the sideline area he had huge splinters in his arm, up through his flesh. The pain must have been horrendous. Just imagine coming into a curve and seeing a broken board, a hole in the track! By a certain point the promoters didn't want to keep investing the money to rebuild the tracks. That wood was not forgiving, especially in the colder northern states, and I think that the economics killed the board tracks as much as anything. But that era was really fantastic.

Harley's founders made the decision to disband the great Wrecking Crew in 1923 as the board tracks were beginning to close. The company continued to sponsor individual riders—Jim Davis among them—but no longer maintained a full racing team. A new Harley-Davidson hero emerged in the second half of the 1920s, and he was our one-man race team through the Great Depression: Joe Petrali.

Joe was just an amazing rider. He won in hillclimbs, he won dirt track, he won board track, he won everything! In the early '30s he was unbeatable—he won national championships year after year. He's the only rider to win the national championship in both hillclimb and dirt track in the same year.

Hillclimbing had been popular for a while by the time Joe hit that steep slope, but it became even more high profile as the board track era ended. It was exciting to watch, different from track racing—it's just one guy at a time, man and machine against the steep hill. They would strip the bikes and put chains on the rear wheel to power up the hill, the rider up off the seat, leaning over the front wheel to try to keep that powerful bike from wheelie-ing and flipping over. And they did flip over at times, roaring and somersaulting and sliding back down the hill. The big hillclimbs drew huge crowds, just like the board tracks. For one thing, there weren't as many forms of entertainment at the time: commercial radio and movies were just beginning; TV didn't exist. For a quarter you could take the family to the hillclimb and get a whole afternoon of exciting entertainment.

And the thing with Joe was, he did it all: he designed and built the bikes, he raced them, he maintained them. In the middle of the Depression when we came out with our great new engine, the Knucklehead, Joe helped design a streamlined Knucklehead-powered speed bike. Then he took that thing down to Daytona Beach and set a new speed record: 136 miles per hour on the packed sand. Smokin' Joe, they called him; he was an amazing man. When he retired from racing he went to work for Howard Hughes, and he was riding on the Spruce Goose the one time they flew that monstrous plane. In retirement Joe stayed involved in racing, leading the officials at the Bonneville Salt Flats verifying speed records, doing anything that involved speed. Long after his passing in 1973, he remains a real legend.

We've got a great example of a DAH hillclimb bike in our museum, the model that Joe Petrali rode to a national championship. Those bikes are really special, like the board trackers—engineered and hand-built for one purpose. The factory built only a couple dozen of those DAH hillclimbers; they're really rare. I should mention that the founders started using letter designations for motorcycle models such as DAH, and those model codes have continued today. Many of the letters in those codes have a meaning. The letter designations were a means to track the model's creation through the product development process. You'll see them in addition to model names referenced throughout the book.

All those early forms of competition played a significant role in motorcycling history, aside from all the records and championships: they brought people together. Riders would gather to ride in groups to the races and the hillclimbs. They'd form clubs to sponsor local hillclimbs, endurance runs, organize races at public courses, or just in a field some-where. There'd be a post-race party, a cookout, an overnight, and pretty soon you'd have a rally, with fun events that everyone could participate in. Clubs started organizing daylong events they called "gypsy tours," combining an organized group ride with picnics and motorcycle games. In the 1920s the motorcycle manufacturers got together and organized an annual national gypsy tour, inspiring people all over the country to put miles on their motorcycles on the same day.

When you combine those fun events with some great riding country, such as up in Laconia, New Hampshire, or out in Sturgis, South Dakota, you've got a recipe for something big. No one would have predicted *how* big it could get. Now, every year, you get hundreds of thousands of motorcyclists spending a week riding and partying in Sturgis, in Laconia, and down in Daytona. All of those rallies started the same way: someone sponsored a race, it became an annual event, groups of motorcyclists started getting together to ride out and watch the race, and everyone shared some great riding along the way. The daylong event becomes a weekend, then a long weekend, then a full week. Now they're gigantic events, but they started with some sort of competition, a race—and any excuse to get out and ride.

CHAPTER 3

WM. H.

That first Harley-Davidson Wrecking Crew had an incredible record of success. Much of the credit must go to the skilled, seemingly fearless riders on the team, but the racing engineers had a lot to do with it. They were constantly reengineering, innovating, refining, and wringing more and more power out of those V-Twin engines. In 1928 the company gave the riding public a taste of what that felt like, introducing a new model powered by a two-cam engine that incorporated the mechanical innovations developed for our racing engines. There were two models of the 1928 Two-Cam Twin, and the bigger one—called the JDH—was the fastest street motorcycle of its time. Harley-Davidson expected great things from that bike, and it delivered.

Nineteen twenty-eight was an exciting year in my family's household for another reason: my father, William H. Davidson, joined the company. My grandfather must have expected great things from his son, too, but his introduction to the motorcycling world didn't receive as much fanfare: he started out working on the shop floor. Harley-Davidson was the industry leader, a big company, and you might have expected that the son of one of the company founders would start in management. But not my father—he was following in his dad's footsteps.

The 1928 JDH would go on to become a highly collectible legend. My dad would be president of our company for three decades, but the timing, from a business point of view, wasn't great. The 1920s were hard on the American motorcycle industry. Small motorcycle companies had started up all over the country in the first two decades of the twentieth century—at least a hundred in total, likely closer to a hundred and fifty. A few dozen of them grew to be quite successful. Then the 1920s started with a recession, and as the economy recovered American life started changing so fast it must have made people dizzy.

Our factory was electrified in the 1910s, but electricity didn't begin to make it into people's homes until the 1920s. What an incredible change that must have been! Things such as refrigerators and washing machines changed people's lives. A nationwide highway system was being built, with gas stations and hotels and roadside cafés springing up. You could ride all over the country on a motorcycle, but more and more buyers were turning to inexpensive Model Ts or more stylish Chevys and Buicks. One by one most of those early motorcycle companies were forced to close up shop. Our sales had taken a dive during that 1920–21 recession, but they'd begun to pick up by the time my father joined the company. Then disaster struck: in the fall of 1929 the stock market crashed and the bottom fell out of the economy.

The stock market crash was a catastrophe that caught everyone by surprise, but the economic forecasters of the time predicted the hard times would not last more than a couple of years. All our company could do was keep going, innovating, doing everything they could to build up the business. We'd debuted another new engine just a year before the crash, the 45-cubic-inch Model D flathead, beginning the switch to the reliable side-valve flathead engines that would help carry the business for decades. The situation was grim at the beginning of the 1930s, but there were rays of hope for the future.

My father, William H., was working his way up to shop foreman, beginning his rise through the company ranks. He was a great rider and rode his motorcycle to work just about every day; he did that for decades until he was in his seventies. He had learned to ride on a unique bike we introduced just after World War I, the Sport Twin, which was a lighter-weight bike with a different type of engine. Where our standard twin has two cylinders oriented in a 45-degree V, the cylinders of the Sport Twin were horizontally opposed, working in a straight line, parallel to the road, one moving back and forth toward the front wheel, the other toward the rear. That was an unusual design for us, cleverly engineered to be smooth, powerful, and trouble-free. Company-sponsored riders set a number of important long-distance records on that little Sport Twin, and it got lots of headlines. Harley-Davidson believed that bike could attract more women riders to the sport and that it would do particularly well for our export market, but sales tapered off as the 1920 recession set in. After only a few years of production, that reliable Sport Twin was discontinued; 1923 was its last year. It was a signal that the transportation world was changing.

By the time the stock market crashed six years later, there weren't many American motorcycle companies still in business. Very few were able to adapt to the changing business environment. Thankfully, Harley-Davidson's founders had done a great job establishing our business, and they tended it well through the difficult times.

In 1930, as everyone was still trying to understand what had happened with the economy and what it would mean, my father took one of our new flatheads to Lansing, Michigan, and competed in the Jack Pine enduro. The next generation picked right up with what their fathers had started, working hard to prove the value and reliability of the Harley-Davidson motorcycle—taking matters into their own hands.

The Jack Pine is rough; it's a good place to prove the toughness and reliability of your motorcycle. It's a two-day race against the clock over challenging terrain with a lot of river crossings. (They still hold it every year.) You start out with a thousand points, and as in other endurance runs, you lose points if you're late for a checkpoint or if you get lost. That might not sound so difficult, but it is. You have to follow arrows marked on trees to stay on the route, so you need to be very observant and find those arrows while trying to maintain a certain speed. If you get hung up, say, at a river crossing, you have to ride wide-open to get your speed back to the right average. The checkpoints can be anywhere, and you have to appear at all of them. You stop your bike, sign in, and they check your time. If your time is off, you lose points. My dad lost three points in two days of riding. His final point total was 997; to lose only three points over that whole two-day course was really amazing. Riding his brand-new flathead to victory in Michigan, my dad had to feel good and have some real optimism for the new bikes his company was developing. Maybe it's a good thing he didn't know how bad the economy was going to get over the next few years.

Having experienced that moment of triumph in 1920 when Harley-Davidson was acknowledged to be the largest motorcycle company in the world, it had to be painful for the founders to read the monthly reports as sales dropped those first years of the Great Depression. After declining more than 50 percent from that 1920 peak, sales had built back up to almost 24,000 motorcycles in 1929, the year of the crash. By 1933 we were at rock bottom, down to 3,700 motorcycles that year. Hopefully my birth, on June 20, 1933, provided a bright spot in those dark times for my father, William H., and my mother, Ruth Godfrey Davidson.

My mother's family owned a wholesale grocery business. Her grandfather, who started the company, was a major figure in our area, running a big operation with an eight-story headquarters on Commission Row in Milwaukee. Among other things, E. R. Godfrey & Sons was said to have been the first to ship bananas to Milwaukee! I imagine the company also struggled during those times, but it survived the Depression and eventually went into the supermarket business.

It took ingenuity and dedication to survive those times, and in 1933 Harley-Davidson made a big move to try to stimulate sales: after three decades of offering little or no choice when it came to color, customers could select from a menu of standard colors and beautiful graphic options when they ordered a new Harley. All of the new graphics accentuated the beautiful side profile of the streamlined tank, and pinstriping followed the form of all the sheet metal, all done by hand. It was our first attempt at major visuals, and I loved that bird design on the tank, that eagle head graphic on the VLD. I'd call it the earliest customization. There's a symbolism there regarding freedom of flight, relating it to the freedom of the road, to being in the wind. And the eagle is America's symbol, so there's a real relevance to the freedom of flight that is intrinsic in our motorcycles.

One significance of those designs is that the founders realized they could use styling to give their existing models a boost, exciting our customers with new paint colors at a time when money to develop new motorcycles was scarce. Over the years we turned motorcycle paint and graphics into an art form, particularly with our tank identity. And 1933 was when it started.

The new approach worked: sales started going up, and they tripled the next year. That was very important because behind the scenes Bill Harley and the engineering department were working on an exciting new project: an overhead-valve engine. They designed and were testing single cylinder and V-Twin versions of this new project, but it was a big change in design, highly innovative, and they were burning through money trying to work out the kinks. That took a lot of courage and confidence, to develop a whole new motorcycle from scratch right in the middle of a worldwide economic depression. Working into 1934, they had to abandon the single and focus their investment on the twin, keeping the whole project secret. Among other innovations, this new engine would have recirculating oil, with the oil moving through the engine, into an oil tank, and back into the engine rather than just dripping out onto the chain and from there onto the road. Cleaner and more economical, this was going to be a revolutionary, modern-looking motorcycle, but as the months went by the engineers dealt with problem after problem; solve one and another popped up.

Sales dipped again after that big upswing in 1934, and the founders were economizing wherever they could, keeping the factory running and trying to avoid laying off workers. A decision was made that the new motorcycle would be announced in the fall of 1935, as part of the 1936 model line. The engineers were still struggling to solve oil-circulation problems with the new engine, among other minor issues, but the company needed something new and exciting to generate enthusiasm in both dealers and riders.

In March 1935 my family had a different reason to celebrate: my younger brother, John, was born. My father was one of the second generation of Harleys and Davidsons at the company. His younger brother, Allan, Walter's sons Gordon and Walter Jr., and Bill Harley's son Bill had all been with the company a few years. Arthur's son, Arthur H., was back East at Dartmouth, soon to return to Milwaukee expecting to join the company and work in international sales. Young Arthur's father told him there were plenty of Davidsons working at the company, and he should strike out on his own, start his own business. Which he did, becoming quite successful—the company he cofounded in 1941 is still in business. John and I would eventually take our place among the third generation at the Motor Company, but we'd both take some major detours before finding our way to leadership positions at Harley-Davidson.

The EL "Knucklehead" received its official launch at the annual dealer sales conference in November 1935, but though it was announced and shown to the dealers, it wasn't quite ready for public release. Engineering was still struggling with the new lubrication system, and there was growing concern that the new bike was too radical of a step for the times. Once the company finally started shipping them, they instructed dealers to avoid placing them in display windows; the suggestion was to put the radical new model on the showroom floor and see how customers reacted to it. This seems unbelievable today: during those turbulent times the company had put so much effort and money into this bike that would play a major role in helping us survive the Depression and become a true classic, an icon among twentieth-century motorcycles. Then they instructed dealers to soft-pedal its introduction, worried at the last minute that maybe it was too much of a departure from tradition.

Not surprisingly, customers loved it. The Knucklehead was both a technological marvel for the time and a beautiful, stylish ride. Harley-Davidson had been focusing more on style since introducing the streamline twin in 1925; all the colors and graphics starting in 1933 were part of that effort. It all came together beautifully in that first Knucklehead.

If you look at the history of industrial design, it doesn't go all the way back to the industrial revolution. A lot of early transportation design, things such as locomotives from the steam era and the first cars, were designed by engineers/inventors who were most interested in moving you from one place to another. It wasn't until the era of streamlining that real industrial design became a common practice. It was engineers who designed our early motorcycles, but they had an artistic sensibility even though they weren't trained specifically as industrial designers. God bless those people, because they understood the intricate mechanical necessities of a vehicle yet were able to put proportions together that worked very effectively. Our proportions: the wheels to the frame, the frame to the engine, the engine to the tank—how it sits, how it feels, how it sounds. That's what makes this brand important from a product standpoint, I believe. The mechanical beauty of our products is something we have to maintain forever, and it started way back with our first bike. The engineers who designed the Knucklehead just took it to another level.

That first Knucklehead is really the granddaddy of all our Big Twin motorcycles. That was a bike that influenced so many things. It had numerous design cues that we held on to and adapted over the years. The teardrop gas tank on the Knuckle was broader and more muscular than our original teardrop, and that's a shape that's endured—a timeless classic. That beautiful engine with the emphasis on the rockers started our tradition of getting engine nicknames from the street. The name *Knucklehead* did not come from the company; it came from the riders. And the same is true for the Panhead and Shovelhead, which came later. Those names all originated from the street, and we just embraced them. If you look at the rocker cover on that Knucklehead, you'll see two large fasteners, and if you look at the knuckle on your hand, the bones that protrude, they resemble the hex nuts in the top cover. Hence, Knucklehead.

The wraparound oil tank on that EL also became a kind of trademark for us—it just beautifully fills that space. If you see it from above, under the seat, it has a half-round shape with the battery hidden inside, which led riders to call it the "horseshoe" oil tank. And of course, when the Knucklehead hit, it had the speedo that's referred to as a "Cat's-eye" console: the switch, the oil and generator lights, the way they're put together—it kind of looks like a cat's eye. That console has carried all the way through to today. Processes change but those iconic shapes remain. The consoles today have taken on all kinds of different cast shapes, where the early ones were stamped metal, chromed, or painted.

All those elements came together in the Knucklehead in a way that emphasized the inherent beauty in mechanical design. That's so important in a Harley-Davidson. We've always had beautifully exposed engines, then we surround those engines with parts that frame the engine: the V-Twin is very nicely framed by the motorcycle frame and the tank hugs the engine; the air cleaner is circular on some models, on others it's kind of a trumpet shape, but none of it is ever meant to be covered, and that's unique. A lot of motorcycles today hide the engine and all the mechanical necessities. On a Harley-Davidson we emphasize the beautiful cam covers and intakes, the pushrods, the valve covers. It's all a carefully designed combination of chrome and aluminum, exhaust systems, transmission, oil tank. All of it fills the space directly under the rider in a way that is just *right*. A lot of newer motorcycles today don't have this kind of form-follows-function beauty about them. We've tried to stay true to that over all these years, to expose that mechanical beauty. Rolling sculpture—I think that's intrinsic in our brand. And so much of that goes right back to that 1936 Knucklehead.

Without the sales and promotional push you'd expect for a major model introduction, the Knucklehead became a word-of-mouth success, and all of those new styling cues made their way across the model line: the 1936 EL Knucklehead had a unique look, with all the other Harley-Davidson models carrying over the established styling of past years, but for 1937 the whole model line was revamped to follow the EL's lead. The motorcycling world was won over, and the Knucklehead was a star.

My grandfather passed away in the spring of 1937. He was the oldest of the original four founders, and the first to pass. I'm often asked if I remember much about him, but I was only four when he died so my memories of him are sparse and not concrete. It had to be difficult for my father, but there could be no question that William A. Davidson was proud of what he and his brothers, along with Bill Harley, had accomplished in building this great company.

Harley-Davidson sales were up and down in the mid-1930s as the Depression eased a bit. The success of the Knucklehead helped, but the economy soured again in 1937, and '38 and '39 were pretty rough.

Fortunately, our company leadership had been working on other angles to shore up sales. Having sold their first motorcycles for police use when the company was only five years old and introduced successful commercial delivery vehicles before it was ten, the company leveraged those parts of the business to help us through the Great Depression. The police still needed to patrol the roads, and though lots of businesses went bust, the ones that didn't still needed to deliver their goods.

Our police business had built steadily though the 1910s and '20s. As motorized transportation became common, our company worked closely with police departments to design vehicles that met the unique requirements of patrolling the roads. During the '20s, as paved roads became more common, Harley-Davidson police motorcycles were a familiar presence both in the cities and on the nation's new highways. People genuinely liked seeing the motorcycle officers, and they got used to them leading parades and things such as presidential processions. By the time of the economic crash there were more than two thousand police and sheriff departments in the US using our bikes. Lots of them needed to upgrade their fleets during the decade-plus of the Depression, and that helped keep our factories moving.

On the commercial side, the company managed to launch an important new vehicle in 1932—the Servi-Car—even while focusing on the design and testing of the EL Knucklehead. The Servi-Car was a utility vehicle, a trike with a big cargo box between the two rear wheels. The first marketing push for it was to automobile dealerships: we built a device for the front of the Servi-Car that converted it into a trailer, so a mechanic could ride it to your house to pick up your car for service, attach the Servi-Car to your car's rear bumper, and drive your car back to the dealership towing the Servi-Car. In those times, when your car needed work you'd call the dealership and they'd come pick it up, do the work, then deliver it back to your home. That was *real* service, different from today. Each trip took two people since you'd need one to drive the customer's car and one to return the dealership vehicle. The Servi-Car cut that in half—pickup and delivery could be done by one person. With sales of "pleasure" motorcycles dropping off, the company banked on businesses being willing to invest in a vehicle that could help them make (or save) money.

The Servi-Car didn't light up sales the way the Knucklehead would, but it helped bridge the worst years until we got that game-changing EL in dealerships. The auto dealership idea for the Servi-Car worked well, and various businesses used them for delivery, but the biggest customer turned out to be police forces. They found they could put that trike to good use in a variety of situations. The Servi-Car made up something like 5 percent of our sales during the worst years of the Depression, which helped keep workers in our factory. But police forces loved that vehicle, and we kept making them until 1973. The last decade or so of production they were mostly used for parking enforcement: chalking tires and writing tickets.

After the surge in sales with all those Knucklehead-inspired designs in 1937, that lull in 1938 and '39 must have made it seem like the Depression would never end. Harley-Davidson was lucky to have inspired leaders, dedicated workers, and resourceful dealers to carry them through those difficult years. Sales started to pick up a little in 1940, and then something happened in 1941 that changed the course of history: the United States entered the war that had been raging around the world for the past two years. World War II came home to American citizens with the bombing of Pearl Harbor. As the industrial might of America rallied to the war effort, military production pulled the US out of its economic doldrums and lifted Harley-Davidson along with it. We were awarded the contract to build motorcycles for the military, and our factories were quickly converted to focus on wartime production. Before long that big factory was operating at full capacity again.

CHAPTER 4

WORLD WAR II: CHALLENGE AND OPPORTUNITY

A s a youngster, if I was a good boy, my dad would bring me down to the factory. I was always excited to go—there was so much happening there. It's hard to imagine today, but just about everything it took to mass-produce motorcycles was contained within that big factory: casting metal, cutting and shaping parts, welding frames, plating and painting. We were a major motorcycle manufacturer, but physically it wasn't that big of a company; manufacturing, assembly, and shipping all happened in one place. The bikes were built up piece by piece as they moved from floor to floor of the factory, ending with testing on the ground floor. Then they'd be crated, carted out to the loading dock, and shipped all over the world.

All the other business functions were housed in the factory as well: administration, publicity, sales, and service. There was even a big photo studio up on the roof. My dad would let me wander around within set limits—I had to stay away from the heavy operations and make sure I didn't get in anybody's way. But I found it fascinating to watch those beautiful motorcycles come together.

Even at the age of eight or nine I would have been aware that we were in the war, but I was more focused on all the activity because the factory was really humming. Our production had finally risen above ten thousand in 1940 as the economy slowly recovered. That probably felt significant, but the next year our focus shifted to meeting the new military contracts and things really shifted into high gear. In 1942, the year I turned nine, we built twenty-five thousand bikes for the military. I wouldn't have been aware of the changes in the economy or the intricacies of the business, not at my age, but I could sure see the changes at the factory. Despite the overwhelming concern for the war raging around the world, there must have been some sense of relief that the big military contract was putting everyone back to work.

All around the country companies were adapting their operations to support the war effort. One big Milwaukee-area manufacturer, A. O. Smith, shifted from building automobile frames and water heaters to making bomb casings and aircraft propellors. Harley-Davidson could have ended up retooling to make generators or something, but we were asked to make motorcycles for the military, thus rebuilding our primary business.

With so many men going off to war, more women took jobs in our factory, operating drill presses and lathes, inspecting and packaging spare parts. That was one big change. And the bikes coming off the assembly line looked different. All those beautiful colors and designs were replaced by military olive drab, and the shiny chrome by black paint. With nearly our entire production being devoted to the military, style was no longer an issue; it was about durability, simplicity, and function. Bikes were still being built, crated, and sent around the world as before, but our focus had changed. We were totally committed to supporting the war effort.

As military production hit full speed in 1942, the primary respon-sibility for managing this new challenge shifted to my father's shoulders. Walter Davidson, who had served as president since Harley-Davidson first incorporated in 1907, died in the winter of 1942. Walter had guided Harley-Davidson from those backyard beginnings through incredible growth to its status as industry leader. With his death leadership passed to the second generation: my father, William H. Davidson, was named president of the company, and Walter's eldest son, Gordon, became vice president.

The war brought challenge and hardship along with opportunity. In addition to navigating the labor shortage resulting from so many working-age men entering the military, wartime production demands across various industries brought rationing of key materials. While Harley-Davidson worked to optimize production, executives and engi-neers had to wade through layers of specifications and repeated testing while developing components to meet requirements for wartime use in harsh environments.

Our primary military motorcycle, the WLA, was adapted from the civilian WL flathead model. It wasn't a high-tech speedster like the Knucklehead; it was a rugged workhorse, and for the military we beefed it up and outfitted it with an array of special-purpose components. The WLA had a heavier frame and thicker handlebars than the WL, and the fenders were flat so mud couldn't build up under them in rugged terrain. The whole bike was military green, with a big white star on the tank and a gun scabbard attached to the front forks. It had blackout lights to camouflage the bikes after dark and make them less visible from the air, along with other heavy-duty components such as a special oil-bath air cleaner to protect the engine from dust in those long convoys.

The gun scabbard on the front made it look like a combat vehicle, but the WLA was primarily used for carrying information, delivering orders and messages. Those motorcycles were great for moving people;

they could get through a lot of areas quicker than a four-wheeler. The motorcycle messengers were called dispatch riders. WLAs were also used for reconnaissance and patrolling. Whatever the task, the machine gun was strictly for protection—anything could happen riding through combat areas. But those motorcycles played an important role in the war effort.

The bikes were shipped with plenty of spare parts to support battlefield maintenance, and every bike carried a repair kit with various parts. Military mechanics were trained at service schools on bases and back in Milwaukee, and there were coordinated rider-training programs as part of basic training for the motorcycle corps. We made tens of thousands of those bikes, with a significant number going to the Allied military—Canada, France, China, Australia; even the Russian army used a lot of WLAs. More than one hundred thousand soldiers were trained to ride and maintain our motor-cycles. After the war a lot of the bikes were left wherever they were when the fighting ended, put to use where they ended up, modified and adapted over the years. The parts too. There were so many spare parts, all packaged to be watertight for wartime shipment—so tight that you can unwrap them today and they're like new. Enthusiasts still use those parts to build and rebuild bikes from that era.

In 1943 Harley-Davidson was awarded a US Army-Navy "E Award" for excellence in military production. There was a big ceremony with a stage set up in front of the factory and military brass in attendance. I always remember a picture of my dad onstage holding up that E Award flag. He was *very* proud of that. We won two more of those awards during the war, which was a real honor. Of the thousands upon thou-sands of manufacturers making war products, not many were honored in that way. My father did an unbelievable job of guiding the company through those years. The company leadership supported the war effort 100 percent, so we basically stopped making consumer motorcycles; the entire company was focused on doing our part to help win the war.

While the factory was working overtime building and shipping WLAs, our engineering department was challenged to quickly develop new vehicles for special purposes. The first order came right at the beginning of US involvement in the war: the military needed a motorcycle that could function in desert conditions. Our military had joined the Allied forces in North Africa, where the Germans were using BMW flat-twins. The horizontally opposed cylinders on those BMWs stuck out to either side and caught the wind so they could cool better in the desert heat. They also had a shaft-drive rather than a chain that could get clogged with desert sand. The US Army asked us to build a thousand motorcycles with those features and deliver them in just over a year. It was a completely different motorcycle from anything we'd made before, but we got it done, delivered on schedule.

While we were building those unique bikes—XA was the model designation—the army ordered a version with a sidecar with a driven wheel for extra traction. Two-wheel drive. We made three prototypes for testing (one of those is in our museum). That one was referred to as an XS. At the time, you had to design vehicles to meet government specs, then take them to an army testing ground where they were put through a battery of tests under government supervision. And there was often competition—another manufacturer would build a competing version for the same purpose. At the end of testing they would approve the contract, or tell you to make changes in the design, or just cancel the whole contract—give it up or go with another vehicle.

They tested a variety of prototypes for those rugged battlefield conditions. Another one we made was called a TA. That was a three-wheeler—shaft-driven, Knucklehead-powered—an unusual bike, like a bigger, more powerful Servi-Car trike with a shaft drive. It was kind of like a cargo/personnel carrier; it had a big, padded box on the back and could fit five people, three sitting on the box and one on the back behind the rider. I've got one in my personal collection. I'd seen pictures of that trike, and I finally found one a number of years ago. After all the testing with those three-wheelers we lost the competition to the four-wheel-drive Jeep. The military canceled the TA contract with us and ordered Jeeps for desert warfare instead.

When the military canceled those experimental contracts, they informed us that they had decided the WLA satisfied all their motorcycle requirements. We were committed to supporting the war effort in whatever capacity was most helpful, so we focused on building as many WLAs as we could and shipping them wherever they were needed. Harley-Davidson, being a proud US of A company, worked hard to give them whatever kind of vehicle they thought they could use.

By the time World War II ended in 1945, Harley-Davidson had built over eighty thousand military vehicles and shipped parts for tens of thousands more. Complete WLAs and tons of parts were scattered all over the world, and over one hundred thousand soldiers had been trained to ride and repair motorcycles. This had a big impact in the period after the war because the young riders who came home after that horrible conflict had really enjoyed riding during their service years. Other soldiers had watched dispatch riders and wished they could be doing that rather than be hunkered down in some miserable trench. So they came home and bought a surplus WLA or maybe a new Knucklehead, and they hit the road. And those WLAs that were kept in use in countries where the war was fought? They just translated to more global riders in the Harley-Davidson family over time.

Without question, our wartime involvement boosted interest in the company all over the world. The role our motorcycles played in helping win that long war reflected well on us. People remembered that. And all the work that was done in our factory to increase production during the war left us in a good position to fulfill the demand for new motorcycles that came with the improving economy and heightened interest in motorcycling.

All those returning servicemen buying motorcycles helped our dealers recover from their wartime struggles, which had been significant: the Depression had been so hard on them, and then with our factory's focus on military production we hadn't been able to provide dealers with new motorcycles to sell during the war. The dealers had to get by on providing service and selling off existing stock and used bikes. When the economy picked up after the war, motorcycle sales rose with it.

Something I don't think anyone saw coming was how motorcycling culture would change after the war. It started with those returning GIs buying surplus WLAs. The first thing they would do is strip off the military equipment. When riders customized their bikes before the war, it usually involved adding accessories: decorative trim, chrome, fancy seats, bags. Lots of riders stuck with that after the war, but for a lot of the new riders coming back from the war, buying those surplus bikes, it became more about removing parts that didn't seem crucial or look right.

The first to go were all the special parts we'd added for the military: the windshield, blackout lights, gun scabbard, toolbox, and that big flat front fender. The rear fender had a hinged rear section; you had to flip it up to remove the rear wheel. A lot of them just took that hinged portion off—bobbed the fender. That's where the nickname "bobbers" comes from. Of course, they'd give the bike a fancy new paint job to get rid of that military green. They took those bikes back to basic wheels and an engine, which made them perform better because they were lighter in weight.

With this new breed of riders, a new type of motorcycle club emerged: many of the ex-soldiers not only rejected prewar ideas about how their bike should look; they also rejected established ideas about motorcycling and motorcycle clubs. The typical club before the war was well organized, got together to sponsor races and rallies, played field games, and competed to be the best dressed. Some of the returning GIs, coming back from the excitement and horror of combat, weren't looking to go back to the farm or to small-town life. They got together to ride and party, looking for thrills and acting tough, maybe bothering the local chamber of commerce a little bit.

The traditional clubs were sanctioned by the American Motorcyclist Association. You joined the AMA when you started riding, joined a sanctioned club, and could participate in sanctioned rallies and competitions. These new clubs were more loosely organized. The returning vets weren't interested in joining the AMA, so the motorcycling establishment called them "outlaw" clubs.

The tension between the establishment and the rebels first hit the headlines in 1947 when *LIFE* magazine ran a story about a commotion at an AMA rally and race in Hollister, California. A few of these "outlaw" clubs showed up, and when they weren't permitted to participate in the sanctioned activities, they spent the weekend riding and partying and getting under the skin of the locals and the AMA clubs. *LIFE* ran a posed picture that made the whole thing seem a lot worse than it really was, and it became a national scandal, sparking a whole raft of sensationalized stories. All of a sudden people were afraid of these "outlaw" motorcycle "gangs."

A fictionalized version of the events in Hollister was made into the movie *The Wild One*, and suddenly Marlon Brando in his black leather jacket became the new image of the motorcyclist. Those clubs that invaded Hollister were mostly ex-military guys, but the stories told about their actions were wildly exaggerated. As time went on, some outlaw clubs really did engage in criminal activities. Lots of them, however, were more like The Booze Fighters, one of those Hollister clubs that now has chapters all over the world; they describe themselves as "a drinking club with a riding problem." That new image of the "rebel biker" was one of the stranger things to emerge from our wartime experience, but it endured, and the changing ideas about motorcycle customization brought on the chopper movement of the 1960s.

CHAPTER 5

MANY POSSIBLE FUTURES

I was only twelve years old when World War II ended, but I was already dreaming of owning a motorcycle. I had plenty of inspiration—motorcycles were everywhere when I was growing up, and my ears perked up every time I heard one go through our neighborhood. I saw new bikes being built on those visits to the factory with my dad and was eager to check out all the workers' bikes in that old garage. My father rode to work every day, often coming home with some new bike or prototype. He rode all year round, adding a sidecar for stability when it started snowing, taking John and me for rides. I examined every new bike my dad brought home in detail, waiting for the day when I could get one of my own.

With the long war finally over, returning servicemen went back to work. America had come out on top, and people were buying goods again after a decade of the the Depression and years of war rationing. The Harley-Davidson factory was operating at peak efficiency thanks to those military contracts, and the company was ready to take advantage of opportunities that developed with the booming postwar economy. For four years our dealers had been starved of inventory due to our wartime commitments. Now they had military surplus vehicles in their showrooms along with shiny new models to sell to riders who'd been pining for a new motorcycle.

As president of the company, my father led the way in mapping out an expansion plan to steer the company through this new era. The first part of the plan was unveiled in November 1947 at the big Harley-Davidson Dealer Convention in Milwaukee. The Department of Defense had built a huge factory west of the city for A. O. Smith to use for military production, fabricating bomb and torpedo casings and propellers for fighter planes. The plant was mothballed when the war ended, and Harley-Davidson was able to purchase it to expand our manufacturing footprint. Our new Capitol Drive factory was right on the train line, and like our Milwaukee plant on Juneau Avenue it had a big railroad siding for shipping. As a special event for the dealers, our marketing people announced an evening "Mystery Ride"—they put all our dealers on a train and took them out to that big new factory. Nobody knew what the destination was, and when they pulled that train up alongside the new plant, they invited everybody in and announced, "This huge factory now belongs to Harley-Davidson, and [it] will allow us to expand to meet future demands." We obtained quite a bit of land along with the factory, which we used when we built our Product Development Center in the 1990s.

As part of the event at the "mystery" location they showed dealers our newest model, the 125cc "S" lightweight. Harley-Davidson built its reputation with big, powerful bikes, but we had also made smaller bikes since the 1920s, recognizing their value for attracting new riders and just getting around town. The S was smaller than anything we'd made to that point; it was actually adapted from a German design made available to us by the US government. The same plans were given to the British and Russians as part of war reparations—distributing German technology to help rebuild Allied industry.

That little S model would play a big role in getting young people like me on their first motorcycle, but it wasn't the bike I was dreaming of owning. I loved the big, customized Harleys I'd see guys riding in our neighborhood. We lived in Wauwatosa, a suburb of Milwaukee that was between the original Harley factory and the new plant in Butler, a few miles farther west. I was fascinated by the Knuckleheads I'd see around town, with the custom seats and bags, unique wheel inserts, horns, all sorts of unique parts and accessories. Each rider added his own interpretation with different paint and add-ons. In my dreams I wanted one of those beautiful bikes, but I couldn't have one at that time. I've still got a drawing of a motorcycle like that, done when I was fourteen. I tried to capture every detail of a custom Knucklehead; I even put my initials on the saddlebags in the add-on letters the way riders would do it at the time.

I was always drawing motorcycles; that's been the story of my life. When other kids were playing baseball, I wanted to be sketching. Don't get me wrong—I enjoyed outdoor activities as much as other kids. For weeks each summer my brother, John, and I went to Red Arrow Camp on Trout Lake, up in northern Wisconsin. We hiked and swam, did woodworking and crafts. Other times our parents would take us to our grandfather's cabin on Pine Lake. I loved the outdoors, but I always found time to draw.

We were especially excited to go to local races and hillclimbs. Those events really fired my dreams of riding. Around that time Harley-Davidson introduced a new stripped-stock racing model, the WR—a sort of racer cousin to the military WLA. One of our Wisconsin dealers, Ray Tursky, was an accomplished racer, and he got one of the first WRs from the factory. We have that bike in the museum collection and it's got a great history. Ray was great to watch, a local legend. My dad would take me to visit the racing department at the factory, and that was exciting because Harley-Davidson was winning a lot of big national races with the WR.

In 1948 I finally got my first bike—a black 125cc S model. I was only fifteen, but with my dad watching over me I learned to ride it on the back streets in our neighborhood, and before long I felt in complete control. I got a black leather motorcycle jacket for Christmas and was a full-fledged rider. I rode that bike everywhere. That was the beginning of my riding days, creating fun memories that are still vivid in my mind. A unique part of that S model was the peanut fuel tank, whose shape was later used on our race bikes and became an instant hit on our late 1950s Sportsters. Versions of that tank were a common sight on chopper-style motorcycles in the 1960s and 1970s; it became an influential classic, but it showed up first on that little 125.

I loved my 125 S and was so excited as a young man to have it to ride, but it stayed stock for only about a week—right away I started customizing it. It took on various shapes of fenders and paint, or no fenders and new trim. I guess I knew from that day on where I was going. I moved up to a 165 within a couple of years and lost track of that 125 S, but many years later my family found a really nice one at a swap meet and surprised me with it for Christmas, so I've got that in my collection and it brings back fond memories.

The new lightweight and the new factory were big news in 1948, but they were just part of the story. With that second factory gradually coming online, the main Juneau Avenue factory was working overtime as we had our biggest production year ever—close to thirty thousand motorcycles—and a new heavyweight engine to replace the Knucklehead. The new engine was given a nickname by our customers—the Panhead—because the engine top end resembled an upside-down pan. That nickname came a little later; back when it was introduced customers called it the "OHV," referring to its overhead valves. The new engine was lighter than the Knucklehead, with aluminum heads that ran cooler than the older cast steel heads. There were a number of other important technological improvements—it was quite a feat of engineering for the time. We made ten thousand of those little light-weights, which was pretty amazing, but we made fifteen thousand Panheads—that was still the meat and potatoes of our business.

The big change for 1949 was both technological and cosmetic: we replaced our springer front suspension with new hydraulic front forks. The first Harley-Davidson motorcycles had no mechanical suspension; it was a hard ride like a basic bicycle. After just a few years we added spring suspension to smooth out the ride, with the springs concealed in the front fork tubes. As the bikes got bigger and heavier, we needed bigger springs, so by the 1920s we added big springs above the fender on the front end. As that front end evolved, it became a great example of functional design: everything in the suspension was exposed; there was no attempt to disguise or beautify it. It had its own practical beauty, particularly the redesigned version used on the Knuckleheads. That springer was a classic—we actually brought it back in the 1980s, and the springer front end has remained a favorite of customizers. But the technology was advancing in the postwar period, and our engineers knew that hydraulic shocks would give a smoother ride.

For the new hydraulic front end we needed a new design, and for the first time in our company's history, we looked beyond our engineering department and brought in an outside designer. And not just any outside designer, but one of the acknowledged pioneers of industrial design: Brooks Stevens, who had his offices right in Milwaukee. Brooks Stevens was one of the first-generation pioneers of industrial design, a founder of the Industrial Designers Society of America. That movement had begun to take hold in the 1920s and 1930s, driven by the idea that products should do more than just work; they should also be beautiful, with a form that expresses their function and makes you want them in your home or office. Stevens had designed everything from furniture to clothes dryers to passenger trains, and Harley brought him on board to help style key parts of the Hydra-Glide, our new flagship model with hydraulic front suspension.

The design that resulted from that effort is gorgeous. The way the big headlight sinks into the upper enclosure and the simplicity of the single tube within a tube of that burly front fork. It makes quite a statement. Stevens's other big design move was the straight cut on the leading edge of the front fender, with the shiny trim to set it off, repeated with the trim on the straight cut bottom of the rear fender. Then the three trim pieces on the rear fender parallel those lines and echo the lines stamped into the cover around the headlight. It all comes together in a striking way, and the front fender being cut straight was quite different for motorcycles. Traditionally the circular shape of the fender followed the wheel. That straight cut was a significant styling treatment that we've never gone away from; it's become kind of a trademark design.

The late 1940s were also a momentous time for me personally. I started high school at Wauwatosa High. I was interested in art, and my school had no art program, but I had lots of other interests to keep me busy. During those years I started dating Nancy Schewe, a girl from our neighborhood who went to Holy Angels Academy, a Catholic high school in Milwaukee. That was the most important thing that happened to me in those years: we went steady through high school and stayed together our whole lives. I don't know how much she thought about motorcycles before we started going together, but she got interested and would ride and go to the races with me. Whatever it was, we did it together.

Of course we did all the normal high school things together, such as going to her prom. Back then, if you had a girlfriend, you'd give her a ring or a bracelet. I gave Nancy a bracelet with a motorcycle on it. I got it at our local Harley dealership, and she wore that bracelet and kept it her whole life. Sixty-four years later, in 2015, the Harley-Davidson Museum curated an exhibit on my life and career—our life together, really—and they made a one-off version of that bracelet in solid gold. They presented it to me when the exhibit opened, and I gave it to Nancy.

During high school I started competing in enduros, and Nancy would cheer me on. I was just extending the family tradition: both my father and my great-uncle Walter had been endurance-run champions. I competed in local events, never in a national, but I won a few trophies. When I traded up to a 165cc bike my senior year I became more of a threat in those competitions.

One great memory from those years is a trip to the Indianapolis 500. That was the major auto racing event of the year, and my dad organized a family trip in May 1949 to attend. My brother, John, and I were excited for weeks before the race. A family outing like that was special because my dad was so devoted to the business; he spent every waking hour trying to make the Motor Company succeed. He wasn't really an outdoors guy like his father, who loved to hunt and fish. There are a number of pictures of my grandfather William A. and Bill Harley posing near their motorcycles with big strings of fish. The pictures of my father show him at work, or on his motorcycle, or at the races. He devoted his entire life to running the business, but he also enjoyed the sport, so it was a real treat to take a trip like that down to Indianapolis.

John and I each came home from that trip with die-cast souvenir race cars to add to our collections. I had begun collecting little race cars years earlier. I've remained fascinated by those aerodynamic forms. I kept collecting them my whole life, gradually bigger and more detailed ones until I could acquire the real thing. I've got a gorgeous Knucklehead-powered midget racer in my collection, toys and models throughout the house, and a couple of beautiful vintage race cars, like the ones they would have raced at Indy in the 1930s. I love the rounded slipper shape of those vintage open-wheel racers—big engine compartment up front, little cockpit in the rear. If you're into speed and racing, I think it's natural to be interested in cars as well as motorcycles. I just find those shapes to be inspiring, along with the finishes, the numbers, the wheels: everything functional, focused on performance.

On the subject of speed, Harley-Davidson came out with an exciting new bike the year after I graduated from high school, the K model. John and I got new Ks, our first big bikes. The K was Harley's answer to the British vertical twins, Triumph, BSA, Norton, beautiful bikes that started flowing into our country following World War II and became quite popular. Those British twins fit with what a lot of young Americans wanted in the postwar period, and they were inexpensive because the English economy was depressed. Wages and expenses over there were lower than in the US, and our government had relaxed import tariffs to help rebuild the British economy. Harley-Davidson's prices were going up due to rising expenses, and sales dropped off dramatically with all these cheaper imports flooding the market. We needed something new to compete in that market, and the K model was it.

Our engineers took a fresh start in designing the K model. It was an upgrade to our early side-valves, but it was a clean-sheet-of-paper design. Like the Sportster that would come along in a few years, it had an integrated lower end—engine and transmission all in one case—and an integrated foot shifter more in tune with what was popular at the time: hand-clutch and foot-shift. Our earlier bikes were the other way around, with a hand-operated shifter on the tank and a foot-operated clutch. We eventually went to the foot shift on all our bikes except some of the police models—police officers preferred the hand shift in some circumstances. But the younger riders wanted that foot shift like the imported bikes had.

Another new feature on the K model was the rear suspension—shock absorbers on the rear wheel. That was a big difference from our other bikes, which had a solid rear frame, because without rear suspension the bike moves with every change in the surface of the road. The seats were sprung on those older bikes, which softened the blow considerably, but the rider still felt the big bumps. Being able to move that rear wheel up and down isolates you from being beat up. It's a safer and more pleasant ride. The only bikes today that don't have rear suspension are the customs. Customizers like to build them that way because the frame can be much lower to the ground, and you don't have the shock absorbers breaking up that long straight line of the frame from the top of the front forks all the way down to the rear axle. Those bikes are called hardtails, which they truly are. If you want to create a nice custom and you want it really on the ground visually, you can do that if you don't have to provide for any movement in the rear tire, but you give up a lot of riding comfort.

None of that would have entered the mind of a young person buying a motorcycle in the early 1950s. The chopper movement was still a decade away; you had hardtails like our Panhead and Knucklehead, the older designs, and you had the new bikes with rear suspension and other new features. The K model was designed to compete in that arena.

Thinking back to the 1950s with my dad running the company, there was tremendous enthusiasm for this bike. They were already working on the racing version, which would go on to be very successful. The big twins like the FL Panhead were still our biggest sellers, but this was the new baby on the block, and everyone was excited about it. John and I were both thrilled to trade up to the new K. Of course, it wasn't long before I started customizing mine. Within a year or so I'd trimmed the fenders and put a different fuel tank on it, then a different seat, headlight, paint, exhaust system. I loved that bike; I wish I still had it!

Moving up from my 165cc single, the K model felt amazingly big and powerful. It had a 45-cubic-inch engine, the same size as our earlier flatheads, like the WLA. That translated to 750cc in European measurement—bigger than most of the popular English bikes, which were 650s. I couldn't wait to get out and compete on that bike. I loved enduros: riding through the woods and rivers and water crossings, like my father did winning the Jack Pine. It might seem strange to want to take your shiny new street bike out in the mud, but competition was in my blood.

Back then you didn't have motocross-style enduro bikes, which are lightweight and agile, with long-travel forks and all that good stuff. Riders competed on big street bikes, which made it more of a challenge. Those runs were often held on farmers' lands; the organizers would explain the nature of the event and the farmers would say, "Sure. You can do that." There's not much of that land left anymore so endurance runs like that are a thing of the past. But I would take my headlight off, attach a competition speedometer that tracked average speed over time, and compete. And I won some enduros on that K, got a few trophies. Then I'd bring it home, shine it up, and set it back up for the street.

My brother and I took our first long ride on those K models. We rode down to Dodge City, Kansas—it's a nice route through the Midwest, and we just had a desire to be on the road and in the wind. Back then there weren't all the events and rallies like there are today; we wanted to figure out a place to go, and we were both racing enthusiasts, so we decided on Dodge City.

If we were going to ride our motorcycles to some distant location, we wanted to go to a race, and Dodge City's was steeped in history. It was the biggest motorcycle race in the US back in the early days of our company. Our factory race team first established its reputation there in 1915–16, so of course John and I were aware of the significance of that track. Anybody who knows racing history has heard of it. The Dodge City race had shut down in the 1920s, but they brought it back in the 1950s, and it was a natural destination for us. That was a neat ride, just John and me. We stopped in Springfield, Illinois, another famous racetrack that we would visit often later in life, then kept going to Dodge City. It was a huge track in the middle of a farm field back then, and it was hot—Kansas in early July. We knew the team racers, followed them carefully, so it was exciting to watch the Harley team run on that famous track.

Back home John and I would go to events at the Milwaukee Mile, at State Fair Park. They ran AMA championships on that dirt mile, one of the more famous mile tracks in the nation. It's long ago been paved over, but John and I being racing fans, we spent lots of time there. One of my favorite photos is of John and me on our two customized K models at State Fair Park. Most Harley riders had a custom bike. I was never without one. It's natural to want to personalize your Harley-Davidson, and we were all at it strong back then.

While all of that was happening I was going to college in Madison, a hundred miles from Milwaukee, studying art at the University of Wisconsin. I spent a lot of time going back and forth between college and home. Nancy was going to Mount Mary College, just outside of Milwaukee, studying to be a teacher. Weekends and holidays I'd come home to spend time with her, see John and my parents, race, and ride. Nancy would ride with me; we'd go to races in the area. It was some-times hard to focus on my studies in Madison when my whole life was back in Milwaukee.

I was learning a lot in my art classes. Our teachers had us work in many different mediums: woodcuts, lithographs, watercolors, oils. I was most intrigued by the watercolors; it's a really difficult medium to master, but that's the one I stuck with. After fifty-plus years, I think I'm getting a handle on it. I love doing it.

Art students all have dreams of becoming successful artists, but the art world is broad, with lots of directions to go in and different ideas of what counts as success. I was becoming a better artist, improving my technique and adding new skills, but my classes weren't totally fulfilling. I was as proud of the design I had come up with for the tank of my customized K model as I was of the best painting I did for school, and my teachers couldn't really relate to that. The art program at UW fell under the School of Education, and as we got further in our art studies there was a lot of talk about going into teaching. That's where many students ended up; very few artists get to the point where they can support themselves through their art, let alone support a family. Nancy was excited about the prospect of teaching. I wasn't. I took my art studies seriously, but I was reading *Hot Rod* magazine, more interested in race cars and motorcycles. A trip to the drag races could be as inspiring as a visit to an art gallery. My two great interests weren't connecting.

Then, during my third year at the university, something happened that changed my life. I saw an article in the *Saturday Evening Post* magazine that talked about a school in Los Angeles called ArtCenter. It was a unique school with different types of curriculum—automotive design, photography, commercial art, fashion design. The article had big color photos of different classes: students making clay design models, plein air painting, all kinds of things that resonated with me. I had been fascinated by the West Coast car culture that I read about in *Hot Rod*, and I was already deeply interested in design. When I found out there was a school out where all that hot rod stuff was happening—where I could study not only art but automotive design—I knew that was where I needed to be. So I showed that article to my mother and father and I said, "You know what, I think that would be a very good place for me to study." We talked about it for quite a while and decided I would do that: leave the University of Wisconsin and go to Los Angeles to study at ArtCenter.

CHAPTER 6

BUILDING A FOUNDATION

Los Angeles is a long way from Milwaukee. From the moment I read that *Saturday Evening Post* article I knew ArtCenter was the place for me to follow my dream. Nancy was finishing her degree in education at Mount Mary and preparing to start her teaching career in Milwaukee. We would be going to school at almost opposite ends of the country, so I wouldn't be able to go back and forth for frequent visits. ArtCenter offered a faster route to graduation if you went through the summer, so we decided that's what I would do: stay at school year-round and finish in three years. That was a difficult trade-off; it cut a full year off my time in Los Angeles but meant I wouldn't be able to spend summers in Milwaukee or see Nancy and my family for any extended period. Still, Nancy and I figured that would be best: work hard, get done, come home. That was the plan.

The ArtCenter School started in the 1930s as a professional training program with just a few students. Enrollment expanded after World War II, and ArtCenter moved out of downtown into a small group of buildings that had previously housed a private school for girls. The *Post* article featured a photo of a painting class out on the lawn in front of the main building, painting plein air. I was drawn in by that image, with a painter's model standing in front of a large building that looked sort of English, except for the bright sunshine and the big American cars in the circular drive. The article described the location as near Hollywood, so that had given me a little idea of what to expect when I got there.

Moving from the University of Wisconsin, a major university with a huge campus, to a small, elite school in the middle of a bustling city was a big change. Growing up in the Midwest, what I knew about Los Angeles was sun, palm trees, and Hollywood, so my first day in the city I headed to Hollywood Boulevard and walked up and down, seeing the sights. My focus in the months leading up to the move had been on working through the requirements to get admitted to ArtCenter and set up my coursework. I knew my life would be different in LA, but walking alone through Hollywood, stopping with the tourists to look at the movie stars' handprints in front of the huge Chinese Theatre, dodging traffic on that busy boulevard, the magnitude of this change hit me. It was a major game changer.

Wisconsin was a great school but so different from all of this. I attended a few parties. I was in a fraternity. I knew a lot of people. I was just an hour and a half from Milwaukee. One long plane ride and here I was in a new world. And I wasn't just visiting—this was going to be my home for a few years. The school was in a nice part of Los Angeles not far from downtown, more of a residential area with big lawns and tall palms. ArtCenter didn't have dorms; I needed to find an apartment. I didn't know anybody. I didn't have my own vehicle. I was excited, wondering what might be next and where this adventure would take me.

ArtCenter had started offering year-round courses after World War II, and its four-year degree program was just five years old when I started in 1954. My studies would focus on transportation and product design, but I looked forward to taking elective courses in painting, studying with ArtCenter's accomplished instructors. The photo in that article that had really hooked me showed students working on one-third scale clay automotive models, with a caption that said something about how most new car designs were being done by ArtCenter grads. The chance to study automotive design in a program that had produced top designers was what I had jumped at. Six months after seeing that article I was in sunny Southern California, one of a small group of talented designers beginning an intensive program, learning rendering techniques and clay modeling. Life can change so quickly.

The courses at ArtCenter were less structured than what I'd experienced at Wisconsin, more project-based and experience-focused. My fellow students were an impressive bunch. There had been some good artists in Madison but nothing like my classmates at ArtCenter. Everybody you met, wherever they came from, had been the best at what they did. Once classes began, I got to know my classmates. That's one of the great things about a place like that—you're inspired by and learn from your fellow students as well as your instructors. And the instructors at ArtCenter were a revelation.

The ArtCenter faculty was made up of artists and designers who'd already built successful careers. They knew what it took to excel in the art world or in the corporate world, and the course of study hit the whole spectrum of skills necessary to do that. I'd been studying art at Wisconsin. At ArtCenter my studies combined art with science and technology. The instructors taught us to see the world differently, to look at things in terms of functionality and possibility, to see the potential for beauty in every object and imagine how to make it better. Then you'd focus on how a person would use that thing you'd imagined, how you'd design it to be simple and pleasurable to operate, comfortable to use.

I'd been forever drawing cars and motorcycles, but at ArtCenter I really learned how to sketch. Keep in mind, this was decades before computers were involved in doing any renderings—everything was done by hand. We'd sketch out concepts and then render them on dark paper using pencils to create highlights and illustrate the shapes. That light-on-dark method of rendering is dramatic, a great way of illustrating form and color. All these years later I've still got a couple of those renderings—an upgrade of a Mercedes Roadster and a one-off pickup truck concept. That type of rendering is a lost art; people just don't do it that way anymore, so I'm glad I saved those. It's a whole different world now; everything is done on the computer. Transportation companies also got away from clay modeling for a while, but that's come back. Thankfully students are learning modeling again. A computer is great, but a designer wants to have a physical model to work with, something they can walk around and modify.

As we advanced in our studies, we learned about materials and specifications for manufacturing. At that time there was a lot of automotive manufacturing in Southern California—it was second only to Detroit in building cars and trucks. And there was aircraft manufacturing, furniture manufacturing; we would go out and see those processes up close, learning about the complex considerations that designers need to understand from real-world examples. I'd been dreaming of designing things that people could really use, and that was ArtCenter's specialty. They were the best at it.

Once I got situated in Los Angeles, I was able to move around a bit and get to know the area. I'd left my motorcycle back in Milwaukee. I'd have it there to ride when I went back to visit Nancy and my family. I bought a used car to get around and set about customizing it. Back in Wisconsin I'd bought *Hot Rod* magazines and developed a fascination with the custom scene. During my last year in Madison two new magazines started appearing on the newsstands: *Car Craft* and *Rod & Custom*. SoCal was the home of all those custom cars and motorcycles, and I loved that creativity. As soon as I got settled I had to find those guys, discover where they hung out, where they showed their cars and motorcycles. I needed to stay focused at school, learning fast and proving myself, but I couldn't pass up a chance to learn from the top customizers of the day, people I had read about in magazines.

I've still got a picture of the car I had out in LA, my '51 Ford coupe, parked in front of ArtCenter. It had a Pontiac grill, Cadillac sombrero hubcaps, the hood was louvered, the trim was modified, and I put chrome side exhaust pipes on it. In that picture it's all gray primer, waiting for paint. One of my classmates at ArtCenter really wanted my '51, so I sold that car and picked up a '54 Ford. One of those guys I'd read about in magazines before I got to California, Von Dutch, pin-striped my '54. He was a character. He was doing some striping and I said, "How come this side isn't the same as the other side, symmetrical?" He gave me some short, gruff answer like "Don't bother me, man." I don't know what happened to that car. It's somewhere. Maybe it's still on the West Coast.

Paying attention to the work those hot rod guys were doing fit right in with what I was studying at ArtCenter. Custom builders worked with different media—sheet metal and paint and proportions—but they were truly artists; it was easy for me to see that and be inspired by it. I guess now I'd call it folk art because they were not trained through professional education, but they knew relationships and proportion, shape to shape to form to wheelbase to engine. That's what it's all about, whether it's a car or a motorcycle. Over the years, I never lost interest in custom motorcycles or custom four-wheelers. As designers, it's important that we keep one eye on what's happening in the street.

I've written a little about some of the bikes in my collection. Of course, I've got some custom motorcycles, including a beautiful custom Knucklehead I did that was featured in some magazines. But I've got custom cars, too, one of which was featured in *Hot Rod* in the 1990s. Being in *Hot Rod* took me full circle back to my college years reading that magazine. The car they featured is a sedan delivery I designed. It's a phantom, which means it was not a production vehicle. But I wanted it to look like it could've been production, and it came out well. The section behind the doors is from a '34 Ford Victoria; the front is a '34 Chevy. It's short coupled—the actual '34 Chevy Sedan Delivery has a much longer tail section. That car has proportions that I was really fascinated by. Again, whether it's a motorcycle or a car, proportions are really everything. If it doesn't sit right relative to wheelbase, it flunks. And you can see it right away. You know it. That's something I had figured out before I went to ArtCenter. They didn't have to teach me that.

Even though I was busy with my classwork and projects at ArtCenter, I still kept up with the motorcycle racing scene, and the mid-fifties were an exciting time to be a Harley-Davidson racing fan. The KR, the racing version of the K model, debuted in 1952 and dominated flat track racing through the '50s. Our primary competitor in pre–World War II racing had been Indian. Of the other competitors in the board track era, only Excelsior stayed in business through the 1920s, and they went under early in the Great Depression. Indian made it through the Depression and World War II, but they finally went out of business the year our KR model hit the racetracks. Faced with intense competition from all those British bikes coming into the US after the war, Indian tried to beat them at their own game and started making vertical twin engines, like the Triumphs and BSAs of the late 1940s. Indian was already struggling, and they pushed those bikes to market before they were ready; they weren't reliable. If Indian had stuck with their flathead the way Harley-Davidson stuck with our beautiful V-Twin, they might still be in business. But they went under in 1953, leaving us all alone as the only American motorcycle manufacturer.

As the proud owner of a K model, I loved following the exploits of Joe Leonard and Brad Andres as they tore up the racetracks on their KRs, dominating the competition. Those guys were my heroes, along with Carroll Resweber, who battled Joe Leonard for the championships until Leonard quit racing motorcycles in 1961. Leonard went on to race Indy cars, where he won some more championships.

Lucky for me, Brad Andres was based out of his father's dealership in San Diego, and we became friends while I was in Los Angeles. Brad's father Leonard was a famous racer in his own right and became a very successful Harley dealer after he retired from racing. He had good connections at the factory in Milwaukee, which was how I met him and Brad. After retiring from racing, Leonard Andres also became well known as a race tuner. He got one of the first KRs and set it up for his son. Brad was a great rider. He turned pro in 1955, my second year at ArtCenter, and he won the AMA championship that year, edging out Joe Leonard. Brad had a record-setting rookie season. I used to go see him race in Gardena and at some other tracks in SoCal. His father even took me to a race up in the Bay Area in his private plane.

I was sometimes able to go riding on weekends by borrowing bikes from Harley dealers in the area, but I didn't have a lot of free time— my studies at ArtCenter kept me working long hours. The demands of those classes were intense, and the instructors had extremely high standards. ArtCenter expected its graduates to be at the top of their chosen profession, and if a student slipped along the way or couldn't make the grade, they had to pack up their pencils and go home. Even with strict admissions requirements and evaluations, many students never made it to graduation.

Art was my minor focus at ArtCenter, and I really enjoyed my painting classes. I'd had good teachers back at Wisconsin, and some of my fellow students were talented, but everyone—instructors and students alike—was at a much higher level at ArtCenter. The sketching and rendering skills I was learning in my Transportation Design work heightened my overall skill level, and the rigor of the art courses really pushed me along. We worked in a variety of media, drawing and painting a full spectrum of subject matter. Our coursework ranged from quick-draw sessions, where a model would sit for half an hour and you had to complete a pastel portrait in that time, to all-day affairs that took us out into the California countryside. Painting on location, plein air, we'd paint watercolors, which became my favorite medium. Oil paintings don't dry quickly enough for outdoor sessions, but watercolors work great. Watercolors are difficult, but I'm fascinated by them. There's a real magic to how the paper takes the water and how the color reacts to it. You must learn how to preserve the white areas—the areas with no paint—and figure out your contrasts, the negative and the positive. You really need a plan; you can't just attack it. Those principles have stuck with me all these years.

I've still got several of the paintings I did at ArtCenter. They take me back to that time. One in particular kind of kicked me into gear and gave me a sense of accomplishment as a painter. An instructor I really respected recognized the painting as a kind of a breakthrough for me, in terms of design, unique color composition, and materials—it's a painting of a freight train and I used watercolor, pen and ink, and some crayon. It's a mixed-media painting, and I saved it all these years because it felt significant at that time, being considered a good step forward by my instructor. (This painting is reproduced in the first photo section of the book.)

When they created my exhibit at the Harley-Davidson Museum, we went through all my files and found a lot of things I'd kept from those years: design renderings, sketches, paintings, even a drawing of Joe Leonard I did back then for my brother's birthday. The design work and the painting went hand in hand, and that's the way it has gone for me throughout my life, my whole career.

My time at ArtCenter was special, and they really prepared me to enter the professional world as a designer. I'm a proud graduate of that great school. So many of their grads have gone on to become well-known automotive designers, top illustrators, top painters. I keep track of some of the alumni. My time there was intense, made more so by going straight through the summers, but once I was done it felt like it had flown by. Nancy had started her teaching career while I was in California. My brother was graduating from college—with my detour from Wisconsin to ArtCenter we ended up finishing our degrees at the same time. I enjoyed Los Angeles, but staying in California was never really a consideration. I got my diploma and headed straight back to Milwaukee.

Nancy and I got married in June 1957, soon after my return from LA. We had no idea what the future would hold, but we knew we would be there together, whatever came to pass. For our honeymoon we went to Laconia, New Hampshire, for the big motorcycle rally and AMA race. My friend Brad Andres had won that race the year before, but Joe Leonard won it in 1957, on his way to another Grand National Championship. I was just an aspiring designer fresh out of ArtCenter, but Harley-Davidson was the big name in racing, and I guess the motorcycle press thought our marriage was a good human-interest story: *American Motorcycling*, *Motorcyclist*, and *The Enthusiast* all ran pictures of Nancy and me together in Laconia.

I had submitted my portfolio to the Ford Motor Company after I graduated. There was a steady stream of ArtCenter grads going to Detroit, with many having served internships there during school. Ford offered me a job, a promising opportunity, but Nancy and I wanted to stay in Milwaukee, so I turned them down in favor of a position in the Transportation and Product Design group at Brooks Stevens Associates. Brooks's offices were right in downtown Milwaukee, and a guy named Gordon Kelly oversaw the TPD group. Kelly made a splash a few years later when a Corvette variant he designed and had built in Italy was on the cover of *Car and Driver* magazine. He was a good designer who also had an engineering background.

Brooks Stevens Associates was a consulting design firm—he contracted with companies to design products, logos, and packaging for established manufacturers large and small. Earlier in his career Brooks had also designed offices and workspaces and collaborated with architects on factory designs. He was one of the pioneers of industrial design, a group that in the 1930s gradually convinced manufacturers that it wasn't enough for consumer products to just serve their purpose—that in addition to performing their intended task, products should also be beautiful, take on a form expressive of their function, and make consumers want to possess them. As the industrial design movement gained traction, far-thinking designers like Brooks also suggested improvements in manufacturing processes and worked to make products easier to use.

Brooks had designed successful products ranging from tractors to household appliances in the decade before he was hired by Harley-Davidson to design components of the 1949 Hydra-Glide. Today his most familiar designs are probably the Miller High Life logo and the Oscar Meyer Wienermobile, but his most significant design accomplishment in that period was the innovative Olympian Hiawatha passenger train. Brooks helped companies realize that good design is a serious business tool. The car companies were among the first to understand this, so it was no coincidence that Transportation Design was a major focus at ArtCenter and that so many ArtCenter graduates worked for automotive manufacturers.

The big auto manufacturers may have been the first to recognize that appearance drove sales, but by the 1950s nearly all consumer products were styled to capitalize on current trends. With cars, the obvious feature from that era were fins. Like the streamline design movement of the 1930s, when even pencil sharpeners were "aerodynamic," fins didn't have any functional purpose. They were for show, and people were loving the show. The point, from a sales perspective, was to change from year to year to convince buyers that they needed to trade up to the new model. Brooks referred to this as "planned obsolescence," a phrase he was much criticized for.

No one was going to put fins on a motorcycle. Motorcycle styling didn't change as radically or rapidly as automotive styling. Riders were more likely to hold on to their bikes and wait to trade up when there was a new engine or some important engineering advance. Harley-Davidson had expected that the front suspension on the 1949 Hydra-Glide would be the kind of major advance that would generate trade-ins and stimulate sales. Wanting to amplify the appeal of the new front end with some dramatic styling updates, the company turned to Brooks Stevens. Consulting design firms existed to perform such services, particularly for companies like Harley-Davidson that didn't have industrial designers on staff.

In 1957, the year I joined Brooks Stevens's staff, Harley-Davidson introduced a bike that made lots of riders want to "trade up": the Sportster, a new design with an overhead-valve V-Twin engine with an integrated transmission. The Sportster release was exciting for me because I had a small part in it—I'd designed the new tank badge, "moonlighting" while I was at ArtCenter. A big change like the Sportster introduction happened maybe once a decade. In between those model releases, if a rider wanted a bike with a new look, they customized their motorcycle themselves. At least that was how it usually worked in the first half of the twentieth century. It's a kind of folk art.

The atmosphere at Brooks Stevens was great. It was a new, modern building and there were twelve of us in a big drafting room, all young guys excited about their work, most of us unmarried and fresh out of school. Everyone worked hard—we were anxious to prove ourselves early in our careers—but we also had fun. There were practical jokes, some long lunch hours. As long as we produced good, creative work and got our projects done on schedule, we were given a lot of latitude.

In my five years at Brooks Stevens I worked on everything from entertainment centers to automobiles. I designed an update to an outboard motor Brooks had done years earlier, and a group of modern appliances for Hotpoint, scaled for an apartment or a small home. The office was full of talent, but I had an advantage because the sketching and rendering skills taught at ArtCenter were beyond anything you could learn anywhere else. The office worked on a lot of day-to-day stuff—toasters, coffee makers—and I sometimes got shifted around to do the presentation renderings for designers whose drawing skills weren't as good. We were always busy. Brooks was a very charismatic guy and very good at pulling in business. Working on such a variety of consumer products provided lots of challenges, and I learned something with every new project.

A young designer named John Bradley had a drawing board near me in our drafting room, and we gradually discovered that we had a lot in common. John had studied Fine Art at the Layton School of Art, a top-notch school in Milwaukee, but because he also showed great potential in his design work, his instructors advised him that a career in design would more reliably put bread on the table. Besides art we both were racing fans. When we had time, we would talk about painting, maybe motorcycles or race cars; we were both into photography, so we'd talk about that. Our work brought us together, and these other shared interests built a strong friendship.

John and I started going to races together. I introduced him to Nancy, and he would come over to the house. We quickly formed a bond, and one day I had an idea: as we were knocking off work I said, "Hey Bradley—Friday, when everybody leaves, why don't we drop our drawing boards down and paint? Bring your painting supplies; I'll bring mine." So that's what we did, and that started a Friday painting tradition. Every Friday we'd drop our boards down, get a six-pack, and paint well into the night. When Nancy and I got settled into a house, I set up a design room/studio in the basement, and from then on, we had our Friday paint nights down there.

Initially Nancy wasn't too sure what she thought about this activity. I had a sound system down there; we'd turn up the rock 'n' roll, have a few beers, laugh a lot, and paint until the wee hours. The more beer, the better the paintings looked. It was a great way to end the workweek, and we kept up those paint nights for many years.

My last full year at Brooks I worked on an interesting Studebaker concept car called the Sceptre. Studebaker was struggling; Brooks had designed their recent attempt to upgrade the product line, the Hawk Gran Turismo, and the Sceptre was one of a small group of new designs they hoped would revive the company. There were three versions of it: a two-door coupe, a four-door, and a station wagon. I worked with another principal designer on the project; my focus was on the coupe.

The Sceptre was a futuristic design for the time, an advanced shape with some outstanding features. It had a horizontal louver grill that concealed a light bar extending across the entire front end instead of your standard headlights, and a light bar across the back end too, under a full-width red lens. The overall design was very striking, with innovative design cues inside and out. Brooks contracted with an Italian coachbuilder, Carrozzeria Sibona-Basano in Turin, to build the prototype, and I was sent over there to oversee the fabrication. That was exciting—the Italian coachbuilding tradition is famous, and it was fascinating to see those artisans at work. The car turned out beautifully. It was shipped back to Milwaukee for photography and presented to Studebaker, but the company was running out of money and the car never made it to market.

Brooks was a car collector. He owned a lot of rare cars, including a 1928 Mercedes SS Phaeton. The same year we showed the futuristic Sceptre, he made headlines at the New York Auto Show with a modern re-creation of that classic Mercedes roadster, built on a Studebaker chassis. It was called the Excalibur, and it became a whole side business for Brooks and his sons—they built them in Milwaukee, using Chevy engines and fabricating their own chassis. More than three thousand Excaliburs were sold by the time the Stevens brothers shut down production in 1990.

Brooks opened his own automotive museum in 1959, and the Sceptre prototype was on display there until that museum closed in 1999, four years after Brooks passed away. That Sceptre is now on display at the Studebaker Museum in South Bend, Indiana. But Brooks's car-collecting activities sent me on an interesting adventure at the end of that Italian trip to supervise the Sceptre prototype fabrication. He'd located an Alpine race car that he wanted for his collection. It was a French car, a special performance coupe with a fiberglass body—light and quick, fun to drive. He asked me to pick it up in Milan and drive it to Monaco, where he had some people who would handle shipping it to the US.

Beyond the fun of driving that car on those roads, I had some extra excitement crossing the border into France. I'd never done anything like that before and had no idea what to expect. I got stopped at the border and the customs agents obviously expected something from me, but I didn't speak French and had no idea what I was supposed to do. I finally figured out that they wanted some documents, and I rooted around the car until I found some papers. I couldn't read them, but they were apparently what the customs guys wanted, so after looking at the papers they waved me through. I'd been afraid for a moment that I wouldn't get past the inspectors, but once I was back on the road it was a beautiful drive along the seacoast into Monaco. I dropped the car off, took a train to Paris, and flew back to Milwaukee. That was a memorable adventure.

One of the other accounts that Brooks Stevens had was Outboard Marine Corporation, the company that made Evinrude and Johnson outboards, which is how I redesigned an outboard early in my time with Brooks. Bradley ended up taking over the Evinrude account, but another Outboard Marine brand was Cushman, the motor scooter company. Cushman had been making scooters since the Depression, and as smaller motorcycles became popular in the 1950s, they needed some new designs, so I got involved with designing Cushman scooters. I did one very modern concept in 1962 that we prototyped, but like with the Studebaker, Cushman was running into financial difficulties and that design never made it to market.

The market for lightweight motorcycles really took off in the 1950s, then exploded in the early 1960s, with Honda importing their scooter-like Cub model. Cushman saw that market increasing and hoped to capitalize on it. Harley-Davidson was in an even better position to benefit from that expanding market. During the years I was at ArtCenter, sales of Harley lightweights kept growing. In 1955 our 125cc and 165cc lightweights made up one-third of our production.

With an eye on the changing market for two-wheelers, Harley came out with its own scooter in 1960, the Topper. The Topper was a classic scooter—it had fairly large wheels, a nice body with two-tone paint, and an automatic transmission, which made it easy for new riders. It had a rope start, like a lawn mower—that was unique. The main body was fiberglass. I worked a little on the Topper design with some of the Harley engineers while I was still with Brooks, kind of moonlighting, like I had with that Sportster tank badge while I was at ArtCenter.

With my dad in charge of the company, Harley was aggressive in going after the new younger market. The Topper came out with a major advertising campaign focused on young people, and that same year Harley bought a 49 percent stake in Aermacchi, an Italian manufacturer of small and midsize motorcycles.

The full name of our new Italian partner was Aeronautica Macchi; they were an airplane supplier to the Italian air force. They had started making airplanes before World War I and branched out into motorcycles after World War II. Our first collaboration was the 1961 Sprint, which looked very Italian. It was the total Aermacchi package; the only input Harley had was tank trim, which I worked on, moonlighting again. The bikes took on a more American, Harley-Davidson look in subsequent years, with a peanut tank like the S model, but they were manufactured in Italy and imported into the US. The Sprint was a 250cc, and we later made a 350cc version. Harley-Davidson had a full line of motorcycles in the early 1960s, from scooters and lightweights through midsize, sporty models, and big cruisers.

All of that was taking off while I was at Brooks Stevens. I was moonlighting a little for Harley and staying in touch with everything happening there. My brother, John, started with the company in 1961, working in the sales department under Walter C. Davidson, the son of cofounder Walter Davidson. I would see John at family get-togethers, and my dad would come to Shorewood every week and we'd have lunch together. By the end of 1962 we started talking about how maybe it was time for me to come over to Harley-Davidson. Harley was pushing the Topper, their scooter, and I was at Brooks designing Cushman scooters. I had to admit that that didn't make much sense. And Harley's product line had expanded to the point where my dad felt the company needed its own design department. With talented engineers and occasional outside input, the company had done well on the design side for sixty years, but with all the new products and stiff competition, it was time to enhance the design focus and bring it in-house. So we agreed that's what we would do: I would leave Brooks and become Harley's first-ever design director.

I'd had a good five years at Brooks Stevens. Designing different products, working with a variety of clients, I was able to hone all the skills I'd learned at ArtCenter. I had to tell Brooks I was leaving; thankfully, it was an easy conversation—he didn't seem that surprised.

With that settled I worked out the details on my new position with Dad. The board approved the plan, and I made a smooth transition.

Nancy was supportive. Our life together was starting a new chapter. In February of 1963 I packed up my office at Brooks Stevens and took my design tools over to Harley-Davidson's headquarters on Juneau Avenue.

CHAPTER 7

W. G.

My first day at Harley-Davidson, walking into the Juneau Avenue factory I'd visited so many times—it just felt right. I was excited by the challenge of establishing and leading an internal design department at a company that for six decades had been turning out great motorcycles without any central design leadership. Harley-Davidson motorcycle design had always been done from an engineering base. But the company was growing, the product line was expanding, and the competition was more intense than ever before. It was time for a change. The company leadership recognized the importance of this move and believed I had the skills and background to lead the charge.

I had been through a couple big changes in the past ten years: moving from Milwaukee to Los Angeles to attend a high-pressure design school, then returning to join a major consulting design firm led by a true pioneer of industrial design. I was pretty sure that with this move I had a better idea of what to expect than I'd had in those situations. I'd grown up with the company, already done a number of design projects on the side, and had many discussions with my father about this new position and what my focus would be. My brother had been with Harley for a few years. I was ready to get started. Walking the halls of the company my grandfather and uncles created, sitting down at my drawing table in my own office, looking out the window to the railroad tracks where hundreds of thousands of Harley-Davidson motorcycles had started their journey to owners all over the world—well, that was quite a feeling.

In 1961 Harley-Davidson had purchased the Tomahawk boat company, a recreational boat manufacturer in northern Wisconsin. That was the same year that the Sprint, the first Harley-Davidson–branded Aermacchi lightweight, hit dealer showrooms. The Tomahawk acquisition was another step in Harley's product diversification, but we didn't plan to go into the boat business. Tomahawk made fiberglass boats, and what we wanted was their fiberglass operation. Fiberglass was proving to be a good material for motorcycle components such as saddlebags, and company leadership was developing plans to go into the golf cart business, so acquiring a company with expertise in fiberglass manufacturing made sense. Since Tomahawk was tooled to make boats and had an established sales base, we planned to keep making boats for a few years while we got up to speed for our saddlebags and golf cart bodies.

A partial redesign of the Tomahawk boat was the first task I took on in my new job. I created a Harley-Davidson/Tomahawk graphic, developed new trim pieces, redesigned the dashboard and some interior elements. Projects like that were fun for me because I loved graphic design as well as 3-D. The 1964 Tomahawk Boats catalog featured the new look and included an article about me and my new position. My last name hadn't drawn a lot of attention back at Brooks Stevens, but my hiring and family connection were news in the motorcycling world and within our company.

Harley-Davidson was a much smaller company back then, and in my new position I was its "resident creative," the go-to guy, whether it was two-dimensional or three-dimensional. I had my hand in everything from advertising and photography to the creation of vehicles. I designed annual reports and retail displays, supervised photo shoots, worked out branding for our new golf carts, and obviously designed motorcycles. For things like those annual reports, I came up with the covers and overall look, picked the type, did the layout, even shot some of the photography. And I'm proud to say I won some nice awards from the Art Directors Club in Milwaukee for those publications.

Another important project I undertook was the design of a new version of our historic Bar & Shield logo. The logo is steeped in so much history, going back to the company's founding era. It's central to our brand identity, but as our product line expanded we needed an alternative logo that would work on vehicles other than motorcycles. The traditional logo read "Harley-Davidson" in the horizontal bar across the shield, with *Motor* above and *Cycles* below. I did a contemporary version with elongated triangles above and below the "Harley-Davidson" bar. It gave the logo a different feel; it played off the original but could work on anything: a golf cart, different utility vehicles, or whatever. We ran with that logo on various products beginning in 1964.

The Harley-Davidson Design Department in 1963 was just me and Ed Saffert, my right-hand man and model maker. I was eager to focus on motorcycles, but bringing all of the company's various design processes together was one of the primary reasons I was at Harley. Without a formalized internal design department, lots of consultants had been brought in for different projects. With the skills I'd learned at ArtCenter and during my time with Brooks Stevens, I could come in and work with all those departments, understand the nature of the tasks, appreciate the challenges, and bring fresh ideas that fit the times but stayed consistent with our brand heritage. I had developed the confidence as a designer to do that work, but it was equally important that I was an avid rider who had a passion for the sport and for the history of the company.

To understand why the drive to diversify was so strong when I joined the company, you have to understand the business environment of that time. In the years after World War II, as I mentioned earlier, our primary competition came in the form of relatively inexpensive middleweight bikes from England. By the time I graduated from ArtCenter, Harley had changed with the times and was beating those brands at their own game, first with the K model, then the Sportster. Our only domestic competitor, Indian, had gone out of business in 1953. But just as it began to seem that things were looking up, a different kind of competition came from a different direction: Japan.

Honda Motor Company was formed after World War II and incorporated in 1948. Its small, commuter motorcycles caught on quickly in Japan's densely populated cities. After a decade of rapid growth, the young company set its sights on the US market, and in the fall of 1959 they established an office in Los Angeles. They sold something like two thousand bikes in 1960, their first full year in this country. Focusing on the scooter-like 50cc model that they advertised as "The nifty, thrifty, Honda 50," sales rose above ten thousand in 1961, close to Harley's total sales for that year. Their sales quadrupled in 1962, surpassing forty thousand. Honda ignored the traditional US motorcycle channels, instead taking out bright, cheerful ads in magazines like *LIFE* and pushing their little bikes into sporting goods stores.

Honda expanded their push in 1963 with the first of their "You meet the *nicest* people on a Honda!" ads. That year, my first with the company, Harley sales dropped below ten thousand, a low we hadn't seen since the last part of the Great Depression, while Honda sales more than doubled, approaching ninety thousand. Harley-Davidson was the motorcycle of choice for the established base of American riders, but Honda had found a way to appeal to a different crowd: total newcomers to motorcycling. Facing such fierce competition, Harley-Davidson had to look for sales beyond its traditional base of motorcycle enthusiasts.

Though big Harley cruisers, the FLs, were the heart of our brand, we'd been making lightweights since the 1920s. The S model, like the one I learned on, evolved over the 1950s, adding a 165cc version in 1953. We reliably sold a few thousand lightweights each year, but with that part of the industry growing so rapidly, the second-generation leadership—my father and William J. Harley—decided that we needed to expand our lightweight line. They determined that the cost of doing that in this country would be too high, so they looked elsewhere, and after considering different options made the deal with Aermacchi. The leadership of the two companies got on well together, and our 49 percent purchase of the company was finalized in 1960.

The Aermacchi factory was in Varese, in the lake country north of Milan. I knew about our new Italian partners from my trip to Turin to work on that Studebaker prototype. I didn't get up there on that trip, but over the next few years I'd visit Varese as our lineup of Italian-made lightweights expanded. It was my job to adapt the styling of the Aermacchi/Harley-Davidsons to be consistent with our brand and appeal to the American market. I worked in the engineering department at Varese for a short time, sketching variations of their bikes and working with my counterparts there.

The Sprint model, our first Aermacchi/Harley-Davidson, did quite well for us through the 1960s. It was a fun bike, and the racing version of it was very successful. Aermacchi had a history of racing success, and it was exciting to add their 250cc and 350cc CRTT racers to our stable. I did the tank logos for those in the mid-1960s. They competed in Grand Prix road racing, which was an arena we had never entered, and we actually won three championships in the mid-1970s on the RR-250. We also produced a Sprint Scrambler in the later 1960s that competed in the smaller-displacement classes of flat track racing, a sort of Italian little brother to the KR and later the XR. We even set a land-speed record at Bonneville with a Sprint streamliner in 1965.

Aermacchi had a simple step-through frame model, the M-50, that would compete with the successful Honda 50, and we brought that into our lineup in 1965. We basically duplicated the Italian version and put a Harley logo on it, and it did really well for us in the mid-1960s. We had an M-50 at home, and as the kids got old enough it was a great bike for them to learn to ride on. Overall, the Aermacchi venture was a success— we eventually purchased the whole company—but our lightweight sales never approached those of Honda, and the Japanese competition kept growing as Yamaha and Suzuki and Kawasaki expanded their US sales.

The M-50 provided a great entry-level option for the first-time motorcyclist, but our big announcement in 1965 was a major update in our traditional big V-Twin line: the Electra Glide. Where the M-50 appealed to someone who might have been considering a Honda 50, the Electra Glide was a highway cruiser for a more traditional American rider. The "Electra" in Electra Glide referred to a small but significant change from the Duo-Glide: a simple, push-button electric start. Kick-starting a big Harley V-Twin is part of the tradition, but it requires some knowledge and skill. The ease of push-button starting removed a barrier that some potential riders found intimidating. As is often the way with design changes, the shift to electric start was more complicated than it might seem. The new electrical system required a larger battery, which meant we had to change the oil tank placement and make adjustments to the frame. It's the kind of domino effect that can get complicated, but I loved attacking a problem like that on our flagship cruiser. The Electra Glide eventually joined the ranks of our legendary models. It's still in production today, a cornerstone of the current lineup.

As the Electra Glide was preparing for launch, we were deep into an even bigger change: a new engine, the Shovelhead, would replace the Panhead in 1966. The Panhead had powered our cruisers since 1948, so this was a big change with another set of challenges. I had my hands full. If you look at a picture of my office from that time, you'll see drawing equipment and drawings on the walls. No computers. We had drafting machines, we had scales, we had pencils. All that changed over time, but during that period it was handwork, and I was always drawing. Each new idea, new product, or product change, the process was the same. I'd start with rough sketches, then move on to a color rendering. When an idea was worked out, I'd do a complete rendering with call outs in a separate panel to describe the details. Then I drew variations, different themes. Sometimes I did renderings on dark backgrounds, like we were taught at ArtCenter, so I could highlight the shapes with pencil—fenders, seats, tanks, exhaust, headlight enclosures. I could do those fairly quickly and would do several. Then I would get together with the people working on the project to discuss the concepts and pick ones that would go into three dimensions. First, scale models; then, if it went that far, full-scale mockups. That was the design process back then.

Fortunately for our bottom line, the golf cart business that we entered in 1962 proved successful. At a basic level, a golf cart is just another motorized vehicle: you're building an engine, putting it on wheels, and trying to design it so that it works well and people like it. To do that effectively I had to learn what those customers wanted, and that was a whole different world for me. I went to some of the big golf trade shows to try and understand what the golfers needed, things such as scorecard holders and golf-bag supports. Then I worked with the fiber-glass folks up in Tomahawk to learn what we could or couldn't do with that body. The whole rear body was one piece, so it had to have draft so you could pull it out of the fiberglass mold. There was a lot of learning involved.

We did seats, I designed the scorecard area, we went through varia-tions for the steering—the first versions had a sort of tiller rather than a steering wheel. That worked well, but we ended up moving to a regular steering wheel later. We experimented a lot. We figured out that if we dropped the rear panel of the body down, you wouldn't have to lift your golf bags so high—that was a popular feature. The work was very interesting, but a golf cart is purely a functional device; there wasn't much focus on styling. Our golf carts were a success, though; they're very popular, and still in use, even collectible. We made three- and four-wheel versions, with an electric version starting in 1969.

Those Harley-Davidson golf carts became the industry standard, and my brother was in charge of that division for a while. We kept making them all through the 1970s, and golf cart sales helped us through some of the difficult times. I designed a related utility vehicle and explored some offshoots that never made it to market. We were trying to build sales wherever we could. During that period I learned a lot about what golfers wanted, but I never became a golfer myself. I spent my leisure time, what little I had of it, riding and with my family.

Working on those vehicles I became very connected with our team in Tomahawk. Golf cart bodies are big pieces of fiberglass, and we moved on from there to some other big forms: a new fiberglass sidecar and a new fiberglass tail section for our Police Servi-Cars. Once we became expert with fiberglass production, replacing those big metal parts with lighter fiberglass forms made perfect sense. Tomahawk had a pattern shop that would take our designs and build wood patterns, then I would go up and critique the result, and they could modify the patterns before going to actual molds. We had good pattern workers up there. Learning to work with that material, developing an understanding of what can be done with it, paid real dividends down the road.

Some other important designs came out of our work in Tomahawk during the 1960s, my first years with the company. In the mid-1960s I changed the profile of our saddlebags, modernized the look, and then in 1968 we introduced a new windshield design, the "batwing" fairing. The "batwing" became a trademark for our Electra Glide–styled vehicles. I'm very proud of those designs because they've proven to be timeless. The original saddlebag profile has been stretched and modified a little, but it's still that same fast form. Both the fairing and the bags got an update in 2014, but the Styling department went to great lengths to keep the feel and profile of the established designs while improving the aerodynamics and functionality. It's gratifying that those forms have lasted so long and are still popular. As a designer, that's what you're shooting for: something that works, with a form that excites people when it's new, then lasts and stays relevant.

I was very busy at work, but I always made time for family. Nancy had given up her teaching job to run the household, and we had three growing kids at home. One after another, Karen, Bill, and Michael learned to ride, and we enjoyed camping up north and going to the races. Spending summers at Red Arrow camp, I had developed a love for the northern Wisconsin lake country, and we eventually bought a motor home, which added a level of enjoyment to those trips. There were lots of races to go to, and the kids learned to love that as much as John and I had at their age. Flat track, drag racing, road racing—those were our sports. Up north, the kids could swim, play, and ride, and I could take my sketchbook out into the woods and sketch. Sometimes John Bradley would come along and we'd sketch together.

John and I kept up our Friday paint nights. The process of putting paint to paper seemed to fascinate Michael, our youngest, who would come down to watch before bedtime. Michael would grow up to be a talented artist and a good teacher—teaching art at the Milwaukee Institute of Art & Design and the Milwaukee branch of the University of Wisconsin. John and I would paint into the morning hours, and I would usually finish a painting in one session. Most nights I'd put what I'd done on an easel in the corner of the dining room before going to bed, and Nancy and the kids would check it out on Saturday morning. Later in life Michael would say it was like Christmas every Saturday, running in to see my new painting. It made both Nancy and me proud that he took that inspiration and became such a talented artist. Karen, too, is artistic in a different arena, with her clothing design.

Through my work with our advertising and publications I became a member of the Illustrators and Designers of Milwaukee, a group of advertising people, commercial illustrators, and art directors. The group had been in existence for quite a while, and I got involved through an artist whom we used for our advertising. He and I became friends, and he introduced me to the group. Some members were interested in plein air painting, and once a year a small group of us would go up to Door County, a beautiful part of Wisconsin, and paint. Door County is on a peninsula that juts out into Lake Michigan, so there are woods and farms in the interior and a long shoreline with boats and lighthouses, beaches, and beautiful rock formations. We would go up in the fall, when the leaves were turning, and spend our days painting and evenings discussing the day's work. There were some very accomplished artists in that group, and it was always inspiring to see other artists' work and get comments and critiques from fellow painters.

I really enjoyed those trips, but after a time I got too busy with work to keep that up. I had to drop out, and a number of the others moved on as well. I kept sketching and would try to find time to paint, but for a while my work took over. Then, after a lapse of quite a few years, I got a phone call from one of that original group. He said, "Hey Willie, how about getting a small group of us and continuing that painting we used to do years ago?" I jumped at the chance, because to paint like that you really need to set aside time, specific dates where that's all that you do for that week. If you think you're going to do it at home with a very intense job, you'll be disappointed. So we started back up again, four of us. We would paint in Door County in the spring and go to different places in the fall—Florida, Arizona, Colorado, some East Coast areas. We had to go to warm weather because we painted outside, on location. For me, my design work and my painting were two sides of a coin because both involve working with form and color and shapes.

I was doing well at work and inspired by all the different projects, but challenges to the business kept coming. The competition got more and more intense and the costs of maintaining and upgrading our manufacturing facilities were rising, both at our Capitol Drive factory and at our Juneau Avenue headquarters and final assembly operation.

We did get a good boost in sales when we came out with the new Shovelhead engine in 1966. Our touring bikes had been getting heavier, first with the addition of rear suspension on the Duo-Glide and then with the new electrical system for the Electra Glide. The Shovelhead's added power made a real performance difference, which riders loved. Still, between the little M-50 and our updated Sprint, our Italian lightweights made up half of our sales in the mid-1960s. In 1967 we introduced a 65cc model with a stretched tank, a look that fit better into our lineup than the M-50. Those M-65s sold well. Our overall volume held steady through that period while our Japanese competitors kept growing, and there were people who felt we should focus more on the lightweights, mimicking what the Japanese were doing. Fortunately, my father and others in company leadership felt the way I did, knowing that the big V-Twins like our new Shovelhead were what Harley-Davidson was all about and that we needed to maintain the traditions that had been nurtured over the years.

It was tough going, though, and it wasn't getting any easier.

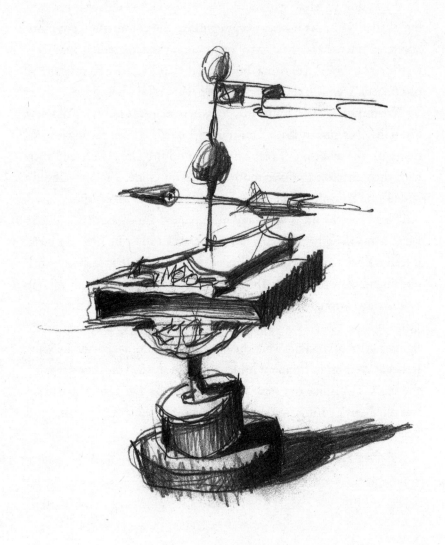

CHAPTER 8

BIG CHANGES

When the Harley-Davidson Motor Company incorporated in 1907, stock was issued to the founders and original board members of the new company. Since that time the company had stayed private, with most of the stock in the hands of the founders' families. That changed in 1965: Harley-Davidson "went public," selling shares in the company on the American Stock Exchange (later renamed the New York Stock Exchange).

The motorcycle market was being transformed as sales of Japanese exports continued to climb. Our sales had risen after bottoming out in 1963, but we needed funds to upgrade both our aging factories and our motorcycle product line. Harley-Davidson needed capital, and selling stock seemed to be the best way to generate it. Going public meant giving up some of the control we'd always had as a family-owned company. It was a big step and there were lots of reasons to be concerned, all sorts of arguments for and against. The arguments *for* won out.

The stock sale went well, from what I understood at the time. I was focused on my work, the design side, and trusted my father and the other company leaders to make the right decisions. There were different ideas about what would be the best way to move Harley-Davidson forward. We were basically a one-product company; motorcycles were our business. Golf carts were a good sideline, but those V-Twin powered bikes were our heritage. In the business environment of the 1960s, some major shareholders felt we should branch out further. As we got into 1967 and 1968, even some members of the founding families thought we'd be better off finding a business partner, merging with a larger business. Mergers were a big thing at that time, and it turned out we didn't need to go looking. One came looking for us.

In fall 1968, a company named Bangor Punta announced that it would pay a premium for Harley shares, intending to take over the company. Bangor Punta was a big conglomerate, one of those holding companies that became popular in the 1960s, buying up businesses of different sorts. Company leadership and family members still owned more than half of Harley-Davidson's stock, and my father spoke out against the deal. Bangor Punta responded by raising their offer—they weren't going away. Realizing that a deal was going to happen one way or another, it was decided that we'd be better off going with a different big conglomerate—AMF, American Machine & Foundry. Bangor upped their offer again after the deal with AMF was announced, and things went back and forth for two months, with Bangor suing the company and the board, trying to force their way in. The AMF deal went to a vote of the stockholders in December, and in January 1969 the sale to AMF was finalized. Harley-Davidson Motor Company became part of AMF's portfolio.

Looking back, it's hard to know exactly what to think about that deal. With all of the business challenges and Bangor Punta trying to take over the company, my father and the board felt we were forced into a corner and needed to come up with a different solution or we'd lose out. My brother was closer to the discussions, and I know he felt we should try to find a way to stay independent, but maybe it was too late.

AMF said they would keep Harley management in place and work with us to preserve our identity. The board was convinced that being part of a larger conglomerate with more resources would allow us to grow and adjust to the times.

AMF had a broad portfolio of products and companies that covered everything from Ski-Daddler snowmobiles to bowling pins. The company thought we would be a big addition to their recreational division, but they really didn't understand the unique aspects of our business. Harley-Davidson was run by enthusiasts like my father, who was an avid rider all of his life; he deeply understood the mystique and the products, where we came from, and what we were trying to do. Our business is built on passion and our unique relationship with our riders. It's different with a big company like AMF. You can lose some of that contact and maybe some of the good relations that have been built up over many, many years. AMF didn't appreciate the heart of what we do or the amount of money it took to keep this thing fired up.

None of that was obvious right away. The top AMF people made statements that sounded good, and at the beginning things seemed OK. They brought in funding, as they'd promised, along with lots of new people with different ideas about how things should be done.

Nothing changed much in my area at the beginning of the relationship, but before long I was feeling it. One immediate change was AMF's control of how our printed pieces would look—catalogs and manuals and packaging. They had a corporate design manual that put a tight rein on what we could do graphically. Our product catalog had to have the same look as the catalogs for their bicycles and swimming gear and golf accessories. AMF publications all had a color block area that came down from the top like a window shade, and all the type was Helvetica. That was specified in the corporate manual. So we could fill in the circular area in their template with product imagery, but we had to use the window shade with "AMF Harley-Davidson" in Helvetica, then "Accessories" or whatever. If you look back at that era, you will see that style of type and layout. It matched all the other AMF recreational product brochures.

It was harder to take when they insisted that we put "AMF" on our gas tanks, right alongside our "Harley-Davidson" name. That's the most valuable piece of real estate on our motorcycles: the place where our name is located. The way we present our trademark is done with a lot of care, never as an afterthought. The stacked "Harley-Davidson" that goes all the way back to the founders and those beautiful graphics from the Great Depression—that bird, the art deco trim with the flying wheel—are an important part of our visual heritage. Whether it's a cast or stamped Harley-Davidson name plate, paint, or a decal, our tank trim is a major design element. I did everything I could to minimize the AMF part of that. You can see that when you look at our bikes from that period.

Around the time of the AMF buyout I was at work on a new design, a bike that would bring more of a custom feel to our lineup. I had been following the custom scene all my life—always very interested, as an artist, in what individual riders were doing to their motorcycles—and it seemed that most of the customs that I was aware of were based on Harley-Davidsons. I think there's a good reason for that: the proportions are right. *Proportion* is a magical word to any designer. It's got to be the right arrangement of wheels, and mass, and color, and form, and shapes, and then the rider's got to look good on it. Harley-Davidson motorcycles, with the way our V-Twin engines are set in the frame, have always had that kind of a look. On the West Coast, customizers were taking that look and following the "bobber" trends, which started with people wanting to go faster. They took parts off that they thought they could do without, lightened the bike, and the motorcycle got simpler. It created more of a performance look because it had minimal sheet metal.

So in 1971 we came out with the Super Glide. It had the big V-Twin and chassis of our Electra Glide, married to the lighter front end of our Sportster. I did a kind of exotic tail section, which I think was pretty extreme for that time frame, and the bike overall had a nice, uncluttered look. I did a red, white, and blue paint scheme that we called Sparkling America. That motorcycle was the first factory custom, and from there the company took on a focus of feeding the custom desire that's been such an enormous part of who we are. The Super Glide became the foundation of a series of bikes that changed our industry, so I'm very proud of that motorcycle.

Harley-Davidson introduced a completely different product the next year—a snowmobile. Midwestern winters are perfect for that type of vehicle. We had been discussing developing a snowmobile before the AMF merger, and then snowmobiling took off in the early 1970s. Ski-Doo was kind of the start of the whole thing, and for a while a lot of manufacturers got into it: Evinrude, Johnson, John Deere . . . multiple brands. AMF had its own snowmobile called the Ski-Daddler. Ours came out in 1972, then we made a more powerful 440cc model in 1974. They were good machines, and well received, but we hit some bad winters in the early 1970s—bad meaning not so much snow, which hurt sales. It just wasn't that strong of a thing to be involved in; it was a complex product and very capital-intensive to redesign, so we got out in 1975.

For me as a designer, though, those were fun to do. I'm proud of the design because in that era, snowmobile hoods had these goofy headlights sticking up, a very awkward-looking feature. I wanted a cleaner shape, so I designed louvers on the hood and buried the headlight underneath those louvers. It still worked as a light but without that strange, periscope look. Louvers are always functional looking, like air scoops, and I could get a side elevation that was really clean—it had a nice slope to the center line. I was the first guy to kind of bury that headlight rather than having pop-ups, which Ski-Doo and all the others had, and I think the visuals worked great. I did a red-white-and-blue graphic, and I designed the clothing for it—boots and mitts and the whole thing. I enjoyed that.

At that time my small design office was on the second floor of the Juneau Avenue factory, where our motorcycles were built. Most of the parts were made out at Capitol Drive and assembled at Juneau. The second floor at Juneau held the offices for the non-manufacturing departments: engineering, accounting, purchasing. There was an early computer system, service, advertising, and of course the executive offices, all on that second floor. Above us on the third floor was motorcycle assembly. Parts would come in from Capitol Drive to the fifth floor for welding and fabrication, then to the sixth floor for treatment, next to the paint shop for painted parts, then down to the ovens in the basement. Assembly was done on the fourth and third floors, then the finished bikes would go down the elevator to the first floor for testing, crating, and shipping. That exciting work was happening all around me.

The founders built that factory in the years before World War I, and when they finished they said they could build twenty-five thousand motorcycles a year out of it. They did that and more in 1920 and for a few years during World War II, but even after adding the Capitol Drive plant we were hard-pressed to maintain production levels much higher than that. We built over thirty-seven thousand bikes in 1971. I don't know how we accomplished that, but AMF wanted us to push harder, keep increasing production. We just didn't have the factory space.

For a while we'd been talking about building a new factory on the land we got as part of the Capitol Drive deal, behind that plant. AMF had deep pockets, and they were helping us with new machining equipment at Capitol Drive, bringing us up to date, but they didn't like the idea of taking on the cost of new construction. They came up with a different idea.

A guy named Rodney Gott was chairman of AMF when they acquired Harley-Davidson, and he was a motorcycle enthusiast; he had been very much in favor of the acquisition. My father and my brother got along fine with him; they respected him. Gott knew that there was a big plant in York, Pennsylvania, that wasn't being used. It was a military plant built during World War II that AMF acquired in the mid-1960s and manufactured various products there. Rodney himself had run the plant. He felt it would make more sense to move motorcycle production to York than to build a new factory in Milwaukee. AMF wasn't getting along very well with the labor unions in Wisconsin, so Pennsylvania might have sounded good for that reason too. So in 1972 they began modernizing that plant for motorcycle production.

AMF had experts in manufacturing but not in motorcycle manufacturing, so they moved some Harley people to York to help set up the new facility. They told everyone it was going to be state-of-the-art, the most modern motorcycling factory anywhere, with an overhead conveyor system that would move the bikes through the assembly process, and a new paint facility. It promised to be a significant improvement on the outdated processes in Milwaukee. Engines and transmissions would still be built at Capitol Drive, then shipped to York, where everything else would be done. New systems and machinery were being installed at Capitol Drive to support the increase in production. It was a major effort and a very expensive project.

Once they got started updating the York plant, that project moved fast. They began producing frames during the 1972 model year, and in 1973 the entire assembly operation was moved there. With everything up and running at the new plant, a complete bike rolled off the assembly line every ninety seconds. Production jumped to more than seventy thousand that year, but the transition wasn't as smooth as AMF had hoped. The move had a big impact on our workers as jobs in Milwaukee disappeared, and we had quality problems with different parts of the motorcycles as the new systems got ironed out. For our family, my relatives, but also the bigger Harley-Davidson family, the move was emotional. After seventy years of making Harley-Davidson motorcycles in Milwaukee, the last bikes rolled out the door at Juneau and the line went silent.

CHAPTER 9

RED, WHITE, AND BLUE

In 1969, Harley-Davidson factory racer Mert Lawwill won the AMA Grand National Championship. He was the top rider on our flat track team, and to celebrate we wanted to create a unique graphic. Every racer has a number plate on their race bike, with the same number on their racing gear, so they can be easily identified during competition. The winner of the Grand National gets to race with the "No. 1" plate for the entire season the following year, so to commemorate Mert's win I designed a graphic with a big number 1. I set bold stars and stripes within the frames of the italicized numeral, with Harley-Davidson across the base. The numbers were italicized on most racers' number plates, so I angled it like that, and the red, white, and blue flag symbolism just seemed right with our brand. The first use of that graphic was as a poster to celebrate Mert's number one championship.

That 1969 title was a big victory for us. Joe Leonard had won the AMA Grand National Championship in 1954, the first year of that competition, and from 1954 through 1966 Harley-Davidson riders won it each season except for one year. For twelve out of thirteen years, a Harley-Davidson rider rode with the No. 1. Then Triumph's Gary

Nixon won it two years in a row, 1967 and 1968. Getting the No. 1 back in 1969 was something we wanted to celebrate, so I created that poster with the big red, white, and blue No. 1. It seemed to be a neat graphic, but I never thought it would go beyond the poster. Lo and behold, that No. 1 grew very, very popular. It became a logo we used in advertising, a part of our packaging, a symbol that was used on a lot of our clothing; it was on banners, hats, and jewelry. The '71 Super Glide carried it on the tank. That No. 1 got good mileage. Rightfully so, because I think it really fits our company as a graphic, and to this day it's still very much used. I'm proud that it has become a timeless part of our history.

From the years I was out in Los Angeles in the late 1950s through the '60s, our race team rode KRs. We had a guy named Dick O'Brien running the team, and he was a genius at finding talent, both racers and tuners. O'Brien was a master tuner himself, and he did an amazing job pushing those flathead KRs to the front of the pack, even as our British competitors started racing updated overhead valve engines. To level the playing field between the older flatheads and the more powerful overhead valves, the AMA placed size limits on the different engine types. Our KR was a 750cc flathead, a side-valve engine; overhead valve engines were required to be smaller, limited to 500cc. As we kept on winning, the British teams, BSA and Triumph, complained about those regulations. Then Triumph won those two years in a row, and things started to change.

For the 1970 season, the AMA lifted that size cap, allowing bikes powered by 750cc overhead valve engines to compete. That caught us by surprise—we didn't have a 750cc overhead valve race bike. With very little time to get something ready for the track, Dick O'Brien's mechanics took the closest thing we had, a 900cc competition Sportster, and modified the engine, reducing its displacement to 750cc.

That Sportster was called an XLR, and the new version became the XR-750. It was quite a thing to accomplish under pressure, and they got those bikes approved and on the track for the 1970 season ... but they didn't perform well. That modified Sportster engine had cast-iron heads, which caused it to overheat under race conditions. Through pure riding skill Mert Lawwill managed to win one race that season, but the unreliable "iron XR" doomed his chances of holding on to that No. 1 plate.

An engineer named Peter Zylstra joined O'Brien's team in 1969, and he got to work redesigning the XR-750. AMF wasn't paying much attention to the factory race team, being focused on revamping operations and building the plant in York. With the team still riding the iron XRs, we had another bad season in 1971, but O'Brien managed to get funding to complete the XR-750 redesign in time for the 1972 season. The new bike was everything the race team hoped for—more powerful, lighter, and with better handling. Factory rider Mark Brelsford rode the new XR through a championship season, recapturing the No. 1 plate for Harley-Davidson.

Flat track racing is incredible to watch; it's a great spectator sport. The tracks are short, a half mile or a mile, so you can see the whole track. The racers go all out on the straightaways, then power-slide through the corners, going almost sideways as they work to keep their speed up and come out of the turn roaring into the straight. Success on the racetrack reinforces brand strength. And the races give riders a destination; it's a series of events that riders attend, and another reason to ride. The excitement of racing helped build the sport of motorcycling, and racing is important to supporting the success of the brand.

It's not surprising, then, that as the Japanese motorcycle brands kept growing in the US, they decided to start competing in flat track, the most popular form of motorcycle racing in America. Our team had a great new racing motorcycle beginning in 1972, but we also had new competitors. The British began to drop out of flat track racing as the Japanese came on, and in 1973 and 1974 Kenny Roberts won the Grand Nationals on a Yamaha. O'Brien's crew was continuing to refine the design of the XR-750 though, and from 1975 on we were almost unbeatable. With great riders such as Jay Springsteen, Scotty Parker, and Chris Carr, Harley-Davidson won the Grand National Championship twenty-five out of the next thirty years. Winning races for almost fifty years—that's hard to believe, but it's true. The XR-750 is recognized as the most successful racing motorcycle ever built.

The XR-750 also became a star outside the motorcycle racing community when Evel Knievel started using it as his jump bike. Evel had started his daredevil career in the mid-1960s riding Japanese bikes. He'd switched to a Triumph by 1967 when he crashed horribly attempting to jump the fountains at Caesar's Palace in Las Vegas. Once he recovered and began performing again, he didn't settle on a particular jump bike until our XR-750 appeared in 1970. Evel tried out an XR and pronounced it the best-handling, fastest motorcycle he'd ever ridden. He loved the idea of riding a US-made motorcycle, and our marketing people thought his tough, all-American persona fit well with our brand, so we signed up as his major sponsor.

Our deal with Evel was to provide him with XR-750 jump bikes along with major promotional efforts. The XR was built for the dirt track, and it required some modifications to adapt it for ramp-to-ramp jumping. No motorcycle is built for that, and if you got the chance to examine Evel's ramps, you'd understand the punishment that jump bike had to take. Evel had figured out the correct angle to launch him across cars, or whatever he decided to jump, but his equipment was primitive, scary to look at up close. Hitting that takeoff ramp at eighty miles an hour had to shake him to his core, and landing, unless he landed perfectly, was worse—for both him and the bike.

Managing our new relationship with Evel Knievel fell under my brother's department. They arranged to deliver the motorcycles and hired an expert mechanic, Roger Reiman, to prepare them for Evel. Reiman had had a very successful career as a Harley-Davidson racer, winning the Daytona 200 three times and the Grand National Championship in 1964 before taking over his parents' Harley dealership in Illinois. Like many successful racers, Reiman had become an expert at setting up his motorcycle for peak performance, making the modifications necessary to meet the demands of different types of races.

One of the first things Reiman had to do was install brakes on the XR-750—flat track race bikes didn't have brakes in that era, relying instead on the rider's skill to control the speed sliding the bike sideways. There were a number of other modifications, and I'm sure they figured some of it out as they went. With Harley providing promotion, Evel started jumping at big stadiums in major cities while keeping up with his standard schedule of state fairs and promotional jumps at dealerships. We featured him on the cover of *The Harley-Davidson Enthusiast* and arranged for other publicity, but whatever we did, Evel always wanted more. He was great as a spokesperson in public, praising the quality of our motorcycles and the company, but in private he could be a real challenge to deal with. There was no denying his promotional skills—he was a master showman—but he was rough on poor Duane Unkefer, the Harley employee who managed our sponsorship relationship. Evel liked to spend money, and there were regular disagreements over the expenses Harley-Davidson should cover under the terms of our agreement.

Through 1971 Evel did more and more high-profile shows at places like the Houston Astrodome and Madison Square Garden, so despite any challenges it was obvious that the relationship was shining a light on Harley-Davidson. Evel had a genius for generating publicity. He was a relentless self-promoter and a tireless performer, traveling all over the country jumping week after week. When he'd crash, you'd think that might be the end, but he'd get back up and hit the road to the next stop. There were times he'd land a jump hard, ride in front of the stands smiling and waving to the crowd, but then, out of sight of the spectators, he'd be helped off the bike and loaded into an ambulance—and later send the hospital bill to Duane Unkefer.

As Evel became a superstar, it became more of an event when he'd visit Juneau Avenue for a meeting or to check out some new bikes. Lots of employees were thrilled to know he was in the building. When he had time, he would come to our home and visit with me, Nancy, and the kids, and we got to know each other pretty well. He was a unique guy. Evel performed in Chicago a few times during those first years with Harley, and I was able to take the family to see him jump. That was exciting, especially for the kids. He was always gracious to our family, and it was pretty neat for Bill, Karen, and Michael to be able to tell their friends they knew him. When Bill was a junior in high school, he signed up for a bike-a-thon to raise money for the American Diabetes Association. He wrote Evel a letter asking him to sponsor his ride, and Evel wrote back with a pledge of $1,000. That was Evel—he could be prickly in lots of situations, but privately he was often thoughtful and kind. Of course Bill ended up raising more money than anyone else in the fundraiser, and he won a little black-and-white TV. Even better, he and Evel stayed in touch. Evel would check in with Bill from time to time to see how he was doing.

In 1973 Evel did a big show at the LA Coliseum that was featured on ABC's *Wide World of Sports* broadcast. That was a big deal. *Wide World of Sports* was a show that families across America would sit down on Saturdays to watch. By that time Evel had also signed a bunch of other sponsors, including Ideal Toy Company. We didn't think much of that when he first started talking about it. Like everything he did, it was going to be the biggest thing ever. That time he was right: it seemed like every young boy in America wanted an Evel Knievel Stunt Cycle toy for Christmas in 1973.

Kids all over the country were playing with an Evel Knievel figure, jumping a plastic XR-750 with the Harley-Davidson No. 1 logo on the tank, just like the 1971 Super Glide. The Stunt Cycle was just the first in a line of successful Evel Knievel toys. Evel had started wearing his famous red, white, and blue leathers in 1971, with a helmet bearing the No. 1 logo on the side, and he used that logo on his other gear and equipment. It matched his whole color scheme better than our traditional Bar & Shield. The toys and the packaging often featured a different version of our No. 1. Ideal Toy didn't ask permission to modify it; they just did it. That version was straight up and down, not slanted, and removed the feet at the base of the numeral. It had fewer red and white stripes and said "Evel Knievel—King of the Stuntmen" at the top. But it was definitely modeled on our Harley-Davidson No. 1 and probably helped popularize the original logo. What's certain is that a lot of kids who played with the Evel Knievel Stunt Cycle or built ramps to jump their bicycles after seeing him on *Wide World of Sports* grew up and bought Harley-Davidson motorcycles.

If your claim to fame is jumping over things on a motorcycle, you've got to keep finding different things to jump to attract attention. Evel started out jumping boxes full of rattlesnakes and riding through burning walls. After his failed attempt with the fountain at Caesar's, he took to jumping over rows of cars or buses. At a county fair or a motorcycle dealership he could get away with a standard jump, a particular number of cars that he'd jumped repeatedly and was almost certain to land safely. For a bigger event, or to make a stir in the media, he had to try to break a record or do something new and exciting. Even with a stunt as crazy as jumping a motorcycle over fifteen cars or ten Mack trucks, if you keep doing it over and over, people will begin to lose interest.

In 1972, Evel started telling people he was working on the greatest, craziest stunt anyone had ever attempted: he was going to jump across a 1,700-foot-wide canyon, the Snake River Canyon outside Twin Falls, Idaho. Harley-Davidson would help fund the development of his "Skycycle," even though it was a rocket, not a motorcycle. It was a crazy enough stunt to gain a lot of attention, and as a key sponsor Harley would share in that. Evel spent two years building excitement for his jump attempt, and as the date approached he was all over the media, on the cover of *Sports Illustrated*, signing a deal for a nationwide closed-circuit broadcast.

Sunday, September 8, 1974, was the day Evel would attempt to jump over the Snake River Canyon. The promotion and advertising had been strong, and there were lots of reporters and cameras on-site for the event. Evel had promised a million-dollar party at the jump site, and fans who couldn't make it to Idaho gathered in theaters in major cities around the country to watch it live. Prior to the jump Evel had come to me for designs for the paint scheme for his rocket, which had the Harley-Davidson No. 1 logo on its tail, and he invited Nancy and me to the canyon for the jump. We flew in with my brother and his wife and went out to the launch site on the day of the jump.

When we got there, we were amazed to see the stark contrast between the jump equipment and the canyon. The ramp on the edge of the cliff looked tiny in comparison to the scale of the canyon. It was built up on a big dirt mound, and the rocket looked like a miniature up against the giant hole in the earth. There were a lot of people crowded into a dusty pasture surrounding the ramp, with security and barriers to keep the crowd away from the rocket. We were escorted into a fenced-in VIP area on the edge of the canyon, close to the Skycycle X-2 steam rocket.

Evel's entrance was typical Knievel showmanship. He arrived in a Learjet, flying low, almost grazing the canyon walls, then shooting straight up to the clouds. It was a star performer's entrance, in a style only Evel could pull off. We couldn't see where the jet landed, but Evel came to the site by helicopter, and we spent some time with him prior to the jump. Other famous people were there as well—I remember seeing Billie Jean King.

The anxious crowd was amped up in anticipation of what was an uncertain outcome—looking at the whole setup, you had to question whether he could complete this dangerous feat. Some attendees had been at the site since Saturday, and everyone became more and more excited as the time for Sunday's jump approached. There was pushing and shoving, and the crowd kept moving closer to the canyon, where a snow fence provided a weak barricade to keep spectators from going over the edge.

Nancy and I stood at the canyon's edge watching Evel get lowered into his rocket. Excitement stirred as he was strapped in and seemed ready to go. According to the plan, the rocket would shoot high into the sky, then parachutes would bring it down on the other side of the canyon.

At least, that was the *plan*. When the rocket launched off the ramp, the force caused the parachute to deploy early. The rocket shot up over the canyon, but when the parachute deployed, the shock ripped the dead man's stick out of Evel's hands. That's a control that turns off the rocket engine if the pilot passes out or lets go of it. The parachute coming out early shortened the trajectory, and the rocket, slowed by the parachute, headed straight down into the river at the bottom of the canyon. When the crowd realized Evel was going down into that canyon, they tried to rush to the rim. There was a lot of screaming.

Nobody knew what was happening, and we all feared the worst. After a bit, an announcement came over the PA system that Evel was safe, and a little while later the helicopter brought him up from where he'd landed in the canyon. If the rocket had gone in the river with him strapped in, he would have drowned (or possibly died on impact). It appeared that he was OK, and all Nancy and I could do was go back to our hotel and wait for word, hoping he wasn't badly hurt.

After all of the lead-up to the event, it was strange just to sit around wondering what had happened—the whole thing was like from another world. A post-launch analysis would reveal a design flaw in the mechanical parachute cover on the Skycycle X-2. This engineering flaw was later proven to be the reason for the jump failure. There was no questioning Evel's courage and willingness to risk the launch. Given all the planning discussions, we thought Evel would be safe, but we later learned that the rocket engineer who worked with him to develop the X-2 had tried to talk him into postponing the launch. Tests with two test rockets had both failed, but after all the build up Evel had decided that the show had to go on.

When the phone finally rang in our hotel room, Nancy thought Evel must be calling from the hospital, but he wasn't. He said everything was fine and he was inviting us out to dinner! We ate together, and Evel acted as if it were just another evening. He and I remained friends for a long time after his jump, and Nancy and I were glad we had been there with him for that amazing and dangerous event.

Evel's fans didn't blame him for the failure at the Snake River Canyon, and he had some great jumps over the next few years, but his willfulness and temper led him to do things that destroyed his career. By the end of the 1970s his fans and his sponsors—including Harley-Davidson—had abandoned him. He suffered from ill health but lived to see a new generation of fans embrace his legacy and relive his glory days. I'm glad to have known Evel Knievel and proud that he rode our motorcycles. Our museum installed a major exhibit covering his career and accomplishments in 2010, and our great dealer in Topeka, Kansas, has created a wonderful museum in his honor.

The red, white, and blue No. 1 logo continues to find new fans too. It has remained popular as a device on clothing and accessories and on more of our motorcycles. Few people remember that it was created to celebrate a specific racing accomplishment. It's taken on its own identity—all-American, symbolizing freedom—and I'm proud that it's still popular and finding new uses.

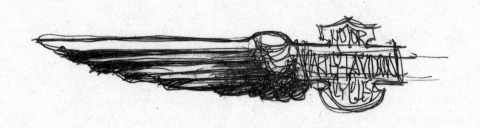

CHAPTER 10

THE EARLY DAYS OF THE HOUSE OF HITS

*I*t was strange to walk through the upper floors of our Juneau Avenue headquarters in 1974, thinking of my grandfather walking the line talking to the workers, and seeing those spaces where our classic Knuckleheads were made be converted to offices. Moving motorcycle assembly to York was the most visible of the many changes that happened as AMF pushed its way into every area of our business operation. AMF had a large executive group back East who ran their various business entities, and though they didn't know anything about the motorcycle business, they figured a motorcycle was a product, so the business principles they believed in should apply to us. The company had experts in labor, so they brought some tough negotiators from that group to work on labor relations. They had a big finance department, so they sent finance experts our way—they had more scorekeepers than you could believe. The company also had experts in manufacturing who got involved in York and at Capitol Drive.

Despite the leadership my father had shown over decades of guiding the company through challenge after challenge, AMF had pushed him into retirement in 1973, feeling that their people could offer more expertise in direction and management. My mother had died shortly before the merger, so she didn't live to see the difficulties of the years that followed or her husband stepping down when he still had so much to offer. My brother, John, was named president and chairman of the board that year, a move that suggested AMF intended to maintain some continuity with our heritage, but he had to deal with layers of AMF management full of people with big ideas for how we should run the Motor Company. He couldn't tell all those experts to go away. He had to work with them, negotiate, sit in endless meetings when he wanted to be out on the floor running the business day to day the way our father had. It was exhausting.

While other areas of our business were being examined and shifted toward an AMF standard, the company didn't seem anxious to push me in any particular direction, beyond insisting that we put their logo on the bikes and conform to the company's graphic standards for catalogs and such. My brother said it was because management didn't understand what was going on "in that back room." They were smart enough to recognize that no one in their company had expertise in motorcycle styling, and they didn't understand our customers, so they mostly left me alone. I felt fortunate in that and did everything I could to keep it that way.

With the FX Super Glide we had added an important new model to our lineup that didn't require a big expenditure in manufacturing tooling. AMF appreciated that. The company liked the good press we were getting and the fact that our sales were up, but they still had some people who thought we should change direction, try to be more like Honda, abandon our V-Twin and all those decades of heritage, and cater more to the customers who were buying Hondas and Kawasakis and Yamahas. We all fought against that idea, and my brother and a number of other people in leadership managed to make the argument that messing with the foundation of the company would be the quickest way to destroy it. But even that was not an easy battle to win.

Our golf cart business was growing, there was a whole line of Italian lightweights to freshen up, AMF was pressuring me to come up with more new models, and I was alone in our design office. Ed Saffert had retired, and I needed a new model maker with some fabrication ability. I talked with my friend John Bradley about the situation over lunch one day, and he somewhat reluctantly told me they had a young guy over at Brooks Stevens who he thought would be a good fit. His name was Louie Netz, and John said he'd be very sorry to lose him, but he was showing great promise in their model shop and was a motorcycle rider. The three of us got together for lunch, Louie showed me his portfolio; he was obviously excited by the opportunity, and I had a good feeling about his potential. With the way things ran under AMF, I couldn't just hire him; I had to wait until the right time in a budget cycle, but Louie didn't seem worried by the delay. He was young, twenty-two or twenty-three, and he took the opportunity to travel for a few months until I could bring him on. It was August 1974 when he walked in as a new employee, and that started a long creative partnership.

It was a long walk from the main Juneau Avenue entrance to my studio—the full length of the building, all the way to the narrow west end of the old factory. The studio wasn't much at the time, just a two-room office across the hall from accounts payable. A set of double doors led into my small office, where I had my drafting board, then another set of double doors opened into a larger workspace set up for small-scale modeling work. Louie was a good clay modeler, and at Brooks he'd made some full-scale mockups. We had to do a lot of three-dimensional stuff to transfer our thoughts to engineering, so we could work with them to take our designs into production. To do that more effectively, we'd need to build out a functional fabrication shop where Louie could work with wood and plastic and fiberglass.

I left the shop build-out to Louie while I kept up with all of the design projects on our plate. Louie wasn't familiar with corporate finance, purchase orders, and things like that. Fortunately Juneau had a petty cash window where he could draw small amounts, which he used to buy used shop equipment that he found through the classifieds. He was anxious to get set up, and within a few months he'd moved in a table saw, a jointer, and a band saw—a good start on a model shop. Louie was a diligent worker, and he honed his skills while fleshing out the shop. He brought in more tools and managed to arrange the space so we had room to build full-scale mockups. Over a couple of years he graduated from spray cans to paint-spray guns to airbrushes, and we had all the capabilities we needed for model making.

The first big project in our model shop was a complicated one. Engineering was prototyping a new front end for a touring bike with a fixed front fairing. Our "batwing" fairing had evolved from our early touring windshields—a partial shell on the front of the bike that shielded the rider from wind and rain. The fairing attaches to the forks of the bike and moves with the handlebars. A fixed fairing mounts to the frame of the bike so it stays stationary when the handlebars turn the front wheel.

The front end for the frame-mounted fairing can be quite complex. The modifications engineering was developing required completely rethinking the shape and form of the fairing. Louie created a full-scale fairing mock-up out of Styrofoam with clay on top and some fiberglass, and got to work. Like most of our projects, we iterated—build a model, modify it, learn something, tear it down, and try again—and try after try, you get closer to a final answer. We worked hand in hand with engineering to resolve issues. It can take a lot of trial and error to get to a solution that looks right and satisfies engineering's requirements. That project became the FLT Tour Glide, the twin-headlight ancestor of today's Road Glide, one of our most popular current models. We moved on from the fairing to the tour pack and saddlebags, and the bike was introduced in 1979.

Five years is a long development time, but some complicated projects take time. Louie and I worked through a lot of other design projects while that one was getting finalized. Even when the modifications in a model from one year to the next are minimal, annual changes to paint schemes and tank logos are time-consuming. Paint and decals can be a solution to create a different look on some models while working through other more complex projects. A great deal of thought goes into color and striping combinations, and we'll occasionally do special editions keyed to specific events. The first really elaborate one of those was the Liberty Edition paintwork and decals we did to celebrate the Bicentennial, America's 200th birthday party in 1976. We did a special paint finish with aluminum chips in the clearcoat and elaborate artwork with a big eagle and a Bar & Shield for a decal on the top of the tank and the front of the fairing.

It was just Louie and me in our Styling studio, but we sometimes got help from the outside, modeling and fabricating. Lou wasn't a welder, and we weren't able to do metal work in our modeling shop due to union regulations. Welding and brazing were union jobs, but engineering's experimental shop was right below us on the first floor, and I would use some of those fabricators in putting a bike together.

I've never had a shortage of ideas, and sales and marketing was crying for new models, so I felt encouraged to push the boundaries a bit in the mid-1970s when it came to product development. One bike that means a lot to me is the Café Racer, which we started on around the time Louie joined. Being a racing buff, it seemed to me that there was a place for a "racerly" looking Sportster, with low bars, a small fairing, and a racing profile. I sketched out a lot of ideas, taking cues from the flat-sided gas tank and integrated seat and rear fender of our XR-750, which was so successful on the track. As I refined my ideas, the details pushed us beyond the Sportster configuration into something that would be more complicated to fabricate. I had gotten to know a talented fabricator named Jim Haubert who'd set up his own machine shop after leaving our racing department. The Café Racer was going to be quite a departure from our other products at the time, so we contracted with Jim to build the prototype. We'd be free to experiment with more radical ideas working off-site, then hopefully we could show an impressive, finished product.

Jim Haubert was very smart, very driven. He was always building exotic stuff and working with different materials. After he left the racing department, my father had hired him to restore one of our early racers, a Petrali Peashooter, which he then donated to the Indianapolis Motor Speedway Museum. Jim did a beautiful job, then took on the first restoration of our 1903 single, "Serial Number One." He had to fabricate some delicate parts while completing that project and proved he could do just about anything. So it seemed like a natural choice to engage him for the Café Racer, and I was lucky to be given the freedom to do that.

Jim's machine shop was down in the old industrial area of Milwaukee. It was an unmarked building with a single door that opened right into the shop, with a machinist's table surrounded by Jim's tools and projects. The Café Racer was born in that shop. Jim would stop by our studio in the morning and give Louie a list of parts that he needed; Louie would gather the material, pull things from our parts warehouse, and deliver them to his shop. Jim would experiment with our standard parts, sometimes turning a part around backward and upside down to make it serve a completely different purpose, because he thought it would work better that way or he just liked the look.

Louie would report back after each trip, and we would go down there to consult with Jim and review progress. As we got into the 3-D forms, the fairing, the fuel tank, and the tail section, Louie got more involved. He learned some valuable techniques from Jim, which was an added bonus of that work. I wanted a big brass Bar & Shield on the gas tank. Louie made the prototypes out of brass printing plates, etching and antiquing them, then Jim showed him how to dolly them into a form to fit the tank using a special hammer and a sand-filled leather bag. I loved the way that proud Bar & Shield looked on that black tank, and when we finished the prototype I stuck the AMF logo down on the side cover, less conspicuous and away from our trademark. That was probably a violation of AMF policy, but I got away with it!

Some things came together nicely on that bike; other parts presented significant challenges. We started with a Sportster frame, but we had to change it to accommodate the unique pieces that made up the Café. We came up with a new triangulated frame that we used on later Sportsters. The all-black look was a significant element of the design that pushed us to some distinctive solutions. We went with cast wheels, which were new at the time, instead of the more traditional spoked wheels. Blacking out the exhaust was a challenge, due to the heat, and the radical "Siamese" pipes were a big part of the look of the bike. On our prototypes the pipes were coated in gloss black ceramic, like the finish of an old stove. That was one process that didn't make it to the final production model, but I was fortunate to be able to acquire that first prototype with the ceramic pipes for my personal collection. I used to ride it to work in the late 1970s.

That was a first: building that bike outside our normal product development arena and then presenting it to leadership as a finished product. I was thrilled that they liked it and approved it for production as part of the 1977 model lineup. I was really pleased with the way the Café turned out. The proportions were right on it, and the overall look with all the black finishes was very forward-looking. Maybe too much for a production bike—it turned people's heads at the time, but it was a little early. It was another step in changing people's ideas about Harley-Davidson at the time, which was important.

In our Styling studio we always had multiple projects in different stages of development, some of them relatively small, like new paint schemes and design tweaks on the Italian lightweights, some of them big, like working with engineering on the FLT. The Café Racer wasn't as complicated as the FLT, but it did require some significant work with engineering and manufacturing—new frame, new finishes, new parts. As the Café moved into preproduction, we were already at work on a new factory custom that built off the foundation of the original Super Glide. I had given the Super Glide the letter designation FX for "Factory Experimental"—a different line between our XL Sportsters and FL touring bikes. The Low Rider would be the next step in that FX line, factory models with the custom look that certain riders were hungry for.

Coming up with motorcycles that rang that bell is where I really came into the game. Being an avid student of the culture, I had a clear idea of what kind of bike would answer that all-important area of custom. We were a smaller, less complex company in that time, and I had a certain amount of freedom to experiment. I could create these vehicles in our model shop in the Styling studio, or working with Jim Haubert in his shop, and they could be approved for production by just a few people. I was able to create the Super Glide and the Café Racer and the Low Rider. Those models were extreme for the time and they told the motorcycling world that Harley-Davidson wanted to be in the custom business.

The Low Rider was a custom Big Twin with different trim and wheels and paint. We found ways to create a statement by combining different pieces—a lot of elements that already existed—analyzing them, trying different combinations, bouncing ideas around, continuously evolving where we were headed. As always, it was a matter of proportions. When you look at the overall motorcycle and how it relates to the ground, you find the proportions that work as a Harley-Davidson. Proportions are everything. A bike should be like a painting on a wall. A rolling sculpture.

With the Low Rider, we made it low to the ground and put together components that worked very well so that when the whole came together, the entire statement worked. We used drag bars—dragster-style straight handlebars that pull the rider forward into a more aerodynamic riding position—and extended the forks slightly to give it a custom performance look. We did some finishes on the engine that were significant, blacking out the cylinder heads and the cast engine covers, then buffing the edges of the fins on the cylinders so they showed silver. We used cast wheels like on the Café, black with silver highlights, which worked well with the engine treatment. The big touring-style tank was topped with a unique speedometer/tachometer console. The whole combination felt right, and it looked right.

That was the first time we'd ever called out for engine finishes, and that triggered all of the blacked-out parts and polished fins and other finishes that are fairly common today. Now the polished fin edges are done by machine, but those first ones were done by hand. The cylinders would be painted black and then the worker would hit the edges with a sanding block. That Low Rider was a turning point, a design project that I am very proud of, and it set the stage for the whole FX line of factory custom models to come.

To create the full-size Low Rider prototype, we worked with Jim Haubert again. By that time Jim had moved his machine shop to the basement of his home out in West Bend, about forty miles northwest of Milwaukee. Jim was busy creating clock mechanisms, trying to make a mechanical clock that would run on its own once it started, with no outside energy force. He was fascinated by that idea. Jim would make his own tools because he found a function that no existing tool served. It was the same with materials—he had an old foot-pedal-operated forge with a type of coal that he could get up to a high enough temperature to make unique alloys to serve specific purposes. That level of creative craftsman is rare, and he helped us build another great motorcycle in the Low Rider.

After a few months of intense work, we completed the running prototype, and Louie and I left Juneau on a Friday afternoon to pull it out of Jim's basement in West Bend. Louie was having a party at his house that night with a bunch of friends who were riders, and I rode it over there to get a reaction before taking it home to show my family. I always loved pulling into our garage on a new prototype and showing Nancy and the kids what was coming next.

On Monday I rode it to the office at Juneau for a presentation to executive staff, and they flipped over it. Everyone agreed that this was the right next step for the Super Glide line, and they loved that we'd managed to use so many off-the-shelf components. Minimizing the amount of new tooling required to manufacture the bike would save money and shorten the time it would take to get it into production.

The Low Rider was the right bike at the right time, because AMF had been analyzing our product development process, trying to figure out how we could get new products to market faster. They'd been sending Jeff Bleustein, a top engineer for AMF, to Milwaukee to assess our people and processes, and he came out full-time as vice president of engineering around the time the Low Rider got the green light. The FLT project was in motion but not progressing quickly, and we were beginning to discuss other long-range projects. At the same time, we were trying to address performance issues with some of our key components as well as encountering increased quality problems at the factory. With all of those things happening, an exciting new model that could go into production without a lot of new work was greeted with a combination of enthusiasm and relief. Jeff helped put systems in place to streamline the process, and in something like eighteen months we were building those bikes in York. That laid the groundwork for more factory customs to come.

As the first Low Riders started coming off the assembly line in early 1977, Louie and I decided we would take two from our factory in York and run them down the East Coast to Daytona for Bike Week. This would be a first for the Motor Company: ride a brand-new model into one of the world's biggest gatherings of our riders, give them a sneak peek at what was coming, and see how they'd react. Louie and I had become tight friends working together and we did a lot of riding together, so this seemed like a great idea.

It was early March when we flew out to pick up the bikes, and leaving from York, Pennsylvania, for Florida at that time of year can be a challenge on two wheels. You can hit ice and snow, which we did in the Blue Ridge Mountains. That delayed us a little, but we had a lot of fun and it was another motorcycle experience that I will always remember. We both fell in love and bonded with those motorcycles on that four-day ride. There's an instant connection when you finally get to spend time with your thoughts at seventy miles an hour along an inter-state, and I think both Louie and I were feeling that we'd gotten it right with those motorcycles. You get to look at one another going down the road at speed—there's nothing that can replace that, I think, in terms of an artist evaluating his work, seeing his work in context. We both got the sense that we were on to something big as we approached Daytona because we could see how many heads we were turning: in traffic, with people along the sidewalks, when we rolled in to park somewhere, or when we stopped for gas.

When we finally pulled onto the beach in Daytona, people came up and started asking questions. That event is packed with judges who have an eye for whether you've succeeded with your design or not, and they crowded around these bikes and were asking us things like, "Who built it?" as if it were a custom one-off. And that to me was a high point in my life because we were trying to create something that did in fact look like a one-off, yet produce it in volume. So we were happy to tell those riders, "These aren't one-offs. You can buy them, with this finish, and with this low seat height. And with this exhaust. With this unique tach-speedo." I will never forget that because the bike turned out really well. It was like, "OK, we did it. Let's go have a beer on this one!"

That Low Rider had a significant impact based on its design and how it looked. My passion for riding and all the rallies I attended had convinced me that there were a lot of people out there anxious for models they could purchase that had a certain *look*. They wanted a custom-looking bike they could buy from a dealer. The Low Rider lit a fire under that part of the motorcycle market, and its success showed AMF and the Motor Company the potential of what styling could do for the business. Dealers across the country told us the Low Rider really helped their business, because when those bikes came in, they immediately sold.

The Harley faithful tend to look at AMF as the big, bad wolf, but they did a lot of good, keeping our company going through difficult times. The problem was, it seemed like every positive came with a negative in some other area. With Jeff Bleustein leading the charge in engineering, AMF was pumping a lot of money into rebuilding our capabilities, bringing in people with valuable expertise from other industries, looking at problems we were having with our brakes, with our clutches, trying to improve the performance and reliability of key components. The quick turnaround with the Low Rider was proof that our product development processes were improving. Discussions had begun on a redesign of our big V-Twin, maintaining our trademark engine architecture while improving performance, reliability, durability, and fuel efficiency. During the first few years of Jeff's run as vice president of engineering, he was given all the resources he needed to make major improvements.

At the same time, when it came to manufacturing, AMF was obsessed with hitting unrealistic production numbers. While they were spending money on engineering and product development, they were dissatisfied with revenue from motorcycle sales and pushing for more volume. AMF instituted monthly production targets, and manufacturing was expected to get that many motorcycles out the door no matter what.

Quality suffered. Bikes were being shipped to dealers that were missing parts, that required work just to get them to run like they should. We had service representatives operating in the field who carried parts with them to help the dealers out. The workers in the factory knew what was going on, and it was difficult for many of them because they wanted to build quality motorcycles. They complained to their managers, but the managers had to meet the numbers.

In many ways, the dealers saved us during that time. They just wanted motorcycles that would take their customers down the road with smiles on their faces. They would get in a shipment of bikes, and instead of moving them out to the showroom floor, they'd test ride every one of them and often spend a day or a day and a half working on a brand-new bike before they would consider putting it out on the floor. That ate into the dealer's profit margin, so nobody was happy—AMF didn't think they were making enough money, so they were pushing problems out the door that made it harder for the dealer to make money. But our dealers were loyal to Harley-Davidson and they cared about their customers. They did everything they could to make sure their customers had good experiences.

One of the new executives whom AMF brought into our engineering department in the mid-1970s was Vaughn Beals. Vaughn became a key leader for our company, and product quality was one of the first problems he tackled when he came on board. As an effort to address the obvious quality issues, an audit team had been set up at York. Space had been designated on the factory floor, and the auditors would pull bikes coming off the end of the assembly line to run them through a thorough quality test. They'd identify specific issues and point out the problems to the managers on the line. They had been making progress but were encountering some resistance because the process slowed production.

Vaughn Beals got involved in the effort, looked at the audit program, and said, "This is good, but we're going to take it another step." We were going into production on the Café Racer, and Vaughn announced that we were going to stop production until we got the quality right on that bike. So we did a complete quality audit on every one that came off the line, ran through a full quality check, and test-rode every bike on the York test track. As a result, the Café Racers went out slowly, but they went out very, very good, and the feedback from the dealer network was, "Hey, this is fantastic, I didn't even have to adjust the chain." We were literally building quality into the motorcycles. The factory couldn't run a full test on every bike coming off the line like we did for Café Racers because it was important to keep production flowing. However, Vaughn saw to it that the audit program was expanded, and quality started to improve across all models.

With the Low Rider and the Café Racer in the new model lineup, 1977 was a big year. In Styling we completed the FLT work and moved on to the 1978 designs, with growing expectations that we'd begin developing new models to add to the FX line. Nineteen seventy-eight would be the 75th Anniversary of Harley-Davidson, so we developed some special paint and badging for anniversary models. Then, after eighteen years of making lightweights in our Aermacchi factory in Varese, Italy, AMF sold Aermacchi off to another Italian motorcycle manufacturer. I had enjoyed working on the lightweights, and those bikes got a lot of people on Harleys who later traded up to our larger models, but the relationship wasn't profitable enough from AMF's point of view.

Aermacchi was out of the picture, but a big new project with a different partner had been added to our plate. A decision had been made to develop a new, liquid-cooled line of motorcycles that would compete directly with our Japanese competitors. Engineering was partnering with Porsche Engineering Services on the engine design, beginning with a big V4, a four-cylinder engine. The thinking was that we would ultimately do a twin, a four-cylinder, and a six-cylinder, all liquid-cooled; the code name was Project Nova.

Nova involved both a touring and a custom, or standard, model. With an entirely new motorcycle to design from scratch along with our ever-expanding product line, we needed additional staff in Styling. Soon after we returned from Daytona I hired a designer named Dan Matre and got him working on new hand-control designs. Another talented designer, Vern Hunt, followed. Both Dan and Vern were multi-talented guys who knew motorcycles very well. As the projects piled up, we added a fifth member to the team, Gene Ikeler, to help from a model-shop point of view. It was tight in our small Styling studio, with three designers jammed into our model shop with a couple of 1940s steel desks along with tools and full-scale mockups, but we made it work and we all got along well.

I enjoyed being surrounded by creative people. I gave direction but made sure everyone had a lot of freedom to do their best work. Working in such close quarters it was easy to track what was going on. We were moving fast, and we often went from ideation sketches straight into 3-D. Sometimes I'd need polished renderings for a particular presentation, or if we were going to do some market research, but for most presentations we showed prototypes.

Going from drawing to modeling just meant getting up from your drawing board and walking across the room. We would either do full-size clay models or smaller prototypes out of acrylic and styrene and wood. For the full-size prototypes we would make what you call a clay buck, which is a structure built on a rolling chassis. Engineering and the great mechanics downstairs would put together a frame with an engine and two wheels, roll it in, and say, "There you go." We would build up a Styrofoam form to carve into a rough shape, pack clay on top, and then we'd start working, carving and shaping the clay. Once we were happy with a design we'd go back and forth with engineering, develop a running prototype, and start testing—everyone on the team would ride the motorcycles. Then we'd work with suppliers, the factory would tool it, and it'd go into production. There were of course many other steps and people involved, but I was fortunate to be able to stay focused on our design work. The Nova, with a totally new powertrain, would be even more complicated than the FLT, so that was going to take a few years. We'd complete a number of major model upgrades and a few new factory customs before anyone rode that one.

Working with the mechanics and machinists on the first floor, there was one guy that caught my eye. Louie and I both noticed that Earl Golden, a fabricator, took his work an extra step, adding aesthetic input to the basic fabrication of parts needed for engineering. Earl was also the only fabricator in that shop whom we saw doing real free-form modeling, like an outer shape for a fairing or a golf cart body where there are compound curves and surface development. Earl had a process with foam and plaster or Bondo for building up those forms. Louie and I started assigning projects to Earl, taking up more and more of his time, and gradually we absorbed him into our department. Earl ended up working with us for a long time, and Louie would later point out that he was the only guy he'd ever known besides Jim Haubert who progressed from working with existing tools and material to making his own tools and materials. Like Jim, he saw possibilities for things that required something that didn't yet exist.

Things were running smoothly with our expanded Styling team. We were working hard but in a positive atmosphere. We were having fun, and I truly believe the designs benefited from that. Working closely together in that way, injecting fun into the process, doesn't mean you work less; done right, it means you work better. Everything we did in the studio was informed by our experience with and on motorcycles. As a result, 1978 turned out to be a significant year for us.

We had to do something special for the Motor Company's Diamond Anniversary, and I was pleased that the main event was a ride. Our PR folks organized Harley-Davidson's first executive ride, with sixteen members of the leadership team—including me, my brother, Vaughn Beals, and Jeff Bleustein—taking part in the cross-country trip. We split up into groups of two or three and started from different parts of the country, riding to Louisville, Kentucky, for the AMA flat track race at Louisville Downs.

I drew a good route, leaving from Key West, Florida. There were three or four arranged stops each day, usually at dealerships, and I loved connecting with our dealers and our great riders. I had fun introducing myself to people and talking with them—they got a kick out of meeting a Davidson. Some of them recognized me from an article in our *Enthusiast* magazine or a story that one of the magazines had done about the Low Rider or the Café Racer, but not that many. By the mid-1980s I couldn't go to a motorcycle event without being recognized. That was nice too; I'm honored by that, but I enjoyed the low-key events on that 75th Anniversary ride. Once we all met back up in Louisville, we rode around the track at Louisville Downs and then watched our great and amazing race team compete. The XR-750 was running strong, and Jay Springsteen was carrying the No. 1 plate. Jay won the Grand National Championship that season for the third year in a row.

We all rode up to Milwaukee together after the weekend in Louisville. Most of the individual groups had picked up some riders along the way, so we had a good caravan for that last leg of the trip. Riding into Milwaukee with a big group of dealers and Harley enthusiasts was an appropriate way to celebrate the legacy of my grandfather William A., my Uncles Walter and Arthur, and Bill Harley.

It was early June when the Executive Ride rolled into Milwaukee, and two months later, in August, Louie and I rolled back out on our way to Sturgis. I had received a Special Achievement Award from AMF and had been made a VP: Vice President, Styling. Making my first trip to Sturgis seemed like a great way to celebrate that. Back then the event was much smaller. It was mainly a bunch of hardcore enthusiasts who loved to ride in the Black Hills. I had read about it and was fascinated, and I said to Louie, "We gotta ride out there. We gotta do this." I was really following the custom world and where the riders were going and what they were doing; I was very much interested in that and wanted to be part of it personally. That's been the story of my life—and it's been a good life.

Riding through South Dakota is really something special. Rolling across the Great Plains, the simplicity of that landscape and the way the light plays on the fields, being with a group of motorcyclists and watching that stretched-out caravan roll through a long curve, then feeling the power, the pulse of the V-Twin as you accelerate into another long, straight section of road—it's just something that strikes you emotionally. Those memories get inside you and stick with you.

Sturgis is unique, but any big ride you go on is memorable. You get excited the night before just packing, deciding what you're going to bring along. The weather is always unpredictable on a long ride, but you know that no matter what happens, you're still going to have the ride. We've been in hail. We've been in windstorms, heat, cold…I don't think there's anything I haven't ridden in yet, including mud and snow. Nature is exaggerated when you're on a motorcycle, but that's the stuff that makes the memories, and that's what the sport of motorcycling is about to me.

Sturgis began as a racing event, then gradually grew into something much bigger. Pappy Hoel was a dealer out there—I believe he was an Indian dealer—and he got together with a group of riders and started racing dirt track. He was part of a club called the Jackpine Gypsies, and he started hosting races in the late 1930s. He would let riders camp for free in a lot behind his dealership on the weekend of the races. Then more and more riders discovered the beauty of the Black Hills, and the rally grew. Anybody who's been there will tell you about the incredible visuals out there—the Black Hills are just gorgeous.

Black Hills is a translation of the name the Native Americans gave them. Approaching the area across the plains, from a distance, the hills look black because of the shadows from the sun. And from that first time I could just feel the atmosphere out there; it was a melting pot of beautiful scenery, interesting motorcycles, and great history—Native American history—steeped in the hills. When I think about it, the mixture of the motorcycles and that riding country and the Native American heritage all seem to blend in my head. Native Americans moved around, following the land, and motorcyclists are in a way a modern version of that.

Camping the first few times I went was at City Park, which was pretty wild back then. But there weren't thousands and thousands of people; it was just a small, hardcore group. I loved it. I really loved it. For a motorcyclist, it's a dream destination. Riding through the canyons, the scenery is staggering from the seat of a bike. By word of mouth, those little Sturgis races became a bigger rally and turned into a gigantic event, with people riding in from both coasts. There's tremendous riding—the Badlands, Mount Rushmore, Crazy Horse, Devil's Tower. It was obvious to me from that first time that it was gonna become a big deal.

Riding back to Milwaukee I kept thinking about all the beautiful motorcycles I saw out at Sturgis. There's something about riding that clears your head and gets ideas flowing, and what stuck in my mind was a lot of those motorcycles had sort of an essence of the Wild West. They were covered with leather and were black on black, and they had a different character from what you'd see somewhere else. I said to my friends, "You know what? We gotta do a motorcycle and call it the Sturgis." I could picture a beautiful black motorcycle that we'd name after that rally. We stopped at a wayside somewhere in Minnesota where I found a paper bag in a trash can and started writing some notes down, describing a mixture of finish treatments—dull black, wrinkle black, gloss black—and which components would get what finish. Then when I got back into the studio we got to work.

A blacked-out vehicle like I was picturing for the Sturgis, that's somewhat common today, but you have to take yourself back to that time and understand that we were the first ones to do it. The Café Racer was all black, but for the Sturgis we took it a step further. We added some subtle orange highlights—we put *Sturgis* on the front fork in orange script along with an orange Bar & Shield on the tank, with just a few subtle orange lines elsewhere. The overall look shows you the impact of less is more. That bike had a visual that I thought was really connected to Sturgis.

One thing that took a lot of work, a lot of testing, was finishing the engine covers in gloss black. We did a wrinkle black on the rocker covers and cylinders, which contrasts with the polished fin edges on the cylinders. Those fin edges are like jewelry when you cut them—they have a nice reflectivity that contrasts with the dull black paint. We wanted a gloss black on the engine covers, and engine finishes are complicated because of the heat, but the factory made it work. Exposing our beautiful engines as the centerpiece and heart of the motorcycle is a design philosophy that's unique to our company. That dedication makes us different from lots of the competition where the motor is hidden. For a Harley-Davidson, the engine is the jewel and the motorcycle is the setting, and the factory has always been very helpful in working with Styling to achieve that. The factory understands that our visuals are a competitive edge that we have versus other brands. The V-Twin and the way it sits in the frame, we pay a great deal of attention to how it's finished, right down to styling the fasteners. Our different models have different levels of finish, and we combine finishes and materials in unique ways, blending style and form and technology—that's a Harley signature. Those finishes on the Sturgis powertrain really pushed us down that path.

The Sturgis introduced another new technology for us: it was our first model with belt drive since those first Harley-Davidsons that were driven by leather belts. The modern belt is a much different animal: rubber with a synthetic fiber that toughens it up and keeps it from stretching, and teeth that turn on a sprocket. There are real advantages to belt drive: it's dry, so it's clean and you have no oiling problems; it's quiet and strong; and it doesn't require adjustment. Getting it right was an engineering breakthrough for us, but we were worried about doing it because the mechanical interest of a motorcycle has a lot to do with sprockets and chains, mechanical things that are a part of this sport. To take a chain drive motorcycle and drive it with a cog belt seemed like a pretty radical departure.

The motorcycle I rode to Sturgis in 1978 was a prototype with that new belt drive. I wrote some comments about the belt drive on the same bag as my notes about the Sturgis. We hadn't perfected the belt drive yet on the prototype that I rode. That's what prototypes and test rides are for; by the time the new Sturgis model was coming off the assembly line in York, we'd worked out all the bugs.

The custom bikes I saw walking around Sturgis, and the ones on Main Street in Daytona during that rally, inspired another factory custom, the Wide Glide. Talking to the riders, looking at their bikes, hearing what they're excited about, I get all sorts of ideas. A lot of riders were purchasing used Harleys and recreating them in their own idea of a design, and I study those bikes because some of those trends become important. We wouldn't recreate them in the same way, but you have to be aware of what's going on in the marketplace to make good decisions about what our future models might be.

The Wide Glide had a California chopper look about it that came out of that knowledge of customer preferences and some of the chopper things that I saw going on. I wanted to do a bigger front wheel, a 21-inch spoked wheel with a small fender and a widespread front fork center line, extending the front end out, giving the chassis a pitch that rocked it back a little bit. Unlike the high-performance bikes that are pitched forward, kind of in a dive, the Wide Glide was tipped back. That gave it some chopper proportions, with that big narrow front wheel and the high-rise handlebars, then the smaller, fatter rear wheel with the bobbed fender.

I explained to Louie what we wanted and asked him to lead the charge on that design. As students of the motorcycling world, we shared a language to describe those kinds of design elements, so I made some notes for him to get started and left him alone for a little while. I'd been made a vice president and we now had five guys in our studio; I needed someone to manage the team. I was confident that Louie was the guy for that job, and I gave him the responsibility.

In a conversation we had as the project took shape, one of us said, "You know, if we're going to do a hot rod, let's do custom flames." That felt right. Flames on the front nose of a '40 Ford Coupe are iconic—it's basic hot rod stuff. They're also very common on custom bikes. Some of them that you see on vehicles are very amateurish; some of them have a very nice flow. It's something a guy does in his shop, one at a time, but nobody was doing it in a production mode. In production our designs are only as good as what the factory can repeat. We can design all sorts of exotic things, but it's got to be producible.

We decided that we were going to do some type of flame and we had to get the support of manufacturing because this would be the most complex paint job we'd ever attempted. We needed to develop a clear plan or the paint guys in the factory would say, "What the hell did you do now, Willie? How are we going to do that?" We knew it would be a multistep process of masking. The tank starts out black, then a mask goes on that has multiple layers. The next coat of paint covers the part of the tank that's not masked. You spray one color, pull off a piece of the masking, add a color, then another reveal is pulled off, another color is added. Five, six, seven layers; sometimes you put wet paint on wet paint to get a blend. It was going to be a very complicated process.

Fortunately, Louie was excellent at hand-cutting decals and vinyl, and he was able to figure out a workable process. After some experimentation he created four or five hand-cut samples of those spray masks, and we took some representatives from 3M, who made the vinyl product, and a representative from our paint supplier, and we went to York to put on a demonstration. To get the factory's support we had to demonstrate that it was doable. The design we came up with took seven masks to get the orange blended into a lighter yellow on the tips with the white trim. The team in York was being pushed to speed up manufacturing, and it was obvious that this paint job would slow things down. But they had the right people in place who saw it was the right thing to do, and they made it work.

That was really a breakthrough, to have a complex two-tone flame in a mass-production environment. It was a combination of York stepping up to the bar, help from our paint and masking suppliers, and of course Styling—we all worked together on that, came together as a team, and that was a milestone. Louie and I are designers, but in making some things happen in a big company we became salesmen: you have to energize people and challenge them, make them feel that they're a part of a new solution, show them what it can look like and say, "We think you guys can do this!" We work with people in so many areas of the company. It's not enough to get buy-in from engineering; we have to energize and challenge our suppliers, the people in manufacturing, in paint shops, the guys who are polishing our parts, the people in quality—everyone all across the organization. If we make them part of the process, and if the rapport and the relationships are right, then they'll bring even more to the table than we ask for. That's when some of this magical stuff really happens. I've gone through that my entire career because I was always trying to push the envelope. And that flame paint job on the Wide Glide sent a strong message, doing custom flames on a production motorcycle. The impact of that was just fantastic, because it was so right for that motorcycle. I kept one of those tanks on my desk for decades.

Both the Sturgis and the Wide Glide were 1980 production models. Coming just three years after the release of the Café Racer and the Low Rider, that 1980 lineup let the riders and the industry know that Harley-Davidson was serious about the custom business. Our factory customs became a key part of our identity. While the company was preparing for that model launch, in the Styling studio we were building a new custom for my 1980 ride to Sturgis. I had in mind a variation on the Wide Glide, keeping its chopper profile, but with the belt drive and monochromatic finishes of the Sturgis, along with some unique custom touches. There were lots of interesting features to that bike, but once I got it out on the road, the thing people noticed first was the rear wheel—a full-disc aluminum wheel. That was a first for us, and those wheels later became an important part of the look of the 1990 Fat Boy.

I revised that bike the following year and rode it to Sturgis again in August of 1981. I designed a custom air cleaner for it as well as hand-laced leather bags for the handlebars and for the small sissy bar on the back. The bike was a deep burgundy, with the engine covers the same color as the tank and fenders, the rest of the engine blacked out with silver highlights. *Custom Bike/Choppers* magazine did a feature on it with a two-page photo of me sitting on the bike in a field right near Main Street in Sturgis.

By the time that magazine came out, Harley enthusiasts were beginning to know who I was. They had started looking closely at whatever bike I rode, hoping for clues about what might be coming next. The next year, 1982, we modified that bike a bit more and I rode it to Sturgis for the third straight time, then in 1983 we did a special production version of it called the Disc Glide. During the three years that I rode that bike to Sturgis, things at the Motor Company and in my life were turned upside down, changed forever.

CHAPTER 11

INDEPENDENCE AND REBUILDING

*O*ur relationship with AMF had its ups and downs from the very beginning. It was difficult for a lot of us because of the size of AMF and all the divisions—we never really fit in that alphabet of companies. Their senior leadership didn't understand the passion of Harley-Davidson and what it means to so many people. They just saw us as another addition to their list of companies. We were their biggest subsidiary but still just a part of their recreational products empire.

As I mentioned earlier, Rodney Gott, who was chairman of AMF at the time of our original deal, was an enthusiast. I think he had an appreciation for Harleys and pushed for the deal, but it would have taken more of an emotional involvement than that to make the marriage work. You have to understand dealers and riders and our rich history.

Rodney retired in 1978, and things got worse. His replacement was not a motorcycle guy, though I don't know how much difference that made because AMF was changing their focus. They had started out as an industrial company, and during the push into leisure products in the '60s and '70s, the industrial part of the company had taken a back seat. That change in focus hadn't worked out the way the company hoped, and they decided to go back to a bigger emphasis on the industrial side. We'd had a partnership with AMF since 1969, and it just seemed like they'd lost interest and weren't willing to invest more money in us. Our costs were going up and our market share was going down. It all added up to a bad situation.

By 1980, AMF had decided we didn't fit in their portfolio, and the company essentially said "Harley-Davidson, we're going to put you up for sale." Vaughn Beals had risen to the top of our senior management team, and he was involved in all the high-level discussions with AMF. The AMF people like Vaughn and Jeff Bleustein, who had really gotten inside our company, had developed an appreciation for what made Harley special. They saw the potential that the AMF brass didn't. Vaughn felt that the best thing at that point would be for AMF to find some good, strong US company to buy Harley-Davidson, one that had money to invest in turning things around. From what I understand, they tried for quite a while to find a buyer, but we weren't looking good to potential investors at that time.

With our options running out, Vaughn approached AMF with the idea of a leveraged buyout by a group of investors. He got together twelve of his leaders—I was lucky to be one of them—and said, "Why don't we try and buy the company?" I thought that was really a fabulous idea because I didn't want to be part of a group that wasn't willing to invest in this opportunity. I thought, *If the ship is going to sink, I'm going down with it.* I really believed in the company.

Vaughn was my good friend and a great leader, a visionary, and I was ready to commit, but I wondered where we would get the money and how a leveraged buyout would work. He explained that we'd have to get together around a million dollars, and the rest would be financed by the banks. He showed us how we could do it, and we all got caught up in the idea of being free from AMF, able to make our own decisions without being second-guessed by people who didn't know our riders or our business.

The economy had gone into a recession at the beginning of 1980, but it looked like we were coming out of it. Our sales were way down and we were losing market share, but the economic forecast didn't look that bad. We all knew that pulling our company out of this slump wouldn't be easy, but we also knew what the name Harley-Davidson meant—the heritage, the camaraderie, the passion. We had customers who remained loyal to us despite all of our problems, and dealers who had sacrificed to keep those customers on the road. More than any of the people in that room, I knew we wouldn't just be buying a company. Harley-Davidson had persevered through so much and it meant so much to so many people. We had an opportunity to extend that legacy and we all committed to do everything we could to make it happen.

AMF agreed to the idea, but they weren't going to give us a lot of time to work out the details. There were thirteen of us, and we all had to go home and figure out how to pull the cash part of the deal together. The risk became real as people started talking about things such as taking out second mortgages on their homes. I knew I had to pool everything we had, and Nancy and I went to the kids and said, "Look, your dad's going to put it on the line. This is extremely high risk. The investment could turn to sand. Or it could put the company on a great path to success." But there was nothing in my mind that would have convinced me not to do it.

For weeks we were on an emotional roller-coaster ride. It was exciting but scary. Scary because we were all going to be in debt up to our ears. There were people who didn't believe that this thing would work—the motorcycle market was not anywhere near the size it is today, and our sales were not anywhere near the volumes that we have today. Some of the lawyers we met with thought we were nuts, and getting the bank financing was not easy. This was early in the days of leveraged buyouts, and ours was going to be one of the biggest deals that had been done. Vaughn ended up getting Citicorp Industrial Credit to commit as the lead bank, then three other banks bought in, and we were able to make it happen. At the end of February 1981, we held a news conference in Milwaukee and AMF announced that it had signed a letter of intent to sell the Harley-Davidson Motor Company to a group of current Harley-Davidson management team members headed by AMF's vice president, Vaughn L. Beals Jr.

The timing of that announcement was good because Louie and I were getting ready for our annual ride down to Daytona Bike Week. We had designed a special Heritage edition FLH that would be introduced later that year, and we were in York to pick up the bikes when the deal was announced. The Heritage felt like the perfect bike for that ride: It had an unusual olive green and orange paint scheme that made it unique and nostalgic, with the stacked Harley-Davidson logo on the gas tank from the 1910s and '20s. I added a long leather fringe on the seat and the bags—Big Bertha bags I called them—had a great vintage feel. It was a vintage-looking bike for a historic moment.

The weather was pretty nice for that time of year, windy sometimes, but dry. Riding is usually good to clear your head, but I couldn't get all the activity around the buyback and everything it meant off my mind. We'd announced the deal, but it would be months before all the papers were signed, and the bank terms were still being negotiated. Every day we'd pull in somewhere for the night and I'd call Vaughn Beals or Charlie Thompson (one of the VPs on the investment team) to discuss some part of the deal. This was before the days of cell phones, so the calls sometimes happened in cold phone booths and often went on for quite a while. But everything was moving forward, and any amount of effort was worth it to get our company back.

When we got to Daytona, we went straight to a famous biker bar called Boot Hill Saloon and parked our bikes right out front. The tank decals on our bikes had an "AMF" next to the "H" in Harley-Davidson, and I was so excited about our new venture that I had put a piece of masking tape right over that AMF logo. Then I went into the bar and said, "Come on outside, I wanna show you guys something." And I could tell them the story because it was hot off the press. That was a big thrill for me, to be able to ride in and say, "Hey, guess what? We bought 'er back!" It felt so good, that big piece of masking tape over the "AMF." I'll never forget that—that was a high point in my life.

Three months after I got back from Daytona, the baker's dozen of us sat down with the lawyers in York, Pennsylvania, and signed all the papers that made the buyback official. It was June 16, 1981. A picture was published in a lot of places of the thirteen of us, gathered around a big conference table with smiles on our faces. I kind of stick out among that crowd—everybody was in a suit and tie but me. I'm standing behind Vaughn, our new chairman and chief executive officer. I have an open collar and a beard and hair over my ears and the biggest grin of the bunch. The buyback was a business item in the newspapers, but for my family and the Harley-Davidson nation it was world-changing news.

We had a celebration with our workers at the York plant, and one of those Heritage editions rolled out as the first bike off the assembly line in our post-AMF era. The bike had a special commemorative statement on the point cover of the engine and a gold oil dipstick, and we made sure to cut the AMF logo off the tank decal before it was applied. That bike is on display in our museum in Milwaukee.

After the events in York, we continued the celebration by riding from York back to Milwaukee. The thirteen of us had matching bikes, black with gold trim, with our names and the date engraved on a brass point cover. We took our wives, and a couple dozen press people, and we picked up more riders all along the way. We took it slow, stopping at dealerships and partying with our great riders and dealers. For twelve years those dealerships had big "AMF Harley-Davidson" signs, and dealership employees were taking out ladders and climbing up to spray black paint over the "AMF" part; that was fun to see. The company had come up with the slogan "The Eagle Soars Alone" and we had T-shirts that said that. At one dealership, I found a black T-shirt with the date and the AMF Harley-Davidson logo with the "AMF" crossed out, like the bike I rode to Daytona. I got my picture taken in it.

That was an incredibly emotional ride for Nancy and me. For all of us. We were excited, of course, and it was really something to feel the enthusiasm of everyone we met along the way. To this day, I've never forgotten it. A new direction was set. Our company was back in our control, even though to a major extent the banks were the ones holding our hands. But at least Harley-Davidson was Harley-Davidson again. I was proud that our great company was returning to its roots and its heritage, and I was thrilled to be able to be a part of it. Many saw it as significant that a Davidson, a guy whose name was on the gas tank, was part of the group that brought it back. That felt good, and everyone just wanted to share in the moment. I was one of the guys who helped make it happen, and we were the guests of honor at all those open houses, but when we were shaking hands with riders and egging on that guy on the ladder with the black spray paint, we all were celebrating our independence together, rider to rider.

There was some other symbolism in that buyback ride: we were carrying flags from our York plant to raise back in Milwaukee, to cement that connection, that York was an equal partner in our liberated company. When we arrived in Milwaukee, we had big events with our employees at both Juneau Avenue and at Capitol Drive, and we raised those flags. We were back to the company that my grandfather founded and my father led for decades, with roots in York as well as in Milwaukee. We were going to work together and show the world we had a bright future ahead of us.

We all returned to Milwaukee full of hope and excitement, stoked by the overwhelmingly positive response to the buyback and the hero's

The beginning—in 1963 I painted this watercolor of the original 1903
Harley-Davidson shed as a gift to my father, William H. Davidson

The founders of Harley-Davidson outside Juneau Avenue, from left to right: My great-uncles Arthur Davidson and Walter Davidson, William Harley, and grandfather William A. Davidson

Arthur Davidson (left), my great uncle, an avid motorcyclist and outdoorsman, is shown here in 1917 after a successful day of fishing

My great uncle Walter Davidson is in front of the Juneau Avenue factory in 1924

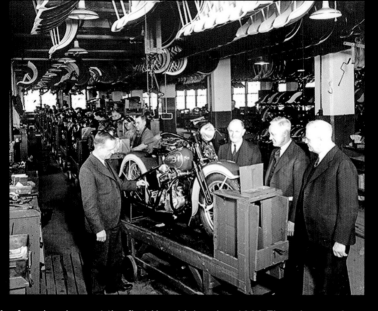

The founders inspect the first Knucklehead, a 1936 EL at Juneau Avenue

The founders, including my grandfather William A. Davidson (left),
were involved in the day-to-day activities of their company

William H. Davidson, my father, seated on a sidecar rig
in 1930, two years after he joined the company

Visiting with friends (I'm second from right) sometime in the mid-1940s

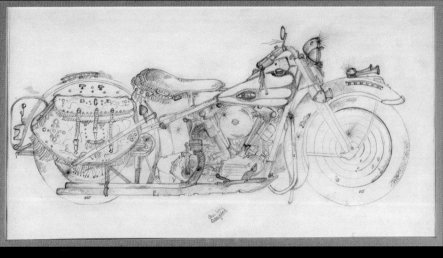

The bike I was dreaming about—a custom Knucklehead drawing with my initials on the saddlebags and my name on the tank—was completed when I was 14

My first bike—a 1948 S model

My wife, Nancy, and I on my K model at Union Grove
Drag Strip in the Milwaukee area

My brother, John, (right) and I with our custom K
models at State Fair Park in Milwaukee in 1953

Competing in an endurance run on my modified K model

An early plein air watercolor created while I studied at the ArtCenter College of Design in California that received recognition from my instructor

In my office at Juneau Avenue shortly after I started at Harley-Davidson in 1963

As the new design director, one of my first bold moves: creating a new logo that was used on a variety of products and is still in use today

Working on
motorcycle
designs in
my office at
Juneau Avenue

My brother, John,
started working at
the company in 1961
and became presi-
dent both of Harley-
Davidson and the
American Motorcyclist
Association

My father, William H Davidson (center), received a Diamond Anniversary award from the AMF Corporation recognizing Harley-Davidson's 75th Anniversary and my brother John (left) and I (right) joined him as he accepted it

Louie Netz and I at the factory in York, Pennsylvania, getting ready to hit the road for Daytona Bike Week on pre-production 1977 FXS Low Rider motorcycles.

The Styling team had lots of fun, but they were also serious designers

Inspecting new tank graphics in my office at Juneau Avenue

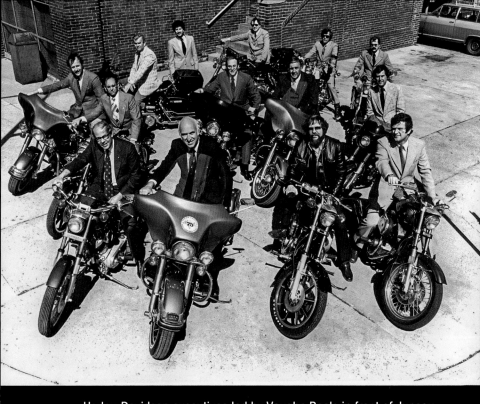

Harley-Davidson executives led by Vaughn Beals in front of Juneau
Avenue in 1978 ready for the 75th Anniversary ride

The thirteen executives from the buyback team in York, Pennsylvania.
I'm standing behind the chairman and CEO, Vaughn Beals (far right).

I joined other executives and employees to celebrate the first
bike off the line after the buyback from AMF in 1981

The Eagle Soars Alone—at a dealership stop while riding
to Milwaukee immediately after the buyback

At our Capitol Drive plant, with one hand on the last Shovelhead engine and one hand on the first Evolution engine in 1984

Giving out awards at the Daytona Bike Week Ride-In-Show in 1984

Vaughn Beals (left) and I presented President Ronald Reagan with a jacket during his visit to our York, Pennsylvania, plant in 1987.

On the cover of our 1990 Parts and Accessories catalog with a customized Fat Boy.

WILLIE G.
AND MACHINE

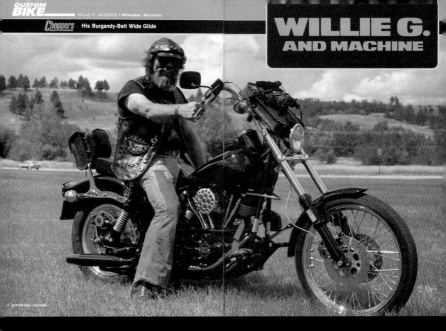

My custom Wide Glide photographed after arriving in Sturgis for *Choppers* magazine

A custom Knucklehead in our Styling office—I still have that bike

The styling team at the Willie G. Davidson Product Development Center in 2009

Designer Frank Savage works with clay to model
surfaces for the 2001 VRSCA V-Rod

My "Willie G" skull graphic is a popular item on motorcycle parts and apparel as well as an occasional tattoo

Greeting riders at the 110th Anniversary celebration in Milwaukee in 2013

Signing one of my Harley-Davidson 100th Anniversary books for a customer at a dealer stop in Mankato, Minnesota, on our way to Sturgis in 2010

Pope Francis blesses Harley-Davidson riders during
the 110th Anniversary celebration in Rome in 2013.

Nancy and I at the 100th Anniversary celebration in Milwaukee in August 2003.

My wife, Nancy, at the 105th Anniversary in August 2008

Nancy and I at the conclusion of the 110th Anniversary parade

Roses in memory of my wife, Nancy, surround the Hillclimber statue at the Harley-Davidson Museum in Milwaukee

welcome we got from the dealers and riders at every stop on our ride. As we settled in and got to work planning our next steps, the economy went into recession again and it started to look like the motorcycle market was falling apart. We didn't have a choice, but we had picked a bad time to buy the company. As 1981 unfolded, sales were declining across the industry and we were losing a lot of money. We had some really grim days, but we knew we had to hang on. There was no way we were going to be the management team that let Harley go down the tube. We had a lot of projects in the works, things that we knew were going to be very positive for Harley-Davidson if we could just give them a chance.

A lot of long-range planning had gone into the decision for the buyback, figuring out how we'd be able to survive and pay the money to the banks that we owed. Watching the market turn, we realized that the projections we had based our assumptions on were not coming to pass. The recession kept getting worse. Unemployment was skyrocketing in the blue-collar industries that were a big part of our customer base. Interest rates were hitting 17 and 18 percent as the government tried to control inflation, and the interest on the debt we'd taken on just tore into any profit that we had hoped to make.

To make matters worse, while all that red ink was flowing, our Japanese competitors were ignoring the downturn and flooding the market with motorcycles. Until Honda started exporting its big Gold Wing in 1975, Harley had had the big heavyweight market to itself. We owned that segment of the industry. Now Honda was leading in that market, battling Yamaha to stay in the lead while Harley lagged behind.

Everywhere we looked there were threats coming at us. We were in survival mode, and we had to keep pushing, not give up. Fortunately we were a tight group with the right talents, the right bean counters, and Vaughn Beals keeping us on course. We had to watch every penny we spent, make sure that the money was going to things that would help us survive. We even found a way to save on tank decals: there were quite a few decals in the pipeline that had the tail on them with the "AMF" in it, and I realized that by just trimming that tail off we could use the Harley-Davidson piece and it worked fine. So Louie sent directions to the factory in York on how to cut the "AMF" part off, and we saved some money. It was a small thing, but all those small things added up.

Harley-Davidson hadn't had an operating loss since the Great Depression, but in 1980, while we were negotiating the buyback, we ended the year just barely in the red. The next year started OK, but in the second half of the year, after we completed the buyback, we lost close to $25 million. In 1982 it got worse. While motorcycle sales were dropping, Yamaha had announced they were building a factory that would produce a million motorcycles a year. A *million* motorcycles a year! Honda had been focusing their investment on their car business, and Yamaha decided they had an opportunity to challenge Honda by outproducing them. It was an all-out war between Honda and Yamaha for market share in the US. Both companies were ignoring the impact of the recession, creating new model after new model, sending more bikes to the United States than our market could absorb. They created a huge backlog of motorcycles and started discounting them, undercutting our prices. As that situation kept getting worse, we began preparations to petition the International Trade Commission for tariff relief, but we knew it was a long shot.

Our losses were mounting and we were having trouble meeting our commitments to the banks that had put up most of the money for the deal. We had to keep making motorcycles—that was the only way out of this—and we had to spend money to make bikes. Parts from our suppliers were arriving onto our loading dock all day long, and invoices needed to be paid. Vaughn Beals and Tom Gelb, who oversaw our manufacturing operation, started taking drastic steps. Vaughn said, "We're gonna stop receiving. We're gonna pay the bills and we're gonna do it on time." They figured out how much we could afford to spend every day, and they sent a controller out to Capitol Drive to monitor all of the shipments coming in. They set a certain dollar value of inventory we could afford every day.

We had started working on improving our manufacturing processes during the last years under AMF but hadn't made a lot of progress. Now we were on the clock. Tom discovered that we had stock rooms where parts had been sitting for months. We started using all those parts, getting rid of all that extra inventory, which was just tied-up cash. It saved $20 million in cash flow. That money went to our bottom line, offsetting our losses.

That solution—bringing in parts when we needed them rather than stockpiling them—evolved into a new process called just-in-time inventory. Jeff Bleustein had been studying Japanese manufacturing methods, and that was one of the principles in their plants. It was the first of the big changes that helped us keep the doors open. There were other processes that had been analyzed and discussed since the late 1970s but only implemented in bits and pieces. In that crisis situation, our manufacturing and engineering team said, "Hey, we don't have time to fiddle around. We have to push these changes through *now*."

It wouldn't be enough to just cut costs. We had to fix our quality issues, stop building bikes that leaked oil; we had to look at our model line and make sure we were making the right products and getting the dealers the products they needed. With Vaughn leading the charge, Jeff Bleustein and Tom Gelb started a pilot project in York and Capitol Drive. They got our employees involved, encouraging them to contribute solutions and provide feedback, recognize the problems as they happened, and get them fixed. For the first time, employees were able to stop the line to address quality problems when they saw them. Employees on the factory floor were trained in precise measurement and elements of statistics and given gauges so they could tell whether they were making a quality part instead of waiting for an inspection to point out problems.

As the project expanded and those changes worked their way through the system, the line slowed down. But with a focus on quality and precision at every step of the process, the bikes that came off the line were good—fewer problems, less scrap, happier customers.

Making changes that quickly throughout our manufacturing process wasn't easy, but it was easier than what came next. We needed to drastically cut costs, and the only way to do that was to reduce our workforce. In May we announced layoffs and a variety of cost-cutting measures. We cut managers and supervisors and went to a shallower organization. We trimmed salaries for the professional staff, with executives taking the biggest cut. We had to make temporary changes to the employee savings plan. We went to suppliers and asked for their help—could they extend terms, give us discounts? Whatever they could do. We asked our dealers to accept some changes they weren't too happy with. We opened our books to the union so they could understand the need. Every day seemed to bring another tough decision—the economy wasn't improving, the market wasn't improving, and our competitors weren't slacking off. By the end of 1982 we had reduced our total workforce by 40 percent.

Those cuts were devastating, but an amazing thing happened. Our employees, our dealers, our suppliers, the union—everybody bought in. Some relations were strained, but nobody wanted to see our great company go under. We made sure people understood the situation, they recognized our commitment, and everybody was all in.

Our company got smaller, and the hard work continued. Employees buckled down and did whatever was necessary. Many of them took on the responsibilities of two and three other employees that had been let go in the downsizing. Throughout the organization people got together and generated ideas, suggested ways to change a process for the better, improve a product, or generate sales. The strength of that was amazing. We had hundreds and hundreds of people brainstorming improvements rather than waiting for ideas to come down from leadership. Everyone who had a hand in our business pitched in and pushed to help us turn things around.

We made the decisions that were necessary for us to survive, but they wouldn't have mattered without the passionate support of our employees and dealers. They accepted the changes and did what they had to do because they didn't want to see an American icon die. And our customers stayed loyal. I remember the thirteen of us sitting in a room soon after the buyback was completed, and we kind of looked around the room and somebody said, "Hey, we can name this company anything we want. We're starting over, maybe we need a new logo." I raised my hand and said, "You know what? It's got to be the original Bar & Shield. We can put the word *Company* in the bottom shield instead of *Motorcycles* as a corporate logo, but I think we need to go back to that original Bar & Shield because of its history and importance." So we stuck with our historic trademark to reinforce our heritage, just made that small change for our new corporate logo, and proudly relaunched Harley-Davidson Motor Company. It's our name, our history that all of those people fought for. They did what they did, we all did what we did, because we had to keep our iconic brand alive.

Fortunately things started to turn around a bit in 1983. The recession ended, the economy rebounded, and all the painful changes we went through in '82 pushed us into the black. Our quality was improving, we had some new models and exciting products in the works, and everyone in the company was clear on what we had to do to keep up the momentum. Then, in April, we got some good news: the government had approved our tariff request.

The Japanese imports had kept flowing, to the point that Yamaha had more than a year's supply of unsold motorcycles sitting in warehouses. Tim Hoelter, who was one of the thirteen buyback investors, had spent the previous months working with a group of consultants to put together a convincing case showing how the excessive imports were hurting Harley-Davidson and the motorcycle industry. We did a lot of lobbying, a lot of politicking, and the government was impressed by all the sacrifices we had made and the work we had in process to try to bring our business around. It turned out that our timing was great because the International Trade Commission needed a test case to prove that our existing trade laws could work. President Reagan approved the request on April 1, placing a significant tariff on imports of heavyweight Japanese motorcycles. It was a five-year deal, with the tariff reduced every year until it ended at the end of the fifth year. That gave us time for our new programs to take effect.

The tariff caused the Japanese to slow their imports, but they'd already shipped their 1983 models and were still selling them at a deep discount. We weren't out of the woods, but the tariff would help stabilize the market. It sent an important signal to both our competitors and our supporters. Knowing that our government was behind us was great news for our employees and dealers.

With our manufacturing transformation underway, we turned our attention to reinforcing our connections with customers. The passion of our customers and dealers had carried us through the difficult times in our history, and after the issues and problems of the AMF years, we needed to strengthen that bond. There was a meeting with several executives who were working with an outside consultant, Michael Kami. He said, "Harley-Davidson has such a strong relationship with its customers, why don't you consider creating an owners group?" And that was the start of the Harley Owners Group. The group became known as H.O.G., which connects back to a Harley-Davidson racer's famous pet pig mascot and nickname from the 1920s.

Our dealers had kept the faith through the hard times, knowing that their job didn't end when they sold a customer a motorcycle. They got involved with the riders, they sponsored events, their dealerships became gathering places. Everyone who bought a Harley got a membership in this exciting new club, and the dealers worked to sign up existing customers. H.O.G. provided a lot of benefits, including pins and patches, and our riders were proud to show their passion for Harley-Davidson.

We pitched a tent at every major rally or race in 1983, brought a keg of beer and some potato chips, and provided entertainment. H.O.G. had thirty thousand members by the end of that year. The club was giving our customers another reason to ride, and the new H.O.G. members were having a great time. As H.O.G. continued to grow, we saw an opportunity to strengthen the relationship between dealers and customers by establishing local chapters at dealerships. Dealers brought people together at their dealership for H.O.G. events. And they could do it year-round—motorcycle riding is seasonal in many places, but enthusiasts are always eager to get together and swap stories anytime. Local chapters worked together to organize rallies put on by volunteers—members of the Harley Owners Group—but with support from Harley. In 1984 there were two national get-togethers, then regional rallies started in subsequent years, and eventually state rallies.

Those H.O.G. rallies gave us an opportunity to connect directly with our riders. We were all members together—I'm a charter member and so is Nancy; we joined up right away. Harley-Davidson sent an executive to every big rally, where they rode and hung out with the members. While there, they were able to discuss issues and have open conversations with customers about our products. This turned out to be a great way to get feedback. Good or bad. I think the honesty of those exchanges had a lot to do with our ultimate success. H.O.G. membership kept growing and growing, and it spread worldwide. It played a big role in our comeback and brought us back to our roots—company executives and employees and dealers and customers getting together to ride, share experiences, and enjoy one another's company.

H.O.G. was one of our most important new programs, but there were lots of others as we attacked every part of our business. We changed our marketing and ad campaigns, started having more fun with them, and they proved to be very effective. We wanted to start a licensing program, but we had to get our trademark under control. AMF hadn't been interested in protecting it; they couldn't be bothered to go after people putting our logos on counterfeit merchandise. If you don't defend your trademarks, you lose them. Tim Hoelter took on the task of straightening that out.

The trademark work helped on another front as we built up our Parts and Accessories (P&A) business. We had been encouraging our dealers to upgrade their facilities, and while we were at it we worked with them to build up their *Genuine* Harley-Davidson Parts & Accessories business. Emphasizing that paid off all the way around—the variety and quality of the parts made it easy for our riders to customize their bikes, and increased sales of P&A generated revenue for both the dealers and the company.

There were so many programs, large and small, that worked together to turn things around. The big key to success for Harley-Davidson, though, is giving customers motorcycles they want to ride, rolling sculptures that fire their imagination. Often, they don't know they want a particular motorcycle until they see it in the showroom or going by on the road. That was my job, to come up with the right products that flip that switch, and both Styling and Engineering were working overtime to deliver new models that would energize riders and generate sales.

Not long after we completed the buyback, we introduced a new version of the Super Glide, the FXR. That was the big news for our 1982 model year. The FXR was our first custom cruiser to have a five-speed transmission and a rubber-mounted engine, a couple of significant innovations that had first appeared on the 1980 FLT Tour Glide. Rubber-mounting the engine reduced the amount of vibration the rider felt through the foot pegs, handlebars, and seat. The five-speed transmission improved performance, and a new frame delivered great handling. It was a hit, and four decades later the FXR from the early '80s remains a favorite of hardcore riders.

A touring version of the FXR, the FXRT Sport Glide, was introduced the following year. It had the innovative features of the FXR, plus a sophisticated new suspension and a modern-looking fixed fairing with similarly styled hard saddle bags. The FXRT got rave reviews from the motorcycle press. It represented a more direct challenge to the Japanese heavyweight bikes of the time, and it sold well. Perhaps more importantly, it showed that Harley-Davidson was moving forward, fighting through its challenges. Lots of Harley enthusiasts looked at these new products and figured they were coming out because we'd been freed from AMF. Each new model did represent a great deal of post-buyback effort and dedication, but those projects had begun during the AMF time and been in the pipeline for at least a few years. What they did demonstrate was our renewed commitment to quality and fixing some longtime problems. Among other things, reviews of both the FXR and FXRT made a point of noting that the bikes didn't leak a single drop of oil.

The most striking visuals of the FXRT—the fairing and bags—had their roots in a different AMF initiative: Project Nova. I mentioned that project in the last chapter, a clean-sheet-of-paper design—frame, engine, everything new. AMF had started pushing that project in the mid-1970s as something completely different from Harley that would allow us to compete with the Japanese and Europeans on their own turf. We worked with Porsche Engineering Services on the water-cooled engine, but the desire was to do something without an exposed radiator, so we designed a unique fairing with scoops that directed air to a radiator laid underneath the seat. What looked like the gas tank channeled air from the scoops to the radiator, which exhausted through a panel that kept the hot air behind the rider. The fuel tank was pushed back, also hidden under the seat. Keeping that radiator off the front allowed us a really clean front section to show off the engine.

The Nova would have been a revolutionary motorcycle. As originally designed, the engine was very advanced, very powerful. AMF funneled a lot of money into the project; it pushed our engineering team to the limit because we were working on a top-to-bottom redesign of our traditional air-cooled V-Twin at the same time. To keep the Nova project going we put the two- and six-cylinder versions that were originally planned on the back burner and focused on the four-cylinder. We had multiple running prototypes by the time of the buyback.

I rode one of those Nova prototypes. It was a fascinating project, but we needed more money and time to get it to where we wanted it to be, and money became really tight after the buyback. Our customers loved the look, sound, and feel of our Big Twin lineup; Nova was totally different. We never got to market testing so we didn't know what the rider might have thought of it, but it would have been a really big and risky change. We were in a difficult situation financially; we were trying to get our quality and our other products up to speed while working on our next generation V-Twin. That became the Evolution V2 engine, and many people credit its introduction with saving the company. Our other new products did well, too, and getting our quality back in line was critical, which we wouldn't have had the money to do if we'd moved forward with Nova. So as I look back, I think it was good that we held off on it. Looking at it now, some riders will say, "Oh, man, you should have done that!" Other riders will say, "You know what? You probably made a good decision."

The unique Nova fairing and the saddlebags lived on with the FXRT, so parts of it made production. Today there is renewed popularity in the FXRT fairing. Harley enthusiasts were very curious about Nova because they heard all sorts of rumors, but we never showed it or talked about it—until we opened our museum in 2008; it's a popular exhibit there.

The Evolution engine—the "Evo" as we call it—was a different story. We introduced it in the summer of 1983 as a 1984 model and it was a smash hit. We had been developing it on a parallel path with Nova until the buyback, so we had been working on it for quite some time. Knowing that engine was coming was one of the reasons we felt confident in buying the company back. We had planned to introduce it in 1982, but we held it back because we needed more time to make sure it was right. We were counting on that engine to show the world we were back.

When we were convinced we were ready, I went to the factory for a photo shoot. I posed at the end of the assembly line with one hand on a Shovelhead, the engine that had carried us since 1966, and the other on an Evo, the one we hoped would carry us into the future. The Evo had gone through more extensive testing than anything we'd ever produced. We had confidence in it, but nothing is ever certain. We phased it in over half of our 1984 product line, with the other half still powered by Shovelheads.

As we'd hoped, it performed beautifully. We used new tools on that engine: computer-aided design in its development and better tooling and quality processes in its manufacture. Everything we designed into it worked: it had increased performance; it was lighter, cleaner, and ran cooler than the Shovel; it proved to be durable, reliable, and more efficient, using less gas and oil. And it was a Harley-Davidson V-Twin: it just nestled into that frame the way it should, with all the right shapes to paint the right picture and every visible component thought through. You can look at the Evo in the historic lineup of our engines and see that throughout our long history we stayed true to our original thought process on what a motorcycle engine should look like, our tradition of mechanical art. And mechanical art is, to me, basic to motorcycle design.

In Styling, knowing that we had the Evolution coming, we needed a special bike to feature it, and that's where the first Softail came in. Just like with engine design, most of our motorcycle designs in the 1980s took inspiration from our Harley-Davidson heritage. Going back to when I was a boy, one of the first motorcycles I drew was a Knucklehead, and that motorcycle, the EL, has always been one of my favorites: the frame makes a beautiful straight line that extends down from the front, the top of the steering head, to the rear axle. Your eye just follows that line; it's powerful and elegant. That's the classic "hardtail": no rear suspension, handsome but unforgiving, hard on both the motorcycle and the rider. When we first added rear shocks, on the K model and then the Duo-Glide, the riders appreciated the cushion, but the suspension broke that visual line. With the Softail, we brought it back.

The Softail is really just a suspended hardtail. We wanted to get back to that EL look, to take the shocks off the side of the bike and bury them somewhere in the chassis. Its story starts in 1976 when a guy named Bill Davis rode up to Juneau on a bike he had built that had the shock-absorber springs up underneath the seat. He'd been showing off that bike, and people were saying to him, "You've got to take that up to Milwaukee and show it to Willie G." Our Juneau factory had become kind of a pilgrimage site going back to the 1920s, with people riding in to take pictures by the front entrance. In the '70s, someone could still walk up to the receptionist and ask for me, and if it sounded like something interesting and I wasn't busy, I'd go on out.

I saw what Bill Davis had done, and I thought it was a significant visual that we might have an interest in. I didn't like that suspension exactly the way Davis did it but I kept thinking about it, and we started experimenting with the idea a couple years later. We tried putting the shocks underneath, at the bottom of the frame, and that was the beginning of the whole Softail development for us. Davis had continued with his development, refined his design, and started selling frames with that hidden suspension. He had gotten a patent on it, so we contacted him and told him, "Hey, look, we like your idea, and we would like to buy out the patent." We worked out a deal to do that. It was complicated; it had to function like our other bikes with that hidden suspension. We got it right, and the Softail became a huge part of the company, in all different varieties of designs.

One of my favorite stories about the Evo and Harley-Davidson's resurgence involves Jeff Bleustein, our longtime president and chief operating officer. Like a lot of our executives, Jeff liked to ride a bike to and from work.

One day, Jeff parked a new motorcycle in his garage at home. When he went to leave for work the next day, he noticed a big puddle of oil on the floor. His wife, Brenda, told him, "I know you want to ride a motorcycle, but you'd better fix those oil leaks because there will be no motorcycles in our garage until you do."

Fortunately for Jeff and his engineering team, the 1340cc V2 Evolution motor was an instant hit with customers and dealers—and, yes, our engines no longer leaked oil. The V2 Evolution was our first new engine project in two decades, and it proved to be more reliable and fuel-efficient than our previous motors. The motorcycle press called it our greatest engineering feat to date, and it couldn't have come at a better time for Harley-Davidson.

After losing around $25 million in 1981 and $32 million the next year, Harley-Davidson climbed back into the black. In 1984, we had $2.9 million in profits on $294 million in sales. The Gang of Thirteen, which had collectively dumped much of its life savings into keeping the company afloat, started to see light at the end of the tunnel. Word of mouth in the marketplace soon shifted. Our bikes still looked like Harley-Davidsons, but they no longer had the problems that had plagued the company during the turbulent AMF years.

Once again, our management team hit the road to get closer to our customers. For the first time, we experimented with a demo-ride program called SuperRide, which was highly unusual in the industry because of the high cost of liability insurance. We knew some consumers were intimidated by motorcycles, and the only way to attract new buyers was to get them past those fears. We bought TV and print ads to promote the program. We loaded our bikes onto trucks and went to rallies, races, and anywhere else riders were congregating. We knew consumers wouldn't buy a car before test-driving one, so why would they purchase a motorcycle without riding one? More than forty thousand people participated in SuperRide. The demo-ride program was a hit and became an industry standard.

Another important development in 1984: the California Highway Patrol awarded us a big contract, which was another much-needed shot in the arm. That allowed us to increase our field sales staff by 50 percent in 1985, which helped implement the demo-ride program and other promotions around the country.

That same year, one of America's most important symbols of freedom and independence, the Statue of Liberty, was being restored through a public-private effort to raise $265 million. As America's only surviving motorcycle manufacturer, Harley-Davidson believed it needed to do something significant to help. We decided to organize two simultaneous coast-to-coast "Ride for Liberty" fundraising rides in September 1985. Vaughn Beals, our chairman, led the northern route, from Los Angeles to Washington, DC. I guided a southern route from LA to the nation's capital, where the two groups met up and rode to the Statue of Liberty together.

The "Ride for Liberty" was a big success. The effort was warmly received by Harley-Davidson enthusiasts. Thousands of them joined us at various points during our rides, and the company received positive press at many of the stops along the way. Vaughn and I were riding limited-edition Liberty motorcycles with a unique paint scheme and Statue of Liberty graphics. The company introduced three limited-edition Liberty models and donated $100 to the restoration for every bike sold. We also raised money through rider sponsorships and the sale of souvenir kits. When the two groups reached the Statue of Liberty on September 22, 1985, Vaughn presented a $250,000 check to the Statue of Liberty / Ellis Island Foundation.

While things were looking up at Juneau Avenue, we weren't out of the woods yet—nowhere close. A few weeks before thousands of Harley-Davidsons rolled up to the Statue of Liberty, Citicorp, our lead financier on the AMF buyback, informed us that it would no longer allow us extended lines of credit to expand our operations. Even though sales were up and people were excited about our bikes again, Citicorp thought its investment was too risky and it was a perfect time to unload us.

As one of the thirteen investors, I was called to an emergency meeting in Lincolnshire, Illinois, on September 6, 1985. Vaughn informed us that Citicorp was pulling the plug and that if we didn't find another bank we would be filing for Chapter 11 bankruptcy on January 1, 1986. I was stunned. After doing everything we could to resurrect this iconic American company, and at a time when people were believing in us again, our bank was ready to close our doors for good. I didn't know what I was going to tell Nancy and the kids.

I've got to give a lot of credit to Vaughn and Rich Teerlink, our then chief financial officer. They went up and down Wall Street looking for a new lender. But once word about Citicorp calling in its note leaked out, other banks were leery of investing in us. There were a lot of fears about a looming recession, which made matters worse. In October, Vaughn and Rich met with the investment firm Dean Witter Reynolds to draw up plans to begin Chapter 11 proceedings. I wondered if the company my grandfather, his brothers, and Bill Harley founded would make it to New Year's Day. I sure had a lot of sleepless nights.

Finally, in early December, with the help of Steve Deli from Dean Witter's office in Chicago, Vaughn and Rich identified a potential lender, Heller Financial Corporation. Heller's vice chairman, Bob Koe, was an avid Harley-Davidson rider and believed very strongly in the company. Initially, Heller CEO Norm Blake turned down the idea, but Koe didn't let up and finally persuaded him that it was a good deal. Suddenly, there was hope that we could save the company. Traditionally, Harley-Davidson's factories and offices are closed between Christmas Eve and New Year's Day. That year, however, most of the management team was in the office each day, trying to figure out if we could get the refinancing closed before Citicorp's deadline.

On December 23, 1985, we struck a deal with Heller and the three secondary banks that had financed our original buyback: First Wisconsin National Bank in Milwaukee, Mellon Bank East of Philadelphia, and Bank of New England in Boston. They agreed to pay $49 million to Citicorp, which ended up taking a multimillion-dollar write-off in the deal. That's how badly Citicorp wanted out of financing Harley-Davidson.

Two days before Christmas, there was plenty to celebrate on Juneau Avenue. Then, on New Year's Eve, someone from Heller called Rich and told him that he couldn't possibly get all of the required signatures and transfer the money to close the deal. To this day, I don't know how Rich did it, but he persuaded the lender to stay open late. Many of our executives were sitting in a bank in downtown Milwaukee, pacing the floor and praying that the deal would get done.

There were two big stacks of papers on a desk: one for refinancing and another for bankruptcy. We would be signing one of them at the end of the night. Finally, around 11 p.m., all of the required refinancing documents were signed, money was transferred to Citicorp, and Harley-Davidson survived with only an hour to spare. Our executives went into the bank lobby and celebrated by throwing papers into the air. I was at home, counting down the New Year with Nancy and the kids, when a phone call from Vaughn finally came. We did some serious celebrating that night. What a way to ring in 1986!

It was amazing to live through that because the entire company was on the line. Bankruptcy would have financially ruined all of us. After everything we had done to get Harley-Davidson back on the right track, it just seemed kind of bizarre that we were even going through that. In the end, it was a better deal for Harley-Davidson. The new loans had lower interest rates, and we had a lender who truly believed in what we were doing.

Heller Financial wasn't the only entity that stepped up to save Harley-Davidson in December 1985. The Wisconsin Investment Board also agreed to lend us $10 million to keep our assembly lines going. With 1,100 employees, we were one of the largest employers in Milwaukee, and then Wisconsin governor Anthony S. Earl took pride in being the home of the country's only motorcycle manufacturer.

Those decisions proved to be sound financially. In 1985, the company had $9.95 million in profits off $287 million in sales. We had regained a 21.2 percent market share of heavy motorcycles, those with engines of 700cc or more, in the US. After so much heartache, disasters, and nearly losing my family's company forever, things were beginning to take off. Just six months later, Vaughn and Rich, two true visionaries, believed Harley-Davidson was ripe to go public.

Even though the Motor Company would be surrendering much of its independence and would have to report to shareholders, Vaughn and Rich believed selling stock was a good way to raise capital, finance capital expansions, and pay off our massive debt. They hoped enthusiasts would stand behind our brand again by investing in the company they loved. I knew there was an attraction to our brand among our loyal riders. They were and always have been the greatest customers in the world. After so much turmoil, the company was in good shape. Manufacturing costs were falling fast; H.O.G. was thriving and was the largest motorcycle club in the world; we had regained the trust of our dealers and were adding several more; and our quality and dependability rivaled any motorcycle maker in the world.

In June 1986, Harley-Davidson announced a public offering on the American Stock Exchange. The offering was a smashing success; it raised about $25 million more than underwriters had projected. The day of the offering, Vaughn came into my office on Juneau Avenue and gave me a bottle of expensive champagne. He said, "Willie, your investment is working for you." I still have that champagne. Since that IPO, Harley-Davidson has been one of the top performers in the US. I'm happy to know it made a lot of money for our employees, enthusiasts, and others who invested in the company.

The additional money allowed us to do something that analysts felt was absolutely necessary to keep the company financially healthy: diversify our revenue base. The Motor Company was already supplying bomb casings to the US government and making computer peripherals and machining components for Chrysler Marine. In December 1986, we purchased Holiday Rambler Corporation, which manufactured recreational vehicles and delivery vans, giving us another much-needed revenue stream.

Our market share of heavyweight motorcycles in 1986 had risen to 19.4 percent, from a record low of 12.5 percent only three years earlier. Our marketing people came up with a brilliant campaign to allow anyone who purchased a new Sportster to trade it back in during a two-year period for a credit of the full retail price of $3,995. It was the first time it had ever been done in the marketplace, but we were convinced the bikes would hold their value.

The Sportster buyback program allowed new riders to trade up to any FX or FL model, including the new 1986 FLST Heritage Softail and FXLR Low Rider Custom, which were big sellers for us. The Heritage had many styling elements that resembled the 1949 Hydra-Glide, only the Softail had a big 16-inch front tire rim and a traditional large tour-ing-style fender. It combined the latest engineering with the timeless look of classic motorcycles. We owned that American look. We started it, and we recreated it, just like we had with many of our bikes over the years. The FXLR was the second iteration of the 1977 Low Rider. The new version had that rubber-isolated Evolution engine. Because we added a five-speed transmission, the bike required a brand-new frame design. The teardrop fuel tank had a special hand-laced leather center strap, unique graphics, and a two-tone panel, which were nice touches. Of course, there also was a tenth anniversary Low Rider logo debossed in leather trim. It was classic.

After near financial ruin, Harley-Davidson was rolling. So much so that in March 1987, we asked the US International Trade Commission to withdraw the tariff protections it had imposed on our Japanese competitors four years earlier. The tariffs weren't supposed to end until the next year, but we didn't need help from the government anymore. We were profitable. We had diversified. We were confident we could stand on our own against the Japanese or anyone else. The company's decision to end the tariffs was unprecedented and was widely praised by Congress and trade officials. The media hailed the decision and described Harley-Davidson as an "American success story."

We wanted to celebrate the occasion properly. More than anything, President Reagan had to be the guest of honor. He had been so supportive of American businesses in the global marketplace and had stood up for Harley-Davidson when we needed it most. We sent a letter to the White House, inviting Reagan to visit our manufacturing plant in York, Pennsylvania. We told him we believed Harley-Davidson was the perfect example of an American company that took the necessary steps to regain our compet-itiveness in the world markets through blood, sweat, tears, and good old-fashioned American ingenuity. A few weeks later, someone from Reagan's administration called back and said the president wanted to come.

As part of the security plan for President Reagan's visit, there were about a dozen orange and black tractor trailers surrounding the York plant on the day of his arrival. There was no way anyone was getting through. I had designed the graphics on the trailers as a rolling billboard, and I was happy to see that they were being put to good use when I arrived at the plant. As you might imagine, there were dozens of Secret Service agents, bomb-sniffing dogs, and even snipers. A secret emergency escape route had been built into cardboard shipping crates behind the stage where the president was going to speak.

York is only about ninety-two miles from the nation's capital, so President Reagan and his security detail were able to travel via helicopter to the ceremony on May 6, 1987. I could hear the sound of helicopter rotors in the distance, and I looked up and saw one approaching. When the doors opened, the White House press corps jumped out; I didn't see the president. A Secret Service agent standing next to me said that the first helicopter was a decoy and that the president would soon be arriving in a second one. A short time later, a second helicopter landed, and President Reagan climbed out and gave his familiar salute to a cheering crowd, including many people waving small American flags. The president stepped into a limo, which drove him into our plant.

After touring the plant and chatting with a few of our employees on the floor, President Reagan attended a forum with workers, union leaders, and executives in the cafeteria. At the end of the tour, he was invited to start a new Sportster at the end of the assembly line. After he threw his leg over the saddle, he asked one of our executives, "Hey, this thing won't take off on me, will it?" The president started the bike and revved the throttle to produce that distinctive Harley-Davidson sound.

During a speech at the end of his visit, President Reagan told thousands of our workers, executives, and visitors, "After being shown around this plant, it seems to me I've come to hog heaven. One thing is for sure: When it comes to motorcycles, this is the home of the all-American

A-team. Of course, that's not what a lot of people were saying about you just a few years ago. Some people said that you couldn't make the grade. They said you couldn't keep up with foreign competition. They said that Harley-Davidson was running out of gas and sputtering to a stop. Well, the people who say that American workers and American companies can't compete are making one of the oldest mistakes in the world. They're betting against America itself, and that's a bet no one will ever win...

"While others may bet on horses, I'll put my bet on you and on America," Reagan told us. "That was what we did four years ago. You asked us to give you breathing room so you could finish getting into shape to meet unexpectedly strong foreign competition. It was like giving a boxer a few extra weeks of training before a fight.... [W]e could see that everyone at Harley-Davidson was serious about getting into fighting shape. So when I was told that you wanted a little more time to train, I said, 'Yes, kick on the engine, Harley, and turn on your thunder.'"

President Reagan commended Harley-Davidson for cutting the time needed to produce a motorcycle by one-third, trimming inventory by two-thirds, tripling the number of defect-free machines, expanding models from three a decade ago to twenty-four in 1987, and once again becoming a leader in motorcycle technology. The president said he was impressed by our company's "can-do spirit." I was honored to present him with a Harley-Davidson jacket. It was one of the greatest moments of my career.

On July 1, 1987, Harley-Davidson stock began trading on the New York Stock Exchange, which is where America's only motorcycle manufacturing company belonged. We celebrated the occasion by riding bikes from the Harley dealership in Queens to Wall Street. There was a caravan of twenty-five motorcycles, ten limousines, two Harley-Davidson tractor trailers, and a forty-foot Holiday Rambler motor home. We were led by New York City cops riding Harley bikes, and we picked up several riders along the way. I'm sure it was quite a sight for those drivers stuck in rush-hour traffic in Manhattan. It was a very dramatic entrance for the first motorcycle that ever appeared on the floor of the New York Stock Exchange.

Going from the American Stock Exchange to the New York Stock Exchange was like going from the minor leagues to the majors. For Harley-Davidson, the move was a signal to the financial world that our turnaround was complete. A lot of people had been ready to give us up for dead, but we were back, and every single person involved with Harley-Davidson had a role in the comeback. That wasn't just the people in the offices at Juneau and the people on the factory floor. It was our dealers and most of all the loyal customers who stuck with us when times were tough and our motorcycles were having problems. They stood behind our product because it was an American success story and an iconic brand. Between Reagan's speech at York and the celebration on Wall Street, Harley-Davidson's comeback was broadcast to the world. After everything we'd been through in the past few years, it felt like a new beginning.

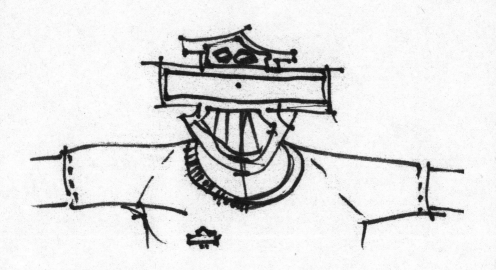

CHAPTER 12

CELEBRATIONS AND RIDING

While we were celebrating the successful New York Stock Exchange listing, we were already planning our next big party: Harley-Davidson's 85th anniversary in 1988. Rides were a part of any major Harley event by that time, and we planned a big one for our birthday celebration. Over the last few years, as the Harley Owners Group grew, H.O.G. had organized big group rides through scenic parts of the country. Those had proved to be very popular, so we had some experienced people to help organize this one. The plan, as it developed, was to have executives lead groups starting from different parts of the US like we had done for the 75th, with everybody coming together outside Milwaukee and riding into the city together.

This anniversary felt particularly special after escaping bankruptcy just a few years earlier and working so hard to make our comeback. Going all the way back to the shed in my grandparents' backyard, through all the years and motorcycles and people and changes, wars and the Depression, good times and hard times, the one constant that carried us forward was the experience of riding a motorcycle, getting together with friends and family and hitting the road. For our big anniversary ride we planned to include lots of stops and events along the way, involving as many of our dealers and loyal riders as possible.

Nancy had been part of my motorcycling life since high school. We'd gone to races and ridden to rallies together, and she'd be there to cheer me on when I was competing. When I'd started riding to Sturgis and Daytona, I did it with Louie or some other colleagues, and Nancy stayed home to be with Karen, Bill, and Michael. When our kids eventually went off to college, Nancy was able to join me on some longer rides and be by my side at public events.

The year before the buyback ride, in 1980, we led an MDA motorcycle parade in Daytona, the first of many MDA rides we participated in. That was Harley-Davidson's first year as a corporate sponsor of the Muscular Dystrophy Association, and that relationship lasted many years. The company, our dealers, and our riders raised over a hundred million dollars for that wonderful organization.

That first MDA ride went from the beach in Daytona over to the speedway for the Daytona 200. We hoped for a big turnout, and there was a lot of planning that went into it. It was the first time Harley had done it, and we didn't know whether anybody would show up. When the morning of the ride rolled around, we rode out to the rally point and saw two or three thousand motorcycles waiting. That was quite a sight—and a relief. Every year MDA picks a child who has muscular dystrophy as a national ambassador, someone with an inspiring story, and that year's ambassador was an amazing kid named Rocco "Rocky" Arizzi. There was a big crowd of riders milling around wanting to talk with Nancy and me and meet Rocky. The atmosphere was incredible, so much warmth and concern—a real feeling that we were all there for a great cause but also to enjoy the moment and ride together. The organizers got everything staged and we led the parade on a bike with a sidecar, with Nancy on the back and Rocky in the sidecar. As people cheered, you could tell it was a special experience for Rocky. It was a special experience for everyone involved, including Nancy and me.

That ride kicked off a great relationship—we knew right then that we were going to do more events, raise more money for MDA. That became a passion of ours, and those rides became an important part of our lives. We got to know a lot of the MDA ambassadors, which was very rewarding. More and more Harley dealers got involved as that relationship grew—there are Muscular Dystrophy Association offices all over the country, so dealers were able to partner with the local offices to organize fundraisers. It's a win-win because the riders are very generous and we raise funds for MDA research, plus the public gets to see that Harley riders have a lot of heart.

We also got involved with a lot of Harley Owners Group rides, and those two things overlap because many H.O.G. activities were fundraisers for MDA. In 1985, as H.O.G. was really growing, my son Bill became the manager of the program. Joe Dowd, who later took over H.O.G. events, had developed a plan to organize "riding rallies," and he and Bill were able to make that program work well. Riding rallies were organized group rides through beautiful parts of the country. H.O.G. members would sign up to participate, and everything was planned out—daily routes, all the stops, where you'd stay each night. The riding rally program became very popular. Nancy loved to go on those rides with me, and that was great because not only did she enjoy the experience—seeing our beautiful country from the back of a Harley—but she could identify with the women on all the rides. She became an inspiration to a lot of women riders. And passengers.

Charitable fundraising rides were becoming popular, and one of the largest in the US was the Love Ride in California. It was the creation of longtime Harley dealer Oliver Shokouh, who became one of our very good friends. Oliver's efforts to help the community started in 1981 as the Bikers Carnival, which was more of a barbeque in the backyard of his shop. Oliver realized one of the best ways to get people involved with a charity event—especially bikers—was to have great live music. The location of his dealership was a bonus; it was right next to Hollywood, so many actors and actresses and musical artists were already his customers. From time to time, someone connected to a celebrity would call Oliver and ask to borrow a bike. It proved to be a fruitful relationship for the Love Ride.

High-profile entertainers such as Crosby, Stills and Nash, Bruce Springsteen, ZZ Top, the Doobie Brothers, and Foo Fighters, along with many other great artists, performed at the main stage over the years. They all wanted to be involved with the meaningful event. Jay Leno was often the event's grand marshal, and actors and actresses also participated such as Peter Fonda, Larry Hagman, Robert Patrick, and so many others. My family and I also became very involved. Out of thirty-two Love Rides, I think I missed only a couple. Nancy, Bill, and Karen were usually with me.

Most of the time, I would lead a group of riders out of Oliver's store to Castaic Lake. One year, with a very large line of bikes behind me, someone shouted quick directions from the sideline at the start to get on Interstate 5. As is often the case with big group rides, there were some riders ahead of me who were working with our police escorts to keep the group together. As those riders stopped and stayed in various locations to manage traffic, I found myself alone in front with a child who had muscular dystrophy riding in my sidecar. One of the police escorts down the road pointed me to the freeway, so I jumped on.

Instead of riding north toward Santa Clarita, I was headed south to Los Angeles. Not much later, a California Highway Patrol motorcycle officer pulled next to me. The patrolman instructed me to stay in the middle lane, so I figured I was going the right way. However, I quickly realized I was leading a mass of motorcycles down an unplanned route.

"Willie, you're going the wrong way!" one of the riders yelled at me.

As I pulled my bike off at the next exit, I looked down at the kid in the sidecar. He had a big smile on his face. From that day forward, Oliver and his buddies liked to call me "Wrong-Way Willie."

Many of the riders who participated in Oliver's Love Rides were members of the UGLY Motorcycle Club. This small club is made up of guys from all walks of life, from different parts of the world. In the early days of the club, one of the members took a bunch of old metal fuses he found in his studio, wrote "UGLY" on each of them, and handed them out to members. These "UGLY sticks" were a metaphor for members being "wired right." UGLY members have a common bond through Harley-Davidson motorcycles, music, and charity. Many UGLY members have joined us on our anniversary rides back to Milwaukee. There is a true brotherhood among UGLYs and I'm proud to be a member, along with my son Bill.

The UGLY Motorcycle Club was just one of several clubs I joined over the years. In addition to being charter members of H.O.G., Nancy and I are life members of the American Motorcyclist Association (AMA). A more local motorcycle club I belonged to was called the Muskego Go Devils. It was a small group of guys who rode together for more than two decades. Along with Louie Netz, the original members included a car dealer, trucker, steam fitter, machine repairman, and another Harley-Davidson employee who oversaw the company's licensing division. The Muskego Go Devils were a microcosm of the Harley-Davidson lifestyle. A common love of motorcycles and riding brought a diverse group together. When you ride thousands of miles across the country together so many times, you develop an unbreakable bond and brotherhood. I came up with the name of our club. Most of our members lived in Muskego, Wisconsin, which is about twenty miles southwest of Milwaukee. I loved those rides with E. J. Salentine, Dave Hense, Don Weber, Tom Parsons, and the other Go Devils.

There were no rules, official meetings, or patches for the Muskego Go Devils. We frequently traveled together to Sturgis and Daytona. After a few years of riding together, someone at Harley-Davidson asked Louie, "How do I get to go on that ride? How do I join your group?"

Louie told the guy, "Somebody has to die."

The planning had come together for the Company's 85th Anniversary ride, our biggest one yet—ten groups, all led by Harley executives, leaving from seven points around the edge of the US map and three cities in Canada, all meeting up to ride into Milwaukee for our big birthday party.

My group's ride started at Griffith Park in Los Angeles, then headed east, raising money for MDA with every mile. Rich Teerlink was leading the ride from San Francisco. Those rides start out with a core group, but people always join up along the way. Sometimes they meet you at events ready to join up, sometimes they're just waiting at a rest stop or a freeway entrance. Some people ride along for the day then head back home because of work or family; some join up and ride all the way. Some who planned to ride only part way get on the phone in the evening to clear their schedule and keep going. You start as strangers, but you're all friends after a day or two.

Our group had gotten big and we all wondered how many riders there would be when the rides converged on Milwaukee. We knew there'd be thousands of bikes but not how many thousands. We didn't have cell phones or the Internet to give us daily updates. The last night we met up with Teerlink's group in LaSalle, Illinois, and there were a *lot* of us. I don't know how many; I was too busy shaking hands and talking and signing autographs to count. Everyone had stories to tell and was excited for the short last leg of our journey.

Our group stretched for ten miles along the freeway, and the groups coming from the south stretched the whole forty miles from their rendezvous point. The last riders left the rendezvous as the first were approaching the city. How many of us were there? I don't know, more than five thousand, less than ten thousand.

Some of the rides had hit a little weather along the way, but the day we rode into Milwaukee it was beautiful and 90 degrees. As the groups came together we were amazed at the number of Harley-Davidson motorcycles stretching down the freeway as far as you could see. Riding in, it felt like the whole city had come out for us. People were crowded on the overpasses with "Welcome Harley-Davidson" signs and waving American flags or just waving, smiling, and yelling. It was incredible. For all those who'd ridden cross-country to get there, it was the warmest welcome we could have imagined.

The party was at the festival grounds, and the huge parking area was already full of bikes when we pulled in. By the time we parked they estimated over twenty thousand motorcycles and thirty-five thousand people. There were concerts that started in the afternoon and ran into the night. Before the final show that evening we celebrated our birthday. Somehow they had made a monstrously large birthday cake, and I stood next to it listening to thousands of customers sing "Happy Birthday, Harley-Davidson!" I was bursting with pride: so proud of every member of the Harley family and all we had accomplished, working through those difficult times to that big moment. We made it!

The 85th Anniversary celebration was such a success that we knew we had to do another in five years. And another after that—this was going to be a new tradition. Styling started another tradition leading up to that big party: we created three special limited-edition Anniversary models, and those were big hits too. We knew that Styling would be designing Anniversary models every five years from then on out.

Harley-Davidson had done a special fender medallion for the 50th Anniversary bikes, and engine cover medallions for the 75th. We started a new tradition for the 85th by designing a special anniversary tank graphic.

The Heritage Softail had extended our string of factory custom hits. Malcolm Forbes, the famous business leader, flew over Main Street during the 1997 Sturgis Rally in a two-hundred-foot-long, eighty-foot-high Heritage Softail-shaped hot air balloon. Malcolm was a big Harley-Davidson fan. He donated the 1980 Wide Glide that he rode through Russia to our museum and commissioned our Styling team to design a special purple Sportster for Elizabeth Taylor when he was dating her. I don't know what happened to that hot-air balloon, but it was certainly the biggest Heritage Softail ever made. I remember a humorous ad our marketing team created with a picture of Malcolm's giant Heritage Softail hot-air balloon hovering over a large enthusiastic crowd with the caption, "Thank god they don't leak oil anymore."

For our new 85th Anniversary bike, I decided we'd take that heritage look a step further back in time and create a new version of the old "springer" front forks. The classic "springer" front end is the one that debuted on our new EL Knucklehead in 1936. It had a great functional look, with two legs on either side of the front wheel, the smaller front leg connected to big springs that extended up on either side of the headlight. We used a version of that springer through 1948, when it was replaced by the pneumatic shocks on the Hydra-Glide, but it remained a favorite of customizers and chopper builders. Putting a springer on the Softail would make a huge statement, but reengineering that front-end design to meet the needs and expectations of the modern rider was a real challenge. Our talented engineers made it work, and the result was a beautiful combination of classic design and modern technology, true Harley-Davidson. The special tank graphic became the signature logo for the event and was used on clothing and merchandise. That also became a tradition for our five-year birthday celebrations.

As we moved through the next five years toward our 90th Anniversary, our sales kept rising and our market share kept growing. After dropping behind our competition around the time of the buyback,

I joined Scotty Parker for a victory lap on his XR-750 after he won the final race of the 1998 season at Del Mar Fairgrounds and captured his ninth Grand National Championship.

Eddie Krawiec and Andrew Hines from the championship-winning Harley-
Davidson™ Screamin' Eagle™/Vance & Hines drag racing team

I was honored to design the 2023 season race suits for the MotoAmerica Mission King of the Baggers Screamin' Eagle factory race team riders Kyle and Travis Wyman

Kyle Wyman from the Screamin' Eagle factory race team aboard his winning race-prepared Road Glide in the MotoAmerica Mission King of the Baggers road racing series at Daytona International Speedway in March 2023

1971 FX Super Glide®

1977 XLCR "Café Racer"

1977 FXS Low Rider®

1980 FXWG Wide Glide®

1980 FXB Sturgis™

1990 FLSTF Fat Boy®

we had fully recovered by our 85th birthday—capturing almost half of the heavyweight motorcycle market. People who had never thought about motorcycling before were getting interested, starting to dream about buying a Harley and riding to one of those exciting rallies. Having famous Harley riders such as Malcolm Forbes and many other celebrities certainly helped.

Back when I joined the company and through the '70s, for many Harley enthusiasts, riding ran in the family, or they started early and it was a part of who they were. Our dealers were avid enthusiasts, lots of them either mechanics or racers. As we entered the '90s, we were beginning to see more and more customers from all walks of life joining the sport of motorcycling. They loved our bikes and wanted to be a part of this brand.

In my grandfather's era there was a period where our sales doubled or tripled every year. That was incredible, and it set us on the path to success, but it's a little different when you're going from 50 to 150, or even 1,500 to 3,000. It wasn't like that in the late 1980s and early '90s, but our growth was steady and impressive—10 percent, 20 percent a year. Between 1986 and our 90th anniversary year in 1993, our sales doubled from a little under 40,000 to just over 80,000, and the planners were projecting we'd hit 100,000 by 1997. We had been continuously building on the manufacturing improvements of the early 1980s, but we were having trouble keeping up with demand. Dealers were putting customers on waiting lists for new bikes, particularly the new models coming out of our Styling studio. It was a situation we were trying hard to fix in order to deliver new models to customers in a timely manner.

Once you start thinking about a Harley, one of the things that hooks you is the history. It contributed to making Harley-Davidson successful, beginning back in that ten-by-fifteen shed. It's American, an American success story, and you're proud to ride it. There's a mystique about it, and you can look at a new bike in a nice clean dealership and see the history in that machine, echoes of someone's grandfather's Harley, but with modern technology built in and hidden from view. Our sales began hitting heights we couldn't have predicted.

We followed the great success of the 85th plan for our 90th Anniversary ride. The welcome coming into Milwaukee was even more enthusiastic, and attendance was estimated at one hundred thousand, with lots of international riders flying over and renting bikes—or shipping their bikes to the US from their home countries. That year, 1993, was also H.O.G.'s 10th Anniversary, and twenty thousand H.O.G. members came to town, most of them a couple of days early for special H.O.G. events.

As the excitement from the 90th grew over the weekend, there was building anticipation for a new element we added—a motorcycle parade. H.O.G. members and invited guests gathered at the state fairgrounds, seven miles out of town, and the state police shut down the freeway for the miles-long ride into Milwaukee. Once we got off the freeway, the bikes rode three-abreast through the city to the festival grounds. Police estimated that one hundred thousand Milwaukee residents lined the interstate overpasses and city streets for the parade—another sunny day with lots of signs and flags and cheers. *Tonight Show* host Jay Leno and Mary Hart of *Entertainment Tonight* joined the parade, along with the members of ZZ Top: Billy, Frank, and Dusty drove the parade in their "CadZZilla" custom car, and my son Bill and Ms. Harley-Davidson 1993 rode two "Hogzilla" custom Harleys that Billy and Frank rode onto the stage later that night to start their concert. Milwaukee police tried to keep the crowds lining the downtown streets separate from the riders in the parade, but both spectators and riders were too excited to pay attention—there were lots of handshakes and high-fives as the parade made its way to the festival grounds. Riders who had been to lots of rallies commented that they'd never encountered a crowd that was so happy to see them. The concerts and parties and riding combined for an unbelievable event, but it was the incredible welcome from Milwaukee's residents that stuck with a lot of the folks who traveled from around the world to celebrate our birthday.

All the attention Nancy and I were getting at events like the Harley-Davidson anniversaries was humbling. We've always just thought of ourselves as fellow riders. We got our first real dose of the celebrity treatment during the buyback ride in 1981. A few years before that I had gotten a lot of media attention as the guy behind our new bikes—the Café Racer and the Low Rider—and during the buyback ride I got more attention because I was the connection to the company's founders, the guy whose name was on the gas tank. Then Nancy and I started participating in all those H.O.G. and MDA rides, and pretty soon we got a request to participate in many big events and charity rides. We were happy when we could raise money for a good cause, spend time with our dealers and their customers, and get out riding. Nancy and I really enjoyed cruising through our beautiful country on a motorcycle and spending time with people who loved our bikes and our brand.

For me, in addition to the riding, I always enjoyed talking with riders about what they'd done to their bikes. I'd get lots of ideas at Sturgis and Daytona, looking at all kinds of motorcycles. I liked to hear what they loved and what they didn't. I'm always fascinated to see how riders have personalized their bikes. When you're out on the road by yourself and you pull into a gas station, there's a natural connection with other riders. You check out their bike and chat about your time on the road, conversations that don't happen between car drivers. When you ride for a few days with a bunch of other riders, those connections naturally get stronger and become a bond, because you're watching out for each other on the road and talking together at every gas and meal stop and in the evenings around the campfire or at the bar.

Wherever we rode, besides wanting their pictures taken with Nancy and me, people were always asking us to sign things. People asked me to sign their bikes or helmets or jackets or their arm or some other part of their body. That was something unique to Harley, I think.

It probably helps that I have a distinctive signature. Around the time of the 85th, the company started using my signature on special versions of the anniversary logo T-shirts. I had been doing special shirts every year for Sturgis and for Daytona for a while by then. I'd create graphics that I thought were symbolic of those areas and events—lots of racing themes and motorcycle parts for Daytona and Americana, and Native American stuff for Sturgis—and they'd include my signature as part of the design. They're available only at those places, during those events, and they became quite collectible. You still see riders proudly wearing their Willie G T-shirt from the '80s, and they're letting you know that they're a veteran of those rallies.

The Motor Company started using my designs and my name as an extension of the riding apparel and Parts & Accessories lines in the '80s. In 1989, the year my daughter, Karen, joined the apparel side of the business, Harley-Davidson formalized its MotorClothes line, and that's been very successful. In 1990 we did a "Willie G" line of riding gear with little brass plaques on the collar with my signature. Sometime before that our legal people decided my signature should be trademarked, so that "Willie G" signature is registered with the United States Patent and Trademark Office. I never dreamed as a young boy that my signature would be registered. Crazy and humbling. Some of my designs became very popular and still are. So then I had even more stuff to sign at events.

It's funny because everybody knew me as Bill up to a certain point. Sometime in the late 1970s, riders started calling me Willie and over time, it stuck. My middle initial got added along the way and Willie G just took hold as a nickname.

As more and more customers recognized that we were enthusiasts, active leaders of the company riding with them, the frequency of autograph and photo requests for myself and the family continued to increase. It's gratifying that enthusiasts look at us as their connection back to this motorcycle they love, that has changed their life. I was intrigued to see how a signature could further deepen that connection. Customers were often emotional when I signed their jacket or bike or whatever they had. Lots of signatures on lots of things—that could be the subject of another book! "Close to our customers" has been a philosophy since the early days of the founders and remains an important ingredient to our success. I've been honored to continue that connection.

Going back to the days of the founders, not only were they trying to build and run a business—they were enthusiasts. They did it. They rode to work, rode their whole lives. That background of being involved in the business and in the sport is important because when you're involved in the sport you rub elbows. The more the merrier. It wasn't just the founders and my father, it was their managers and employees, and in my time it hasn't been just me—it's other executives, employees, dealers, and dealership employees. I think being close to the customer and accessible at various events, showing the enthusiast group that we ride with them, is critical. It differentiated us from our competitors. That connection goes all the way back to the founders. We simply kept it going and hopefully deepened it.

Through the 1990s the efforts we were making in every part of the business kept paying off. We passed 100,000 in sales in 1995, two years earlier than we'd projected in 1993, and we were approaching 150,000 by our 95th Anniversary in 1998. The Harley Owners Group went global, with our first big international rally in 1991, and hit a half-million members by the end of the decade. Sometimes it was all a little hard to believe.

Our grown children were also doing great. Karen was applying her talent and creativity to leading the development of our MotorClothes line, Bill was moving on from H.O.G. into a leadership position in motorcycle product planning, and Michael was working in the art world but keeping one foot in Harley-Davidson territory. Nancy and I would make sure our kids blocked out their calendars when it was possible so they could ride with us. Our family is fortunate because our work is our passion. Our whole family is riding and is also very close to the riders and what's going on.

We were really looking forward to the 95th birthday celebration in 1998, with ten rides coming to Milwaukee. The party promised to be even bigger than the 90th, and our family had something special planned: we gathered some of my riding buddies and extended family and rode together out to Riverside, California, where we met the Anniversary ride and turned around and came back to Milwaukee for the celebration.

The ride out was fantastic, crossing the country with a small group of family and friends, which I love. Nancy was one of those packers who never forgot anything; she'd always have whatever we needed, whenever we needed it. She took care of everyone.

Our little group took a full week to ride out to Riverside, saw some great countryside, relaxed, and had fun. Then we linked up with the Anniversary group, and things really got exciting. It was great to ride with so many different customers and dealers as we crossed the US. It was also cool to be riding with some local media from Milwaukee who were broadcasting our progress nightly. Each evening we had great parties with our dealers and raised a lot of money for MDA. As we got closer and closer to Milwaukee, the excitement grew. The welcome all riders received as we rolled into the city made a lasting memory.

After a great weekend, Jay Leno helped kick off and lead the anniversary parade in Milwaukee with over fifty thousand riders participating, a river of bikes rolling up and around and through the city. We raised something like one and a quarter million dollars for MDA. There was lots of music and more than one hundred thousand motorcycle enthusiasts from all over the world, all in Milwaukee to celebrate Harley-Davidson.

It was also the 15th birthday of H.O.G.—the kind of round numbers we tend to commemorate—and the 17th anniversary of the buyback. Not a round number, but for those of us who'd participated in that and the difficult years that followed, it put everything else in context. Anniversaries are a celebration of success, both looking back and to the future. We had achieved success we couldn't have imagined. We were all excited to see where we'd be by the 100th.

During that time, when our company was coming back strong, there was a Sturgis ride in the early '90s that stands out in my mind. We had left Milwaukee with a group of employees and a few other executives. We learned that ZZ Top wanted to hook up with our group, with that great "CadZZilla" custom car. Billy Gibbons of ZZ Top is a big hot rod guy, and we had gotten to know each other—we knew a lot of the same people, the major custom car guys out in California, and Billy and Dusty, the bass player, were also Harley guys. That car, Billy's CadZZilla, was one of the most famous cars ever built, and the same man who did the CadZZilla had built those two extreme Harley-Davidson motorcycles called Hogzillas and painted them in eggplant purple, the same color as CadZZilla. So we arranged to meet him at Wall Drug and ride together into Rapid City, with him driving CadZZilla and the two Hogzillas on each front fender of his car.

Just picture those three vehicles in front of this group of Harleys, headed toward Sturgis. As we planned this pseudo parade to Rapid City, we connected with a H.O.G. member who was based at the nearby Ellsworth Air Force Base. We asked if one of their famous B-1 bombers could do a flyover. Not surprisingly, we were told no, that they couldn't do a low pass over the interstate. Despite that, we still had a cool ride into Rapid City with the CadZZilla and Hogzillas. But then an amazing moment occurred. As we were approaching the Air Force base, we could see a B-1 staged on the runway, and just as we were riding by, it took off.

I thought, *Wow! This is the coolest thing!* The bomber took off and launched straight up in the sky until it was out of sight, and the sound was just awesome.

What a combination of things that all came together, all those riders, those famous people, that famous airplane, because of one reason: Harley hyphen Davidson. That, to me, is just part of the magic of our great brand. That will never happen at other companies. Being a part of Harley-Davidson is very special.

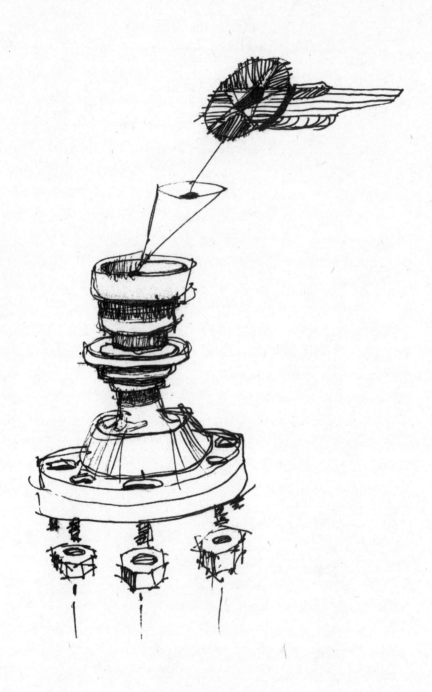

CHAPTER 13

INSPIRATIONS

As a designer I've taken lifelong inspiration from the beautiful motorcycles built by Harley-Davidson, going all the way back to the early days of the company. Our motorcycles have evolved, changed with the times, while maintaining a uniquely Harley aesthetic. Fortunately, my grandfather's generation began saving bikes for the archives right off the assembly line not long after they started the company, a practice that continued through all the hard times up to the present day. So throughout my life I've been able to spend time with the fantastic Harley-Davidson Archives collection, revisiting bikes from every era. It's so inspiring to see all that history gathered together, to be able to get up close and examine individual bikes. Studying the handwork of our early models, I think about the workers who fabricated those parts and assembled those bikes with my grandfather stopping by periodically to see how things were going, maybe have a brief chat.

I've got my own beautiful Knuckleheads, but there's something that's hard to describe about looking at the '36 EL model from our archives, thinking about the challenges the founders faced getting that bike to market, wondering how that bike has 112 miles on it, when most of the archives bikes have zero miles, or just a few miles accumulated when being pushed back and forth from one storage spot to another. Spending time in the archives is a renewable source of ideas. The archives collection is now housed at our museum in Milwaukee, but only a small portion of the total collection is on display at any time. The rest of the motorcycles are stored on movable racks in climate-controlled storage. When our Styling team is getting started on a new project, the designers often take a trip down to the museum for inspiration and then go into bike storage to look closely at specific models. The museum team will pull a half dozen bikes that represent different historic approaches to whatever we were thinking of, and the ideas just start to flow.

Design inspiration can come from anywhere—if we're doing a Softail we don't just look at Softails. A finish on a Touring bike, a wheel on a racer, or the proportions of a classic from the 1920s might send us in a new direction. I remember when we were working on a new variant of the Sportster, a beautiful 1956 KR flat track racer caught our eye and became the primary inspiration.

Sometimes a particular ride will put an idea in your mind, as my early trips to Sturgis did for me. You never know where inspiration might come from or when it might arrive. It might be a hot rod show or noticing a new automotive trend, maybe something about a particular airplane, or even a bicycle or skateboard design. Often you're not sure where an idea came from, but being surrounded by art and books and objects always helps.

I'm fortunate to have some historic motorcycles of my own. I've mentioned some of them in previous chapters, and being immersed in the characteristics that define a Harley-Davidson is important. One of the standards that we've worked to maintain is that though our bikes are big, they're narrow. That's a key result of the way our V-Twin engine fits in the frame. Our racing bikes, stripped down to essentials, are great examples of that. I wrote in a previous chapter about our XR-750; I'm very proud of that design and the XR-750's incredible record of success on the track. Vaughn Beals and Jeff Bleustein worked with Louie to get a factory XR-750 to present to me in recognition of my 30th anniversary with the company in 1993. That was something special and I cherish that bike. Louie also presented me with a "hot shoe," the steel shoe that flat track racers put on their left boot, the foot they drag as they slide around the corners.

Attending various race events has been a constant in my life, and as a designer the look of different race bikes has provided a great deal of inspiration. But not as an explicit reference—just the idea of speed and the functional details of a purpose-built racer get expressed in different ways in design. I love drag racing, road racing, enduros, and motocross, but flat track racing has been a strong passion and I'm lucky to have a few mementoes to go along with my XR-750, including a set of Scotty Parker's racing leathers, a signed helmet and a signed No. 1 plate, and a photo of me going around the track on the back of his bike.

There's a great story behind that photo. It was taken in 1998, and Scotty had won the Grand National Championship again that year, one of nine he won in his career. I was down on the track, and at the end of the race the winner will often take somebody on the back of the bike for a victory lap. I had the pleasure of being the flag man for that race, but I didn't do it right. When Scotty came down the straightaway on the last lap in first place, I flagged only him because he's my friend and I was so excited. And the AMA official came at me and said, "Hey, Willie, you're supposed to flag the whole field, not just one rider." I said, "Yeah, I was a little excited I guess." But Scotty picked me up and rode me around the track with everyone cheering. That was great. Then, after the race Scotty pulled in and took that No. 1 plate off his bike and signed it and gave it to Nancy and me. So to have a team bike, and Scotty's leathers and everything, is pretty special for me.

There were so many talented and successful flat track riders whom my family and I got to know and cheer on over the years. Going to the races, we got to know not only them but also their families and crew, and we followed along in the emotional ups and downs of racing. Luckily, we had a lot more ups than downs in dirt track. Riders such as Scotty Parker, Jay Springsteen, Chris Carr, Kevin Atherton, and Kenny Coolbeth, Jr. are just a few of the many we enjoyed spending time with.

Another race bike I'm proud of is the VR1000. That was our entry into the Superbike race series in 1994. We designed that bike's bodywork from scratch to race in that very competitive series, and though we never took first place in a race, we learned a lot in the process, and those races were fantastic to watch—the sound of the V-Twin was exhilarating. The VR1000 racer was unusual for us in that it had complete carbon fiber bodywork, pretty much fully enclosed for aerodynamic reasons. I designed it so one side was black and one side was orange, split down the center line so it looks like a different bike depending on the direction it's going when it passes you. I got to know some of the racers on the superbike team as well, and Pascal Picotte gave me a set of his leathers and a helmet. The riders on our factory teams have always been my heroes, so that's all very meaningful.

Of course, I find inspiration for both my design and my painting in lots of other things. I have favorite painters and sculptors and designers and folk artists. I'm always energized by meeting and talking with artists, whether painters or photographers at a gallery or art show, or folk artists at a street fair or swap meet. And being an artist, I'm fascinated by all sorts of different artifacts.

On our various trips, Nancy and I would visit galleries and spend time walking among the booths at rallies and antique fairs. We'd buy things that somehow caught our eye, attracted by their intrinsic beauty and craftsmanship, knowing that they'd be reminders of places we rode and people we met.

I'm an admirer of folk art and love how it can take so many forms. People often struggle to define it. The person who made a particular piece probably learned from someone in their community or as an apprentice to a local master. I can look at a pair of moccasins and say it's the beauty of the geometric design and the intricate beadwork, but sometimes I'll see a carved folk-art figure, and it's kind of crudely done, but there's just something there that speaks to me—I know there's a real story behind it. Sometimes it's the combinations of colors and designs; sometimes it's how the piece has weathered and aged.

It's the same with motorcycles. If you find one that's customized, someone put their personal stamp on it and you can tell they put a lot of miles on it; it makes sense to leave it that way. Sometimes you want a beautiful Panhead that looks like it just came off the line at Juneau Avenue. Sometimes that's the bike you find at a swap meet, and it calls to you. Like the beautifully restored 1948 S model that was a present from my family. We went to an antique meet and Michael saw that bike and knew right away that it was identical to the one I learned to ride on. It showed up under the Christmas tree that year with a red ribbon on it, and it's been in my collection ever since.

In an earlier chapter I mentioned the die-cast racer replicas that John and I got when our parents took us to the Indianapolis 500. There's a picture of me from about that time with a little model gas-powered racer that has that same shape, the early racer silhouette. That shape has always appealed to me, and I have many other pieces in that form, large and small. It's just a timeless design with beautiful proportions: the long front end of the body with big, exposed wheels and the open cockpit and short tail. Those cars were aerodynamic for the time period, but just like with airplanes then, there was as much guesswork as science in their forms. The racers were designed before wind tunnels were used for testing. It was pure artistry from the talented people who made those cars. They created shapes that they thought would work, and in the process they came up with forms that are absolutely beautiful. We learned more about aerodynamics over the course of the twentieth century, and the shapes of airplanes and race cars changed. Better aerodynamics, but I loved those handmade forms.

You can't fool around on the racetrack—you've got to do whatever it takes to create a competitive advantage. If there's a change to the bodywork that decreases drag at high speeds or provides better traction, you make it, no matter what it looks like. Performance is obviously critical in a motorcycle designed for the road, but it's not the ultimate goal. While designing motorcycles, I've often gone back and forth with engineering when style and function come in conflict. If there's a mechanical innovation that improves some critical function, we will find a way to implement it, but we also have to maintain the visual heritage of our brand. It's the look, sound, and feel of a beautifully crafted rolling sculpture that truly depicts the DNA of our heritage, along with the sophisticated technology, that keeps us moving forward with a lot of excitement for the Harley-Davidson world.

Look, sound, and feel balance strongly into the mix. The people in manufacturing and engineering can get frustrated when we veto certain solutions, but they understand the importance of creating looks that appeal to our customers and reflect our design heritage, and we always work our way to a solution. That's an important part of our process.

A good example of this approach is when we were adding antilock braking (ABS) to our touring bikes in 2008. A couple of competitors had already introduced that capability on some of their models, using what our Styling team saw as an ugly metal ring and speed sensor around the hub of the wheels to detect when the wheel was in motion. That wouldn't work for us. To achieve the right look and the technical capability, our engineering team was able to embed special magnets hidden in the wheel hub. This certainly wasn't the easiest solution, but it delivered the ABS capability to our customers in a way that maintained our strong visuals.

I've always been intrigued by blacksmiths and metal forms, and our Bar & Shield came from that decorative era of metal embellishment in the early twentieth century. I'm attracted to artifacts that reflect our history and culture because Americana has always been intrinsic to our brand. We kind of grew up with this country when you think about it. From the industrial revolution and the time of the railroads on, our motorcycles have roamed the country through all those years. So the eagle symbol, the wings, our trademark, and stars and stripes are a common theme that's in my head a lot. From a thought process focusing on symbolism, putting those elements together is the right thing to do for our brand.

One of our most successful motorcycles ever is a good example of that: the 1990 Fat Boy. It's a big, burly motorcycle that just feels American. For years, the big gas tanks on our touring models have been called "Fat Bob" tanks, and the big front end that was introduced with the Hydra-Glide looks great with that tank. The Fat Boy begins there. We used a unique front fender that was a little smaller than our big touring fender, and monochromatic paint—a silver frame as well as all the silver sheet metal. We used solid cast wheels front and back, and the wheels really set it off. The entire bike has a massive "fat" look.

For the Fat Boy tank emblem I wanted kind of an Americana style, so I used the star with "Harley-Davidson" encircled around it, "U.S.A." on the base, and a contemporary wing shape on both sides. That logo is part of the impact of the bike—it's patriotic and nostalgic. It's all part of who we are, and again it's got a timeless aspect to it. When Harley did a 30th Anniversary version of it in 2020, that logo still looked new. *Fat Boy*—those two words became synonymous with Harley-Davidson. People refer to their motorcycle as a Fat Boy and everybody knows it's a Harley-Davidson.

The original Fat Boy had some unique leatherwork that made up the tank strap and saddle bags, braided edges and a detail with four grommets and a leather lace knot on the tank strap, with a similar detail of leather laces on both sides of the seat. That idea came from a kidney belt I made. Kidney belts were popular in the 1940s, and they really help your anatomy riding on a hardtail. They just feel good. I have a collection of them; they're unique. I decided to make one because riders back then made their own variations, so I got some trim and some brass pieces and designed a one-off. It had a repeated pattern of crossed rawhide strips with grommets, and those details on the Fat Boy were inspired by that kidney belt.

I rode the first Fat Boy prototype bike to Daytona in 1988. We had done that with some bikes since the first Low Rider, and we knew it was a good way to get one-on-one feedback from the riders. There are of course many ways of getting customer feedback now, but back then we designed a bike, built it, and then took it out in front of our Harley Nation to see what they thought, which was pretty cool. Plus we had great rides.

The year after the Fat Boy came out it was featured in the blockbuster movie *Terminator 2: Judgment Day*, starring Arnold Schwarzenegger. That came as a surprise to us; the factory wasn't involved in the placement. Apparently James Cameron just decided that big Fat Boy was the bike for Arnold's character to ride. The Fat Boy was popular from the moment it launched—like the original Low Rider, they sold as fast as dealers could get them—and the production company had a hard time finding enough bikes for the movie. They needed multiple bikes for stunts and to make sure they had spares if filming didn't go as planned.

With bikes like the Fat Boy we managed to come up with something that matched a lot of people's interests. They saw that bike and they could imagine how they'd feel riding it. But still, as time passed, they'd make changes to it to make it their own. It's fascinating to me how different groups with different interests, all over the world through history, embellish the things they use, the things that matter to them. Ornamentation, intricate handwork, beautification of functional items—those things are very inspiring to me as an artist and as a designer. I believe it's in our genes to change and modify, to augment and customize. We tend to go after distinction and uniqueness. Just one of many examples: motorcyclists through the middle of the twentieth century added glass jewels and metal studs to their kidney belts and saddles and saddlebags.

A motorcycle is so much more than transportation. It's something that makes you feel good going down the road, and in feeling good, you want to individualize it so it's yours. For a Harley enthusiast, their motorcycle is an extension of their personality and interests. They do things with their motorcycle to give the vehicle a personality, to bring it to life. They're all folk artists in their own way. We give them a palette and they use it to express themselves.

CHAPTER 14

FORM FOLLOWS FUNCTION,
BUT BOTH REPORT TO EMOTION

*I*n March of 1997 I was honored to speak at the grand opening of the Willie G. Davidson Product Development Center. That fantastic new facility was built behind our Capitol Drive factory, on land that had been included when my father had purchased the factory after World War II. The PDC, as we called it, brought all of the disciplines involved in developing new motorcycles into one building. I was tremendously proud that our executives and board chose to name that facility after me. Several company leaders shared with me that my designs had pulled us through the dark years and brought us to this moment, when the company could invest in a truly state-of-the-art technical center.

The creation of the Product Development Center reflected my belief that design is a collaborative process. Styling works hand in hand with engineering, testing, manufacturing, purchasing, and product marketing to develop motorcycles that reflect our strong brand and appeal to potential buyers. All those departments have to collaborate for designs to gel because we need to ensure that our designs function properly on a motorcycle. The PDC brought us all under one roof so we could be more efficient with the way people interact.

Whether it's a cam cover, a fuel tank, a logo, or a cylinder head, there's a give-and-take, and our end product is a result of all of our thinking. You have so many things to consider—manufacturing processes, materials and methods, what type of customer you're going after, what price bracket it sits in. It's a very complex process. We'll go back and forth and iterate and iterate until we get it right in a way that's consistent with our brand.

The PDC gave the Styling department an entirely different home to live in, with more space to collaborate, new tools, and enhanced mock-up and fabrication capabilities. It also transformed the Engineering department. The engineering shops had been at Juneau Avenue in a space downstairs from Styling, with numerous functions all squished together—fabricators, testing, and dyno booths—and everybody working, making noise, wishing they had more space. At the PDC, all those engineering groups got brand-new workspaces with leading-edge equipment, and an amazing array of high-tech testing facilities. There were labs to do everything from sophisticated materials analysis to simulating incredible rainstorms for hours on end, soaking a bike to make sure nothing leaked and everything would continue to function correctly in extreme weather. There was a huge soundproof room for doing all sorts of advanced noise testing. We were able to test everything you could think of and all sorts of things that the average person would never think about. We had labs where we could run multiple engines twenty-four hours a day for weeks, putting the equivalent of more than one hundred thousand miles on a bike. We had computerized mechanical stress tests and full-vehicle "shakers" that simulated road conditions, putting more stress on critical components of a bike in a few days than the average rider would in a year. And everything was organized to facilitate teamwork so we could meet and collaborate in ways we hadn't been able to before.

During the 1980s, our design studio moved from the second floor at Juneau Avenue into a larger space on the third floor. We were still on the west end of the building and the engineering offices filled most of the rest of that floor. So our two groups were next door. We collaborated well with the engineering team, but as the business grew and the volume of new product development expanded, we needed to get manufacturing and some of the other departments closer to us. The whole company was growing and space was getting scarce at Juneau, so we started lobbying for a new home. Those efforts and planning culminated in the opening of the PDC.

One development that made a big impact on our work in Styling was computerized rapid prototyping. Back when I started with the company, if I wanted to try a shape or a form or to modify an existing shape, I needed a model maker to make that by hand, often out of wood, sometimes with a combination of wood and plastic, metal, or fiberglass. With the new equipment at the PDC, we can design a part or a component, input the design into a computer, send the file downstairs to the rapid prototyping department, and have a full-scale model on our desk the next day. Then, as the design progresses, we test and make changes to the model until we have a functional design that can go to manufacturing, using the same information that was used to create the model. We still used clay for full-scale mockups, but in combination with rapid prototyping we could move so much faster than we had before.

Similar changes were happening in engineering. They had all the advanced mechanical test equipment and lots of new programs to test designs using computer modeling. They could create computer models to predict the performance of individual components and systems before they built the physical part. Tests to measure durability or performance that used to require us to build and ride a prototype, we could now do in hours or days, depending on how complicated the computer models were.

Of course, we still had to make prototypes and do all sorts of physical testing. The computer models and component tests just meant we were a lot further along in the process by the time we did that. We had acquired a great testing facility in Talladega, Alabama, with all sorts of different road and track environments where our test riders could put prototypes through their paces. Test engineers at the PDC would attach precise sensors to different functional parts of the test bikes and record real-time information as the test riders rode bump courses and simulated road environments. Back in the Structures Lab at the PDC, our testing engineers would then feed that data into the full-vehicle shakers and simulate the wear and tear on the bike in the lab. The test bike is mounted onto a computer-controlled hydraulic fixture that recreates the impact of the bumps and dips of the road, the vibration caused by road surfaces, and the mechanical components of the motorcycle. It's entertaining to watch a bike on one of those shakers. You can tell what's happening as the bike navigates bumps, speeds up and slows down, goes over railroad tracks . . . all sitting a few feet off the ground in a bright, clean lab.

In a few days in the lab, we can accomplish what it took months to do on the test track. And if a problem is found, you analyze it, modify a part, and put the modified bike back on the simulator. Or do a smaller structures test, with similar equipment designed to stress just that one part. Walking through that area of the PDC, it can feel like a crazy clockwork environment, with rooms of machines twisting throttles on partial handlebars, headlights on machined aluminum fixtures violently shaking up and down like they're going over a field of railroad tracks, and hydraulic arms stressing motorcycle swingarms.

Styling was able to take advantage of all the new technology at the PDC because we'd grown by the time we moved over there, adding new people and new tools that made that possible. Through the 1980s, Louie and I used a number of contract designers, but the two of us were the only full-timers in the department. We were very careful when it came to bringing in someone new because of the way we worked together, the fact that we needed to be equals and respect each other. That cohesiveness, to me, was everything in our department. I didn't want an empire; I'd rather have a group that's too small than a group that is not working together as a unit.

In the mid-1980s we started working with a young designer who would become a core member of our team as it began to grow: Ray Drea. Ray had attended high school with our son Michael. He had grown up with motorcycles and started doing custom paint and learning to pinstripe at a young age. Nancy and I went to a high school art show that Michael had some work in, and there was a Sportster tank in the show that Ray had painted. I told Michael to have him give me a call, and I asked him to stripe the prototype of the Heritage FLH, the first version of the bike I rode to Daytona just before the buyback. Ray had started doing commercial art during high school, and after he graduated, we would sometimes hire him to do tank graphics—I would give him a sketch of what my idea was, composition and proportions, and work with him from there, guiding and critiquing. Ray is very talented, and the results of those collaborations were inspiring. Pretty soon he was doing other work for the company, art for H.O.G. and for Karen in MotorClothes. Then he went to work for a local company that did custom paint for Harley, and I had my eye on him that whole time.

In 1993 Louie and I decided to give him a project as sort of a test. We had in mind a new blacked-out version of the Springer Softail and asked Ray to come up with a design for it. We dropped off the bike at his home shop and he went to work. He created a unique design with scallops that started on the tank and then picked up again on the rear fender. We went back and forth on it, he passed with flying colors, and eventually we offered him a job. So he became just the third full-time member of the Styling team.

That bike went into production as the Bad Boy, and even though we did it for only three years, 1995–1997, it became quite collectible. That was another design that led to some real learnings with our manufacturing partners. The scalloped graphic that Ray created ran across the whole bike, and the company had never done anything like that before, where you had to have parts line up perfectly from the tank through the rear fender. That was the key to that design—those individual parts working in concert. Ray created the design on a completed bike, but in manufacturing the parts are painted individually and then assembled, and manufacturing said, "There's no way we can do that." But our great people in York took on that challenge and they figured out how to get it done using laser sights to line up the details, to make sure the elements of the graphic were going on in the exact same spots every time. Because of that challenge, figuring that out, Harley-Davidson added a new capability for creating custom graphics in a volume production environment. We raised our game.

The workers and technicians in our factory were willing to take on that kind of challenge because they recognized that if we could pull it off, it would be worth the extra time and effort to create something our customers would love. That's something that sets our bikes apart. Paint and graphics are areas where we're the best in the business, and Ray Drea helped push that forward. He's a graphic designer who's a gearhead, a motorcycle and hot rod guy with an intimate knowledge of paint and how you achieve certain finishes, like our candy colors and our great combinations of striping and paneling. That's a whole science in itself.

For Harley-Davidson, the color and graphic scheme starts with the tank. Fuel tank shapes are fascinating to me, and we're always paneling or striping or two-toning and locating our logo there. The most valuable piece of real estate that we own is where our name is located on the fuel tank. So the nameplates on our bikes require a sensitive lettering talent, and Ray had that in spades, combined with an understanding of form, shape, and color.

I've always had a great interest in letters, in lettering forms, in the negative and the positive areas of a nameplate, in how letters flow together, and what the flourishes are on the strokes. I think that's very important to a beautiful piece, and I'm not sure a computer can do that. I go way back, prior to computers, so if you think of lettering experts, sign painters, people who do hand-lettering for graphics for printed pieces, that is a tremendous talent that is harder to find today because it's been taken over by computer. Sign painting as an art form is of high value to me. That understanding of type and what looks good and how you pack the letter forms or expand them to make a beautiful name plate is critical. I think you should do that on a drawing board with a paintbrush in your hand rather than a keyboard. I am very proud of the designs we've created and what we've done with various nameplates and lettering, with how we handle the Bar & Shield trademark and lettering variations of our name, Harley-Davidson. Paul Martin, another talented designer who later joined our team, shared the same appreciation for type and had a background in old-school custom sign painting. He helped expand our leadership in paint and graphics over the years.

Going back to the 1930s, we created beautiful tank designs and intricate paint schemes. People become excited in the showroom when they see a great color combination and a great trim piece design, whether it's a cast or stamped Harley-Davidson name plate or an elegant flowing script or a decal. You look at the "Tank Wall" at our museum, a hundred different tanks from across our history, and it shows the depth of our design team and what they're able to do with graphics and color, and the feeling of motion that is so much a part of our brand. With Ray, Paul, and Louie, we were able to extend that tradition and translate that painterly craftsmanship into a modern production environment. The pinstriping is done by robots now, but it's real paint going onto metal, not tape or decals.

Ray took on the development of a team that works on that aspect of things, and they're at the top of the field. As the technology has changed, they've continued to push into new techniques and finishes. We designed the Styling studio area with an outdoor balcony so we can push a bike out there and look at it in the sun, and we can test the durability and colorfastness of the finishes in the PDC's Materials Lab. When you look at a new Harley, you see how special it looks. It's a real marriage of traditional craftsmanship with cutting-edge manufacturing technology. It's an enormous challenge to come up with new graphics, unique designs on similar sheet metal year after year, and nobody does it like we do. Those unique tank logos have become a central element of Harley-Davidson style.

As design technology changed in the 1990s and computers became more and more important, we knew we had to add that capability in our studio. Louie did some research, found a very sophisticated program that seemed like it would work well for us, and we purchased the hardware and software around the end of 1994. Computer-aided design (CAD) had been around for a couple of decades by that point, and the use of 2-D CAD systems had become common in architecture. I never used it, but I understood that working in 2-D CAD was similar to drawing. As we found out, 3-D CAD was a completely different animal. Developing computer-based 3-D models required a different way of thinking. Engineering was fully committed to using CAD, so adding computer-modeling capabilities in Styling would allow us to better integrate with them.

So much was happening, with our sales rising rapidly and the planning for the PDC moving forward, that we knew we had to embrace the new technology, but we didn't want to move too fast. With Ray on board there were three of us full time; we had model makers and contractors whom we worked with, and we'd been very careful selecting those people because we needed to maintain the right atmosphere, keep the synergy going. True collaboration can work magic, and I got a tremendous amount of energy from working with artists, developing ideas and iterating, going back and forth until you're not sure which idea came from where, but you know the right solution when it appears.

We started searching, but there weren't a lot of industrial designers out there using that software, certainly nobody we could find in the motorcycle industry. Then, through the software company, we found a guy who was working in a small transportation-design company designing trains and buses—people movers—and he happened to be a lifelong motorcycle enthusiast. His name was Kirk Rasmussen, and when we brought him in for interviews we all just clicked. He was excited about the idea of working for Harley-Davidson and designing motorcycles, and he talked about all the capabilities of the new systems, how we could build 3-D models of our engines, spin them around, make parts, put the engine in a motorcycle and see it from different angles. We would be able to make photorealistic 3-D renderings and integrate with the engineering team's CAD software to have them produce rapid prototype parts. Those were all the things Louie and I felt we needed, so our team grew by one more person.

Adding two new people—doubling the size of our department—was a big deal, but the volume of new work was growing faster than we were. Harley sales just kept climbing, enthusiasts were on long waiting lists for bikes, and the demand for new, exciting factory custom models was soaring. The Fat Boy had been a huge hit in 1990, and we followed that with a new version of the Sturgis in 1991 that created a whole new branch in our model lineup—the Dyna platform. The big change with the Dyna Glide Sturgis was a completely new frame. This was the first model that engineering designed from the ground up in CAD, and the new frame was stronger, with a sturdy single backbone. It was easier to manufacture, with forging replacing welded joints. There were other engineering advances that combined with the styling to produce rave reviews, and the Dyna line of cruisers became extremely popular as we added new models.

In 1994 we introduced a new touring model, the Road King, that filled an in-between spot in our product offering: a more stripped-down version of a touring bike, with just a basic windshield and saddlebags. No fairing or luggage pack, with a big headlight that recalled the classic Hydra Glide. The Road King was as good for cruising around town as for riding long distances. That proved to be the right bike for a lot of newer riders, and longtime enthusiasts loved it as well—it became the biggest seller in our touring lineup. We kept introducing new models, building on our past with new technology and advanced manufacturing, thanks to the continuous improvement in our factories. We were increasing our manufacturing capacity at the same time, but we still couldn't build bikes fast enough to reduce the waiting list.

Alongside the planning for the PDC and improvements in manufacturing, we'd overhauled our product development process, tightening our collaboration with Engineering and Marketing. Our long-range plan included a major new engine project to replace the Evolution and a new performance-focused, liquid-cooled model from a clean sheet of paper—a totally new bike. That would require additional staffing in Styling, the way the Nova project had twenty years earlier. But this one wasn't going to be canceled before going into production. It was going to be a dream project, and we needed the right people to make it happen.

With so much happening in every area of the company, Louie and I were spending a lot of time in strategic meetings with other departments, helping to ensure that our motorcycle heritage was expressed consistently throughout the company. That work went well beyond the motorcycles themselves, into what our brochures looked like, our marketing and advertising, communications, you name it. I was also involved in lots of leadership meetings and decision-making, along with our ongoing product planning. I wasn't able to sit at my drawing table all day anymore, and Louie no longer had time to immerse himself in design solutions and make mock-ups. Ray was handling most of the graphic work while Kirk added elements of our new design projects into the 3-D CAD system. We needed more design help and someone to take on the full-scale modeling work. The computer drawings and models were a great tool, but they weren't able to give a sense of the proportion that a designer really needs. We needed both: computer models that could be communicated to engineering and used to create rapid prototyped parts, and full-scale physical vehicle mock-ups, clay that we could hand-shape and experiment with, walk around, critique, and modify.

We found a guy named Frank Savage who had studied industrial design and was working in Milwaukee for Dan Matre, who had worked as a contract designer for us during the Nova era. We had been using Dan's firm to design some motorcycle accessories, and we met Frank when he was assigned a headlight fairing for our Softails. Frank had impressed us, and after our first meeting he called regularly, making sure we knew he'd like to work with us at Harley. Somehow Frank had heard that we were starting a new project, and he wanted to be a part of it. As we got to know him better we decided he'd be a good fit, and we knew him to be great with clay, a skilled modeler. So we brought Frank on and he began working on the new liquid-cooled motorcycle project, eventually named V-Rod.

Frank came on while we were deep in the planning of the PDC. Work on the building was underway, we had defined our space needs and projected how the department would grow, and we were working with the architects to lay out our workspaces. We identified the need for an executive assistant and found the right person close to home, working a few miles away at Milsco, our seat manufacturer. Her name was Christine Eggert; I'd met her at a rally a while ago. She was over-qualified but so excited about the position that during her interview she said she'd work for a week for free so we could see what she could do. We hired her, and I'm pretty sure she got paid for her first week. She quickly proved to be invaluable, wrangling my schedule and working with Louie to streamline our design coordination, taking on all sorts of things that freed up valuable design time.

Our Styling team of six filled up our Juneau Avenue studio. I had my office, we had a little conference room and a small shop, Frank had a space in a corner where he was building the clay mock-up for the V-Rod, Ray and Louie had their desks and drawing boards, we found a desk for Christine, and Kirk took up the narrow end of the studio with his computer equipment. We were just upstairs from our original smaller studio, where the west end of the building got really narrow as the back-side followed the railroad tracks.

With so much packed into that small studio, it could have been a problem for another group, but it was great for us. Working on the V-Rod project, Christine said that the five of us were like a family developing something that we had a great passion for, something we wanted to give to the riders—this great new bike. We would have the engineers in on a limited basis, but it was really the five of us working together, in and out of Frank's model area, back to our desks or into the meeting room to explore ideas, then back together to create solutions. We'd sketch an idea, fill that in with clay on the mock-up, critique, refine, and refine-critique-refine. There was something really special about doing that work in the old brick factory, feeling the history of that building. With our small group we got a lot done in a short time, and it was very collaborative. We'd walk around the model, step away, come back, and I'd say, "OK, this looks good but tweak that." Frank would make the update, and at some point we'd realize, "OK, that part is ready."

Interaction was unavoidable in such a small space, and we had a lot of laughs, a lot of joking. I feel that a lighthearted atmosphere is good for creativity, and we had a real family feeling, but we got an incredible amount of good work done that way. That group really had a great time, and we did a lot of things together. I'd have everybody out to our house and Nancy would make a great lunch. We were excited about the move to the PDC, but we knew the atmosphere would be different. Juneau Avenue was the heart and soul of the company, and there was such a diverse group of people down there, so much history.

Leaving the factory where my grandfather and great-uncles built our company was bittersweet, but moving to the PDC was exciting. We had designed the best garage in the world for building motorcycles. Looking around our new Styling department, I thought, *What the heck are we going to do with this big space?* But I knew the projects would pile up, we'd settle in, and in a year the space would be full. It couldn't have been more different from those days when Louie bought our shop tools through the want ads. Everything was new and we had designed the space for our workflow—we had multiple fabrication bays to replace the cramped model shop at Juneau. We'd made the Juneau process work by building models down in the mechanic's area, but in our new studio we could work on multiple designs at once, which was really powerful. Then, as we continued to grow as a team, with more players and fresh designers, we could move designs forward simultaneously for all the platforms.

I made sure we brought some history into our new studio to provide inspiration. I rolled in my beautiful Knucklehead bobber and it sat near the entrance, outside my office. It was a constant reminder of our heritage, the DNA of Harley style. We hung a beautiful grouping of classic gas tank designs from the late 1930s through the early 1940s on the wall next to my office. They were original paint samples from those years, the right half of gas tanks, painted and striped by hand, that had been discovered in the old rooftop paint area during one of the renovations at Juneau.

Our design space was bright with natural light, with high ceilings and room to spread out. We had a huge, long wall to cover with drawings and sketches and design inspirations, and room to line up a dozen bikes for review. The fabrication bays for building prototypes were expansive, with all the modern tooling and hydraulic lifts, next to a large modeling studio. As time went on we were able to hire two dedicated fabricators to work alongside us. There were aspects of the old studio we would all miss, but I couldn't help but be energized, thinking of what we'd be able to accomplish with our new space and all of our product development partners nearby.

When I reflect back on those days of building that talented team at the Product Development Center, it's a love affair. The world of design, the PDC, the brand, our company, the products, the riders, the people, the dealers, the whole gigantic package is really a love affair. I enjoyed it, and I think that feeling was infectious. We put together a hugely talented group, and that was because as we grew, we searched hard for talent that would really understand, have a feeling about our brand, and be capable of massaging the brand without losing it. It turned into a pretty happy family, I'm proud to say. The designers were all riders, and being riders, they knew what two wheels were all about. To excel they had to really understand this whole motorcycle thing, and they took off with their creative ideas from there and did a very good job.

Passion and emotion are such an important part of what we do, and the designers in our department had that feeling. They were constantly barraged with motorcycling, whether at a rally or at an event, whether looking at a trade magazine or involved in one of our historic birthday gatherings. And we had fun, a lot of laughs. I always wanted the design team to feel comfortable and creative. Humor was a big part of it, respect for the brand was huge, and doing your best as a designer was critical. It was an atmosphere that kept the creativity at a high level.

Team members would sketch—some at their drawing board, some on their screen—and then we would get together to talk. Through discussion and group critiques we'd gradually develop designs where everyone was happy with the output. Sometimes that would take quite a while, a number of iterations, but we had a synergy. It was a collaborative group of individuals who had unique and diverse talents. And there was a mutual respect for the approach that each person took, whether it be computer modeling, or clay modeling, or renderings in two dimensions, or color and graphics. By bringing that team together, we achieved great design.

A big part of my role as the department grew was to encourage and guide the younger designers. I'd walk up and put my hand on their shoulder and say, "What are you working on?" Just showing a genuine interest in what they were doing went a long way. Pointing out what worked when things magically came together and just felt right, helping them see how that happened. And of course, pointing out when that wasn't happening, trying to provide some insight into where a solution started going wrong. "Yes, that's good, but you need to look at this area again, that's not quite working." Being able to tell them *why* we needed to do it that way was critical. It might be something broad, and we'd walk over to that Knucklehead outside my office and focus on where the line goes from the rear axle all the way up to the tank, or how the tank is rounded at the front and terminates at the back. There had to be a story; you can't just say, "No, that's no good."

We always had regular critique sessions, asking, "Who's the customer?" and "What's the spirit of the bike?" The designer explained what they were going for, then we looked at how it related to our heritage, what parts of the DNA from our past motorcycles were present and how they were expressed. "How does this bring that heritage forward to create something new and exciting for the customer, a graceful evolution that resonates with the current rider?"

One constant through all the change and growth of the department was my partnership with Louie Netz. We were together so long, we had lunch together every day, we worked so well together, it evolved into something truly special. Sometimes I knew he could read my thoughts, and we really shared an aesthetic viewpoint as well as a firm dedication to extending the brand while maintaining continuity with our heritage.

As the team grew in size and responsibility, Louie took on a lot of the business responsibilities, but he also had his mind in design. He was great at establishing relationships with people on the business side of the house, because there are a lot of things in a big corporation that you have to do; it's not just a small studio cranking out designs. Louie was able to build those relationships so we could keep the studio flexible and a little rebellious, a little crazy at times, and that really gave the designers the freedom to create great bikes. When new people came in, they interviewed with both of us, then interviewed with everyone else in the department, because the team had to work together, the personalities had to mesh. For us to be successful we all had to get along, and we managed to assemble a great group that just had a great time together.

One thing all of our designers had to understand was that styling and engineering is a marriage, because form follows function. Then, what I added to that equation is that form follows function, but they both report to emotion. A Harley-Davidson motorcycle has to have a visual level that, when you look at it in your garage, is proportionately right—all the elements come together perfectly. So we build mock-ups that are full scale and we're able to sit on them, walk around them, get a long view—that means backing up a distance and really looking. Then the prototypes are ridden so you can see how they look with a rider on them. We look hard at every part and how they fit together. Because everything is visible on our motorcycles, it all has to have a beauty and work well together. Lights, taillights, turn signals, license plates—those are always a challenge. They're required, but they're not easy design solutions. We've moved turn signals and license brackets around. What we're looking for is a pure, simple, handsome motorcycle that *says* Harley-Davidson. That's critical, I think. You should be able to walk up to it and say, "Oh, that's a nice Harley."

We talk about being customer-led, and that's always been a key to our success. For me, that was about truly being with the customer, going to the rallies. We learn from our riders, and then we take it in a unique direction. We're building custom motorcycles, staying true to the essence of what makes a Harley a Harley, but moving it forward. In some ways I felt like the "keeper of the flame," building new forms that retained the essence of the original recipe, something I've always had my hand on and my mind around.

We know that people are riding motorcycles because they're looking for the spirit of adventure and escape from their daily routine. It's such an emotional aspect of their life, and their Harley-Davidson is the vehicle for that. Riding a Harley-Davidson connects a customer not only with other riders locally but with a huge international group that understands and celebrates everything that riding a Harley represents. All of that is wrapped up in the emotion part of the "Form follows function, but both report to emotion" equation. It's gotta work, it's gotta look great, and people have to want to buy it. They have to walk in that dealer showroom and say, "I've *gotta* have that bike."

As we grew and added designers, we made sure that stayed in the backs of their heads. That's what we design: bikes that make a visual impact, with the promise that pointing it down the road might change the rider's life. And that has literally been the case—many riders have said to me with a grin, "Harley-Davidson has changed my life."

CHAPTER 15

THE HITS KEEP ON COMING

"Welcome to the house of hits!"

That's how I'd greet visitors to our Styling studio after we'd settled into the PDC. We'd started off the 1990s with the Fat Boy, a smash hit, and followed up with the Dyna Glide Sturgis the next year. Our factory customs had changed the motorcycle industry, and Styling kept busy rejuvenating the lineup. We brought back a beautiful Dyna Wide Glide in 1993 along with a Dyna Low Rider, and a new Super Glide in '94. These were busy times, with new customers lusting after our new models, often waiting months for their bike to get from the assembly line to their dealership.

I mentioned the 1994 Road King before, and that bike added a jolt of energy to our Touring lineup. We worked to add other new models and enhance the Touring platform, but the Road King remained the best seller. One other hit was the Road Glide, introduced in 1997. It was a redesign of the fixed-fairing Tour Glide. I rode a new Road Glide on the 95th Anniversary ride, and it's a great long-distance runner. As it evolved over the next decade, it became a favorite of Harley enthusiasts.

Our Sportster platform had gotten its version of the Evolution motor in 1986, with a change that became a real winner: a smaller version, a return to the 883cc engine size of the original Sportster back in 1957. Our Sportster engines had increased in size over the decades, gaining power, and the larger 1200cc models remained very successful, but the return of a smaller Sportster, lighter and easier to handle, was another hit.

We were keeping the product lineup fresh by introducing special models that appeared for just a few years, had a good run, and then retired in favor of something that gave a new look to the dealership showroom. Harley had been around for so long; we had ninety-plus years of heritage to draw on for inspiration, and our enthusiasts loved the combination of advanced technology and heritage styling. We'd proven to be pretty good at nostalgia, but with each model, there had to be a new element. It had to relate to the past, but it also had to be new.

The Heritage Softail Nostalgia, which we introduced in 1993 and made for four years, is a good example. It had a long name, but everyone called it "Cow Glide" or the "Moo Glide." The design idea started to come together when Milsco, our seat supplier, showed us a new saddle idea with black and white cowhide inserts. I pictured those with some whitewall tires on big, spoked wheels, and that was the trigger point. We added cowhide inserts on the saddlebags, a black-and-white paint scheme, a Hydra Glide–inspired front end, and long shotgun exhaust pipes with shark-fin tips that were popular in the 1950s. It evolved into a fairly extreme statement, with a lot of nostalgic ingredients and excitement. Our riders loved it.

The V-Rod model that began over at Juneau had advanced quite a ways by the time we moved to the PDC, and progress accelerated once we had all of our product development partners close by. Frank's clay had taken on an exciting form, and Kirk's work with our 3-D design software allowed us to collaborate with the rapid prototyping engineers downstairs to produce quick, accurate prototype parts. That was a real time-saver. Those machines worked by laying down a thin layer of powder, then a laser would harden the portion defined by the 3-D design and build it up layer by layer until you had the 3-D part. Nowadays 3-D printing has become almost commonplace, but back in the '90s it felt pretty magical.

The prototypes those machines produced were precise to our specifications, extremely accurate. With our handmade prototypes, the parts would come back, sometimes from different people, and we'd often have to take time to modify things to make them fit. With the new CAD systems, the precision was phenomenal. Kirk did the work in 3-D and everything fit the first time. That efficiency was another tremendous time-saver. Eventually a whole department developed at the PDC called Styled Surfaces, and they handled the big 3-D CAD projects. As technology advanced they could make incredibly detailed, full-scale digital models with the ability to zoom in and go inside all the individual components, look through the cylinder into the pistons, through the pistons into the connecting rods and all the internals, all over the entire bike—incredible technology, and necessary as our bikes became more and more sophisticated and advanced.

Even with rapid prototyping available, handmade models and prototypes remained critical for our styling work in the early stages of development for many parts. Everything still started with ideation and sketching, and we'd been able to move Earl Golden, our ace model maker/fabricator, to the PDC with us, so we had a creative full house. I sketch on paper, and I'm able to depict dimension and texture using standard rendering techniques. Earl sketched in three dimensions, using Bondo, Masonite, and other materials. I could show him a sketch and talk over what we were trying to achieve, and he could then picture it in his head, go into the shop, and create a full-scale 3-D model that we could fine-tune. He had a great design sense, and the synergy between

Earl, Louie, and me resulted in some important innovations. Earl's name appears on a number of our patents from the '90s, along with mine and Louie's. We had to patent things such as our now-classic oval air cleaner cover to deter the copycats. Our competitors realized that we were on to a visual that attracted buyers and we had stayed true to that, so they started zeroing in on our look. Some of them had pieces that came close, but overall they weren't willing or able to expend the resources to do it right. It was sort of a backhanded compliment, but I wished they'd have told their designers, "You guys have a clean sheet of paper; create whatever you want, but don't make it look identical to a Harley." I mean, how many people want to wear a phony Rolex? I want the Rolex, and that's who we are.

The PDC had only a short run as Harley-Davidson's newest facility. Less than a year after its opening ceremony we opened a new factory in Kansas City and followed that with a new powertrain factory north of Milwaukee on Pilgrim Road in Menomonee Falls. Harley-Davidson was determined to reduce the waiting lists for enthusiasts wanting one of our new bikes. Our sales volumes were hitting numbers that my grandfather and my dad wouldn't have believed possible, but I knew they'd be very proud if they could see where we'd taken the company.

Our snowballing success wasn't just due to the great bikes we were building and the improvements in our manufacturing processes and general quality. The US economy was booming, consumers were confident and spending money, and our marketing was doing a good job of getting potential customers off the fence and into our dealerships. Just as importantly, there'd been significant upgrades in our dealership network around the country. The new Harley dealerships were bright, clean, well-organized, and welcoming. And profitable. With customers on waiting lists, sales pressure was negligible, and dealers who may have once catered almost exclusively to longtime riders were working hard to turn curious non-riders into first-time buyers.

Adding all that production capacity would allow us to get new models to dealers more quickly and shorten those waiting lists. That wasn't the only reason for the expansion though. We'd developed a larger strategic plan, and product development was a big part of it. Looking ahead into the twenty-first century, we knew we needed a new engine.

The Evolution powertrain remained popular and was still going strong. It had played a big part in our comeback from the AMF years, proving that we had the engineering and manufacturing capability to build a modern, powerful, reliable engine while maintaining our classic V-Twin architecture. But technology kept moving and we'd developed a list of improvements that we knew were possible. First on the list was a significant increase in power. Surveys showed that our customers wanted more power, and talking with riders at rallies and events confirmed it—lots of riders were buying aftermarket kits to increase the displacement of their Evos. Wanting a bigger engine just seems to be a part of being a motorhead. Motorcycles or cars, you want more power than the next guy.

Given everything I've written over preceding chapters, you know that a new Big Twin engine is a big deal for Harley-Davidson. A completely new engine is a huge investment in engineering and tooling and is probably the most significant upgrade driver for repeat customers. It's something we must get right, and this new engine would power the 100th Anniversary bikes, taking us into our second century. As always, there was back-and-forth as we progressed toward a design that *worked* the way Engineering needed it to but *looked* the way Styling knew it could and should.

The new engine was called the Twin Cam 88, the "twin cam" referring to two cams that drove the valve actuation, and the "88" referring to the larger displacement, up to 88 cubic inches from the 80 cubic inches of the Evo. The Twin Cam was not only more powerful; it promised greater reliability, easier maintenance, and quieter operation. Other engineering changes made it quicker to assemble, speeding up the manufacturing cycle to support increased production. And it would be built in our new Pilgrim Road power-train plant in Menomonee Falls.

Our new Kansas City plant would manufacture and assemble the Sportster as well as the V-Rod when it went into production a few years later. With all these changes, we'd be able to produce the new engine while shipping more bikes faster to our dealers.

The new engine was the big change for 1999, and it had an immediate impact. Our sales had been growing between 11 percent and 12 percent over the past few years. With that new engine powering half of our '99 product line, sales increased more than 20 percent from 1998. Styling focused on one model to highlight the new Twin Cam—a sleek, blacked-out Super Glide Sport. The powerful new engine made a big performance difference in the relatively stripped-down Dyna, and we showcased it in a black-on-black package that emphasized the performance and handling characteristics of the Super Glide. The Softail version of the Twin Cam was coming for 2000, and we had a more radical new custom in development for that model launch.

Putting the Twin Cam in our Softails for the 2000 model year was both a critical and popular success, as our overall sales surpassed two hundred thousand for the first time. Think of that: we'd gone from selling twenty thousand motorcycles in 1980, the year before the buyback, to two hundred thousand, in just twenty years. Our showcase Softail for the new Twin Cam was called the Deuce; we thought of it as the second generation of the original Softail Custom that had helped with our recovery in the mid-'80s. Our line of factory custom motorcycles, going back to the original Super Glide in 1971, had redefined Harley-Davidson motorcycles and driven our unprecedented growth. The Deuce was our most radical statement yet, setting a new benchmark for factory customs.

With the Deuce I wanted to present a new look for Harley-Davidson, something that would carry through to other models in the future. We started with different proportions and worked hard to get all the lines just right. We stretched the tank, giving it a longer, thinner shape, and that set the tone. The tank blended smoothly into the saddle, then into a short rear fender, with the taillight buried in the fender, creating a long, flowing look that defined the bike. Every piece of hardware received styling attention, from the front forks to rear fender braces—we played with forms and reshaped elements until we got them absolutely perfect. Nothing escaped our eye, so most of the individual hardware was unique to the Deuce. Lots of people had a hard time believing it was a factory bike. But as we do with all models, we left room for individual riders to make it their own—we made it a canvas a creative rider could work with.

Our custom models had become a big part of the business, and they really differentiated us from the competition. We kept pushing the envelope, and building a bike like the Deuce required buy-in from every area of the company. Changing the shape of a part required support from engineering, and everything had to be tested for strength, reliability, and proper function. Unique parts meant more inventory, more complexity in assembly. Our Harley-Davidson organization supported that work because they knew how important it was to our customers. And designing new customs provided a constant challenge for us in Styling.

The designers in Styling are all artists, with different ideas and unique strengths. It's the nature of the work, and as we added new designers, we added new talents. Like me, many of them are fine artists in their work outside the Styling studio—painters and photographers and sculptors. At work they need to maintain that creative individuality and drive, but they've also got to think like commercial artists. We weren't designing one-off customs; we were designing customs that could be reproduced thousands of times. That's not a compromise—that's the reality of doing cool, factory custom motorcycles. You have to really think through, *How are we going to be able to do this thousands of times, and have it look like that bike was done just for you, that person seeing it in a dealership showroom?*

In 1999 we had started a program that took our custom designs to another level. We announced two limited-edition versions based on our old FXR platform. With those limited-production bikes we were able to enhance the custom element by identifying a special team of technicians working in the factory who would hand-build each bike with exclusive styling, special paint schemes, and unique accessories. That first year we made just under a thousand of each model and had a special assembly line just to produce those unique motorcycles.

The Custom Vehicle Operations program grew from those first two FXRs. Every year we'd announce a small number of new CVO models, rolling works of art that appealed to customers looking for something unique. Each CVO motorcycle represented the pinnacle of Harley-Davidson craftsmanship, quality, and performance, and our customers loved them.

The V-Rod, a bike that would be introduced in 2001, was moving quickly by the time we moved to the PDC. It had been exciting to start with a clean sheet of paper, and we were able to have Kirk and Frank focus on just that task. We moved Frank's clay model into the studio, and it was really helping us picture where the bike needed to go.

The genesis of the V-Rod was a desire on the company's part to enter the performance and custom market space. We knew we needed to branch out and look at other areas of the market, and our Product Planning Committee felt that a performance-focused street bike would appeal to potential new buyers and be a draw for European customers. We'd had some discussions earlier about building a street bike based on our liquid-cooled VR1000 racing engine. They hadn't gone far at the time, but they came back up as we laid out plans for the V-Rod project.

We had an enormous following for our air-cooled V-Twins, but we had never wandered into a water-cooled motorcycle. So number one, we decided that this motorcycle would have a high-tech look, with forms and shapes that would give it a strong identity, different from our air-cooled models. I wanted this vehicle to have a presence where you walk up to it say, "*That's* a new Harley-Davidson. Wow."

The first concept mock-up had been a total failure. Engineering thought, *Well, we have Softails; would it be something like that?* So the VR1000 engine went into a Softail frame, just as an experiment. It was so awful we didn't even take pictures of it, we just took it apart. But it was important because we learned what not to do. It confirmed my instinct that a liquid-cooled engine demanded a different look.

This was going to be a performance bike with a very powerful engine. That brought the idea of a dragster to mind. Drag racing vehicles have a distinctive look—low, long, and aggressive—so that idea set a direction. We started from there, stretching out the front end like a dragster, lowering the bike, giving it a fast, mean look.

We were building off of the VR1000 engine, but that was a race motor, built for specific performance characteristics. Our racing program had proven the architecture and design, but the VR1000 wasn't designed to balance the competing needs of a production powertrain—durability, fuel economy, emissions. It provided a model, but building a street version would require a top-to-bottom redesign. Our engineering department had all they could handle with the Twin Cam 88 projects, so we decided to get outside help and turned to the Porsche contract engineering arm that we'd worked with on Project Nova. A dedicated team of Harley engineers began working directly with the Porsche group in Germany on the new design.

We were just about to phase out our Evolution engine, replacing it with the Twin Cam 88. As the new engine took shape, we started working on a name for it and landed on Revolution. That felt right—going liquid-cooled was a revolutionary step for us, but we took pains in the design to reference our V-Twin heritage. The Revolution was a wider V, a different architecture from our air-cooled models, but if you look at it in the bike, it looks like an extension of our engine heritage. You can see the connection to our history. As a clean-sheet motor we could have taken that thing in any direction, but we wanted to maintain a relationship to our air-cooled engines.

The next challenge was the frame. None of our current frame designs would work with that engine and that bike. We started putting tubes around the engine, experimenting, sketching, covering a wall with ideas. We brainstormed with the engineers and went through dozens of computer models, testing ideas against functional requirements. After a lot of experimentation, we came up with a frame that would wrap tightly around the engine and have two upper rails running along the outside of what looked like a fuel tank but was actually the airbox cover. We were able to slim that down to enhance the low dragster look. The fuel tank now resided underneath the seat. The proposed design gave us the opportunity to really make the exposed frame part of the styling. That's where "hydroforming" came in.

You can bend a steel tube only so far, and engineers like straight lines because they're strong. Curves mean joints and welds. For our first prototype we made a welded version of the frame with a VR engine. We could see that it would work, but it wasn't attractive. If we were going to show off our exposed frame, it had to really wrap the engine and the tank; it should flow almost seamlessly under the seat and down to the rear wheel.

Through our partners in engineering, we learned that there might be a way to accomplish that: hydroformed frame tubes. Hydroforming uses high-pressure fluid to reshape metal. The technology had been around for a while, and with recent advances it was capable of forming stainless tubing into fluid, complex forms without joints and welding, just elegantly curved continuous forms. Beautiful and very strong. That was a breakthrough. We could begin to see the overall form coming together. Another new metal-shaping technology solved an issue we were having with the exhaust requirements, allowing us to create muffler shells with a continuously changing conical section, to get the muffler volume we needed.

Those new technologies enabled us to do things that wouldn't have been possible fifteen years earlier. With every new bike design we looked for a unique solution to what a rider wants. What's their desire? We were looking at attracting some different riders with the V-Rod, and the tools helped us come up with a Harley-Davidson answer to those questions.

Blending style with form, materials, technology, and performance is what has made Harley-Davidson distinctive from a styling standpoint. We combine those elements and work to create a feeling that starts with what you see with your eye but travels to your heart. That's what separates us and keeps us Harley-Davidson. We work to create an intangible emotion through hardware that has beauty and function. Artistry in iron. Rolling sculpture. So we're always looking to push materials, methods, and engineering's ability to make it look the way an artist wants it to look but also perform the function that the engineer has to have. With increased collaboration and all the new tools at the PDC we were able to achieve some truly unique solutions, but we kept our history and heritage top of mind. The V-Rod was a stretch for the company, but the design remained in line with our tradition: a unique Harley-Davidson look, sound, and feel that sparks an emotional response in the rider.

By 1998 we had a new engine and were able to put it in our new prototype chassis, so I was finally able to take our ideas for a ride. Those early prototypes include lots of handmade parts and are not as durable as a factory bike, so you've got to be a little careful riding them. I was familiar with that; I've tested lots of prototypes. But with the Revolution, I got excited and managed to lock it into fourth gear. I broke it and had to bring it in. I got enough of a ride in to know we had a winner though. I was grinning from ear to ear.

We were in the home stretch, but there were still a lot of details to work out. The radiator was a particular challenge—we'd never had one. We needed a solution that complemented our beautiful, exposed engine. Our competitors did the obvious thing—they hung the radiator out in front of the engine. That wouldn't work for us. We had to find a way to package it and integrate it into the look. The first one we did was tiny, and we loved that, but it didn't have the airflow to cool that powerful engine. The front tire is directly in front of the radiator and deflects the air around it, which complicates the problem. You need a lot of airflow to cool that engine, so the radiator had to be a certain size. It was a classic collaboration between Styling and Engineering. We kept drawing, experimenting, modeling, testing—trying one thing, going back to the drawing board, trying something else. Others wouldn't have taken it as far as we did, but we had to get it right, so we kept working until we did. We made that radiator feel like it belonged, a unique statement that enhanced the overall look.

The bodywork gave us another opportunity to innovate. We wanted a finish that would enhance the performance look, so we came up with the idea of raw aluminum. When you think of aluminum, you think high-performance materials. And we knew aluminum would look good with chrome. The engineers told us how difficult it is to form aluminum, to make the kind of curved shapes we needed. Again, we believed it would be worth the effort, and our engineering and manufacturing people worked with us to make it happen. Developing something that is unique and beautiful, that demonstrates craft, and putting it all together into a form that will immediately attract the rider—that's our heritage.

The amount of work and dedication it took to bring the V-Rod to market was way beyond what anyone would normally expect. We had set out to do something that had never been done before, and to do it in a different way, pushing and trying different approaches. It was harder work than any of us had faced on other models, but we all believed in that project. We stretched to the limit and beyond to make that motorcycle, every department at the PDC and the people in manufacturing tasked with building it. I can't say enough good things about everyone who worked on it.

In the end, I believe we came up with a masterpiece. It had been half a century since we'd introduced a model with a completely new engine, transmission, and frame, and we pulled it off. The V-Rod was a new type of Harley, but it was Harley-Davidson through and through. The muscular lines of the perimeter frame complemented aluminum body parts and beautifully framed the gleaming Revolution engine. Every component was sculpted, from the way the headlight and instrument cluster meshed gracefully with the raked-out forks to the broad flare of the exhaust, and we managed to integrate the radiator into the overall profile—low, sleek, and fast. It was a true performance custom, with the look of a dragster but the comfort, ride, and handling of a highway cruiser.

Our first reveal was at the 2001 Dealer Show in LA. After six years of intense, collaborative work, Bill and I rode matching V-Rods onto the stage, entering together from either side as the employees and dealers in the audience stood up and cheered with excitement. It was an honor to represent teams from all over the organization that helped develop and launch the V-Rod. That's something I'll never forget.

I'm proud to say that motorcycle won thirteen awards worldwide, and the one I'm most proud of was voted on by a group of motorcycle designers from other companies. At a European show they picked the one vehicle that they thought had the most interesting forms and shapes, and we won with the V-Rod. And that was from competitors who were designing motorcycles, like myself, from Japan and Europe, so I'm very, very proud of that.

The motorcycle press loved it, too, amazed that Harley-Davidson would build a liquid-cooled engine and come up with something so radical but so beautiful and rideable. Every trade magazine featured it, and it made all the "Best of..." lists, including "Motorcycle of the Year." It was the perfect triumph to lead us into our 100th Anniversary year.

The year 2001 brought the attacks on 9/11. Our country was hurting, and at the company, many felt helpless. We wondered if there was anything we could do. How could we play a part in helping? A small group of employees were brainstorming ideas, and after hearing from Jon Syverson from the Police and Fleet sales team about the number of police motorcycles lost in the collapse of the twin towers, the recommendation was made to donate thirty police motorcycles to the New York City Police Department, Port Authority of New York, New Jersey Police Department, and New York State Police. In addition, we'd make a donation to the Red Cross to assist with relief efforts.

The need was immediate, and we were able to secure some police bikes that were being used in Milwaukee for training and get them ready to be put into service. To get the bikes out to New York quickly, we held a lottery for a couple of employees from each of our facilities to ride to New York and deliver them. Just ten days after the attacks, we held a small ceremony in the courtyard of Juneau Avenue to send the group off. It was an emotional moment for all of us. Different than most of our rides, this was a solemn mission. The group had a police escort all the way from Milwaukee to our dealership on Staten Island, where the bikes were presented in a small ceremony.

Just as the group was about to depart Juneau Avenue, our chief executive officer, Jeff Bleustein, handed one of the riders, Steve Piehl, an envelope and said, "You'll need this." Steve stuffed it in his jacket before the group pulled out and hit the road. At their first stop, he looked at the envelope. It was a $1 million check for the Red Cross. The group decided to let each employee on the ride carry the check for a leg of the trip.

Moments like these made me very proud of our great company and employees. We didn't do it for the publicity; we did it because it was the right thing and there was a need we could help with.

People talk about "the Harley-Davidson mystique." I think they use that word because it's hard to understand how and why Harley enthusiasts are so passionate about their bikes. The mystique is made up of many different ingredients: events, rides, racing, clothing, jewelry, our big birthday parties, and obviously our motorcycles with that V-Twin engine, which is the heartbeat of everything we do. Understanding that culture and mystique is critical to any artist/designer who's involved with Harley-Davidson. As our Styling team grew over the next few years, everyone was involved in trade shows, events, riding together; we would ride as a group to our various plants in York, Kansas City, and Tomahawk. Experiencing the product, understanding our customers, being students of motorcycling—by that I mean having your face in trade magazines, rider publications, enthusiast books—all of that is understanding a culture. You have to be passionate, and our Styling department was steeped in that passion.

A motorcycle has to look good with a rider on it going down the road, in various situations. A motorcycle has to trigger your emotions. Not everybody needs a motorcycle. A motorcycle has to make you feel good. It has to sound right. *Look*, *sound*, and *feel* are in our vocabulary daily as core descriptors. But what really makes riding a Harley special is more than that. It is about fulfilling people's dreams. Supporting their pursuit of adventure and freedom for the soul. It's all tied in with emotion and passion.

I grew up with motorcycles and with this company, and I think I have a special understanding of motorcycles and how they affect people.

While my situation was unique, there are lots of ways that someone can develop a passion for motorcycles and an understanding of the relationship between a rider, their bike, and how that relates to and influences the rest of their life. I love helping new designers immerse themselves in our culture and grow in appreciation for our brand and products. Our history is so rich, and we're so lucky to have a museum and such a vast archive that documents it all. We can use all of those materials to understand where we've been, so we can build on that past and take it into the future.

The Harley "mystique" is more than just the motorcycle, but the motorcycle is at the foundation of it, because the motorcycle is the key to the rider's experience, and it's a direct tie to our heritage. I could describe the vehicle bolt by bolt, but that's not what it's about. It's how all of those bolts tie together the elements that create a feeling. Our design is evolutionary, based on a deep-rooted understanding of what the company is, what it has done and meant over generations, what it can be in the future, and what all of that means to our customers. We draw on historical cues because those ties to our heritage define us. We're not stuck in the past; we're always looking for fresh takes and watching what's happening in the design world. We've done some pretty radical things—the V-Rod and more recently the electric LiveWire being good examples—and our technology is modern, pushing the envelope, but there is always a "Harley-DNA" that we can't lose, because that's what makes us special.

Defining that "Harley-ness" can seem simple, but it goes deep. We inherited a tradition of mechanical beauty and simplicity. And I say it every time, but our exposed engine is at the center of that. The Harley-Davidson V-Twin has an architecture that demands a certain motorcycle form, and I believe it's the ideal form, visually. By exposing that handsome form and making it the centerpiece, the heart of the motorcycle, it becomes a jewelry piece for us in design.

Then the fuel tank: it's the shape and form that sits on top of that exposed motor; it has a certain statement and feel that will always be there. Then, as we did with the V-Rod, we carefully sculpt all the other engine components and combine finishes of paint, aluminum, chrome, steel, playing with where those finishes are applied until it's right. And because those things are so important—every part that is visible is styled; every part matters—there can be no throwaways. You can make a beautiful form with a unique finish and ruin it with an off-the-shelf fastener or by failing to consider how it works with its surrounding elements. The process is painstaking. But when it all comes together and everything is just right, it's magic.

My friend and design partner Louie Netz paid me the highest compliment when he said that my work had changed the way people relate to motorcycles. I have such a passion for the mechanical beauty I've been talking about, and Louie shared that. The bikes we designed were so different from our competition. We stayed true to our heritage while innovating and moving the brand forward. We took function and added great form; we created forms that pushed the emotion side of function. Lots of Harley enthusiasts will talk about going out into the garage and staring at the pushrods and rocker boxes of their beautiful black-and-chrome V-Twin. If, as Louie says, I can take some credit for making so many people feel that beauty, then I did my job.

Getting that rider to connect with their bike means we succeeded in giving them a vehicle to enable their pursuit of freedom and adventure. What they chose to do with it, the people they met, the places they went, the experiences they had, lots of other things played into that. Many people play a part in making it happen, from our Styling team conceiving of the bike, through the engineers who make it run so reliably and handle so well, to the dedicated workforce that builds it, to the marketers that write the ad copy that catches that rider's eye, or the neighbor who rides by on their new Fat Boy. Then there's a dealer who helps that customer make their dream a reality and a H.O.G. chapter that welcomes them into the family and gives them reasons to get out and have fun on their new bike.

It can happen in a lot of ways, but it happened with hundreds of thousands of people around the world in those years leading up to our 100th Anniversary. We fulfilled a lot of dreams.

CHAPTER 16

LEAVING A LEGACY

*I*t felt like we had just wrapped up the 95th celebration and we were into planning for our 100th Anniversary. The 95th was a triumph, but one hundred years, that's a special number. It's amazing. How many companies can you think of that are in that age bracket? We've been through two world wars, survived the Great Depression, overcome decades of economic ups and downs, fought off determined competitors—and we're still here, more successful than ever. Generations of leaders pushed the right buttons, took risks, endured hardship believing we'd come out the other end stronger. But the true magic of this company has a lot to do with the emotion and the connection to the riders.

For the company's 50th Anniversary my father's generation had designed a beautiful fender medallion and created a special anniversary yellow color scheme. For the 100th we were making much more elaborate plans.

The entire Styling department is involved in designing the anniversary models, but for the logos I worked closely with Ray Drea. We'd talk about some ideas, then just start sketching. There's problem-solving all along the design process, but once we're settled on a direction, the essence of that design drives the decisions. We've got a set of basic elements—the wings, the Bar & Shield, the anniversary number—and we need to make it not just visually striking but also obviously distinct from other anniversaries. When the bike's going down the road, aside from the special anniversary color, how does it graphically mark the celebration? For the 90th we had vertical wings; for the 95th we went with horizontal wings. We had lots of ideas, but I was doodling one day and came up with a solution. I sketched it out and just left it on Ray's desk. He walked in the next day and said, "Look what the design fairy left me." And we ran with that direction.

The 100th Anniversary was a really, really important one, not just for me but for the whole department, for the company. We wanted to do some things with the motorcycles that we'd never done before, make them extra special, and spend a lot of attention on the graphic itself, the logo. There were so many facets to the celebration we were planning, and the logo would appear in multiple forms: on printed materials, signs, pins, patches, parts and accessories, clothing, merchandise. It had to work in different sizes and be producible in different processes, fit in a circle or a square. There were a lot of demands on that one element.

In the end we maintained the horizontal wing for the 100th. We tried so many designs, but the history of those early designs of the Bar & Shield with wings, where the wings were always horizontal, just felt right for 100th anniversary logo. As part of the celebration in Milwaukee, we created a huge display at the Milwaukee Art Museum demonstrating the breadth of designs we'd explored to finally land on that final logo. That was really special, and museum visitors enjoyed seeing the process and all the design options.

We went all out with the anniversary models too. We worked out a silver paint scheme that was stunning. The silver paint was specified to have a depth of translucence equal to custom show quality. These special bikes were designed as a tribute to our century of great motorcycles. They became collector's items.

With our anniversary models in production, I could turn my attention to the pre-celebration activities. Planning had started early for a major exhibit and traveling roadshow called the Open Road Tour—weekend festivals that would travel to a half dozen cities in North America and four international destinations. It was a big event, with three spacious tents of displays focusing on our company history, on the bikes and different aspects of their design, and on the cultural impact of Harley-Davidson. We took some special motorcycles from our archives collection on the road, along with celebrity bikes and lots of artifacts. Displays included specially produced films, multimedia, activities for both kids and adults, stunt and motorcycle shows, and concerts at every stop. The whole production and the logistics were complicated, so the tour visited one venue a month, starting with Atlanta in July of 2002. Nancy and I traveled to most of them, including Barcelona, Spain, in June of 2003, and Hamburg, Germany, in July.

Nancy and I had a wonderful time in Barcelona, which is a beautiful city. The streets were full of Harley-Davidson enthusiasts, and I was surprised to be recognized almost everywhere we went. Even sitting in a van in traffic on the way to the rally site a customer got very excited to see me. Nancy and I led a parade of over eight thousand motorcycles through central Barcelona, riding behind the Spanish Royal Guard—who ride Harleys and usually escort the king of Spain. It was hot, but the spirit of the riders was incredible. Afterward we signed autographs and took pictures with riders from all over Europe. It was great to feel the excitement and enthusiasm for the brand among our international customers.

We had some free time in Barcelona and took the opportunity to visit works of the architect Antoni Gaudí. I had seen his work in books and had been fascinated by the organic, shifting shapes and intricate embellishment of his buildings. Seeing the majestic constructions up close was truly incredible. We visited the Park Güell and Sagrada Família cathedral. I could stare all day at the geometry of those structures; they're so complex but natural, with every detail just growing somehow logically out of its surrounding elements and forming coherent form, completely free of the rigor of traditional architecture. Very inspiring.

From Barcelona we traveled to Hamburg, for the last stop before the Open Road Tour packed up and made its way back to Milwaukee. It was another great Harley-Davidson party and further evidence that our motorcycles and the Harley-Davidson camaraderie was alive and growing in Europe. Once again, Nancy and I were treated like rock stars, recognized everywhere we went, signing autographs and taking pictures, checking out the bikes, and enjoying the extended Harley community. The last evening we led another fantastic motorcycle parade that stretched along a thirty-five-mile route lined by spectators waving and high-fiving the riders. There is a local flavor to every rally, but wandering through the sea of personalized bikes, seeing the vests of the local H.O.G. chapters, feeling the excitement of riders gathered to celebrate their love of motorcycling and Harley-Davidson, it felt like home away from home.

The 100th Anniversary year was filled with events and activities and excitement, but a real highpoint was riding with my family. The company again organized a "Ride Home," with executives leading group rides from different points in the US, launching with a big party, stopping at dealerships and events along the way. We led the ride starting in Las Vegas, but what made it really special is we all rode out together from Milwaukee. Nancy was on the bike with me; Karen, Michael, and Bill were there with their significant others. If you're a close-knit family like we are, riding together, seeing our beautiful country, and doing it with close friends—it doesn't get any better than that.

When we're out riding together, it's just us and our bikes and the road: riding up on one another with big smiles on our faces, stopping for gas and meals and talking about what we've seen and where we're going, enjoying the family time before we join the big group. Then we got to Vegas and it was a big party, and we turned around and came back.

After a week of riding with the family and friends, the group ride home is a different experience. As usual, the group picked up riders along the way. Our first day out we came up on the Hoover Dam. Pulling to a stop to gawk at that engineering feat with the group lining the road behind it, I felt pride in the incredible things this country has achieved and the part our company has played in some important points in that history.

We rode through the Southwest—Arizona, New Mexico, into Texas and up through Oklahoma—great scenery, great times, lots of stops to hang out with customers. We spent a night in Kansas City, and everyone got a special tour of the plant, got to see V-Rods being built and coming off the assembly line. The next night in Illinois, we connected with three other big groups and rode into Milwaukee together. It was an emotional crescendo leading to that amazing sight of thousands of locals gathered on freeway overpasses with signs and flags, lining the streets to welcome us home.

We had been at so many Harley events—rides, rallies, H.O.G. events, anniversaries of various kinds, international celebrations—but there's something special about events in Milwaukee for both riders and the company. This is Harley-Davidson's birthplace, where we've been for 120 years. My grandfather's generation would have marveled at how far we'd come. Our loyal enthusiasts feel that connection when they visit Milwaukee. They can go see Juneau Avenue, in the same location as the original shed from 1903. The connection to the company's origin and base in the Midwest, the unbroken thread back to the shed where the first bikes were built; that authenticity and continuity are powerful, a source of pride for everyone who rides a Harley-Davidson motorcycle. The family is part of that heritage, and it's a responsibility that is rewarding and that we take seriously.

We were busy as soon as we got off our bikes. Nancy had been attending events with me for several decades, and she was as recognizable to many enthusiasts as I was. Among other things, Nancy spread the love of riding. It's in her blood, the same as mine. Both Karen and Bill had become global brand ambassadors, and Michael joined us at signing events too. He had been working on strategic planning for the Harley-Davidson Museum and was very much involved with the company at that time.

The riders are always respectful, and everyone wants a handshake, an autograph, a chance to show me their bike—their pride and joy. That emotional bond with the riders, people from so many walks of life and from different geographic areas, that's unique to our company, and it's everywhere you look at these big events.

All of that was amplified at our 100th birthday party. An estimated 250,000 people joined us to celebrate in our hometown. Milwaukee was filled with smiling riders, proud to be a part of the Harley-Davidson family. The whole Open Road Tour was set up by the lakefront. There were factory tours, events at the art museum, music on different stages, parties all over the city. That was an amazing three days, and we were busy every moment of it.

One thing that always inspires me at big Harley gatherings is looking out at all of the parked bikes. Thousands of Harleys, and no two alike. I've said it before, but it's a constant source of amazement: our riders make their motorcycles their own. From minimal paint or a chrome part, to a complete radical custom bike, there's a little bit of everything. I find that fascinating. They want that motorcycle to be a part of their life,

WATERCOLORS

EST. 1903

YESTERDAY

FOREVER

PARKED

STORAGE

EXTREME

LONG-TERM

TRANQUIL SNOW

SUNDOWN

RIFLE

CHICAGO

MIRROR

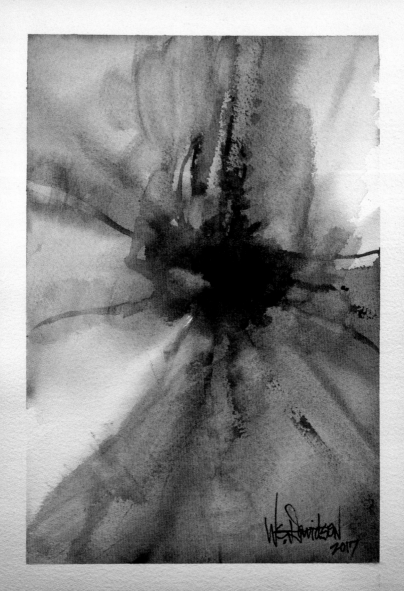

and Harleys have a way of becoming essential to what they do and who they ride with. I had a lot of riders come up to me and say, "Thanks. You changed my life." It's pretty amazing that our motorcycles can change lives. But that is what our product does. As an artist, I am fascinated by the creativity of our great riders, and I'm proud to have led the team that designed the bikes they use to express their own creativity.

Our months of anniversary activities culminated in the big Sunday night concert on a beautiful stage along Lake Michigan. I was asked to address the crowd, which I was proud to do, and I got an amazing response. There was so much enthusiasm and love. I was up there with my family celebrating a century of Harley-Davidson success at a moment when we had reached unbelievable sales and popularity. I don't remember everything I said, but at the end I raised my arms and yelled, "We Ride With You!" and with that, the crowd roared in unison.

It feels strange, talking about something I did, to call it an epic moment, but that was an epic moment. Standing in front of hundreds of thousands of Harley faithful and local Milwaukee residents, looking out over that huge crowd on their feet and cheering, and repeating the phrase that has defined a big part of my life with Harley-Davidson: We Ride With You. I have always believed that we connect with riders because we are riders, and at that moment I could feel that all those miles, all those events and handshakes and one-on-one conversations, had made an impact beyond my wildest dreams.

Back at the PDC after all of the 100th Anniversary festivities, my inbox was filled every day with letters from enthusiasts, packages containing items their owners wanted autographed, and occasional tributes and mementos. Lots of requests and letters from people all over the world.

I was always happy to hear from customers. I loved getting letters where people talked about what they were doing, where they were riding, where they were going. I received invitations to weddings and retirement celebrations, letters from veterans who had just purchased their first bike, pictures of people posing proudly with their Harleys.

Those hours of signing things was my way of connecting with people when I couldn't be out at events. I was honored that they wanted to share their thoughts with me and cared enough about our company to want my autograph. Those connections kept the company small and relatable and brought excitement to our enthusiasts.

In the studio, we were busy as always. With annual updates to every model and the popularity of our Custom Vehicle Operations limited editions, we needed to expand the team but do it carefully. Our spectacular run of success and the reputation we had built had made Harley-Davidson Styling a place designers wanted to work, and there were a lot of talented designers out there. Motorcycle designers have a passion for what they do; it's not just a job. I can always tell someone who truly has gasoline in their veins. You ask them about their hobbies, what their passions are, and they're into drag racing, or hot rods, or dirt bikes.

The other major factor in finding the right person is a commitment to understanding and designing for the customer. We need to always be thinking about the customer. That's the heart and soul of our brand, and it goes all the way back to the founders.

As the team grew, I knew I needed to give others more responsibility, chances to stand on their own. Louie did an awesome job of keeping everything running while of course contributing his own significant design input. Our work had always been highly collaborative, and I made certain that the individual designer's voice and their ideas always mattered.

One of our big hits a couple of years after our 100th was a bare-bones bagger we called the Street Glide, a bike I designed because it was one I'd want to ride and I knew others would too. Kind of like the Road King had, this one took off and became a big seller. The next year we introduced a redesigned, back-to-basics Sportster called the Nightster, which made waves. The level of talent in the Styling studio working on those models reassured me that as we continued to move forward, the design team would continue to create stunning new motorcycles.

We had a lot of fun and made some great design statements between our 100th and 105th anniversaries. We reengineered the Dyna line in 2006 and celebrated it with a 35th anniversary of the original Super Glide, the bike that started our factory custom journey. We had a new version of the Twin Cam motor in 2007, which was a really big deal, a more significant upgrade than lots of people realized. Ray spearheaded the logo design for another beautiful lineup of anniversary models for our 105th birthday. We customized a special version of our new Softail chopper-like Rocker motorcycle for me to ride to Sturgis. I had a special "Rocker Willie" kidney belt made for that ride. Then I created a custom version of the Street Glide for our 105th anniversary ride. That was a real beauty—one-off paint job, custom leather with a special storage bag I designed, copper leaf trim throughout with coordinated color on the wheels. The family rode with us again on the 105th ride, and that bike really turned heads.

Not long after our 105th birthday party, we introduced a whole styling lineup we called "Dark Custom"—stripped-down, blacked out, designs that really connected with many of our enthusiasts. Kirk led the design of the most dramatic version of that, the Cross Bones, a sinister-looking throwback that had the look of a post–World War II bobber married to the high-tech engineering of the twenty-first century. By that point we had a dozen designers in the Styling department. Frank and Kirk and Ray each had their own teams, and we were all busy, all the time, with a lot of exciting design projects.

After 2003, lots of people wondered how we could possibly follow up our fantastic 100th birthday bash. We did it with the 105th by opening our Harley-Davidson Museum. We'd dreamed of that museum for decades. Every time I walked through the archives, looked at all of those beautiful bikes we had saved over the years, I couldn't wait to finally give them the appropriate showplace. We'd gone through different stages of planning at sites around Milwaukee but finally landed in the perfect spot: twenty acres on the river at the end of the Menomonee Valley, the area that was called "The Machine Shop of the World" when my grandfather was young. Most of those machine shops and foundries and factories and tanneries are long gone, but we would help bring that pride back with our new development.

Initial planning for the museum had begun in the late 1990s, but things didn't really ramp up until we settled on that site in 2004 and hired some museum professionals to lead the charge. We broke ground in 2006 and gave the world a sneak peek at what was coming. Our construction company presented us with some beautiful chrome shovels for the ceremony, but we went in another direction: my friend and racing legend Scottie Parker did a "groundbreaking" burnout in front of the assembled executives, dignitaries, and politicians.

I, of course, took great interest in every aspect of the museum's development, and in particular was involved with the building architecture. We had hired a talented, accomplished pro named Jim Biber as the lead architect, and he also happened to be a great guy. He and his team worked through a lot of design variations, trying to come up with a metaphor to drive the design. I just kind of dipped into the process at first, reviewing progress and making sure the big ideas were consistent with our brand. I got more and more involved as the team homed in on a design scheme and began to work out the details.

That was a fascinating process to be involved in. The form our building would take was an open question. We knew what it had to do, but we had twenty acres and the building could take any form we chose. Once we settled on a direction, we were into design and making decisions, committing to specific ideas and elements, and moving on from there.

The team settled on "factory" as a metaphor for the building, which made perfect sense both with our brand and our location. We talked a lot about materials and methods and how the building might reflect our motorcycle design philosophy while maintaining a factory simplicity. Some things fell naturally into place: factories are honest, functional buildings, and we've always strived for simple, honest design with our motorcycles. Jim knew motorcycles and our brand, and we had a great rapport. We're both visual people. He had ideas for how we could expose the structural elements of the building the way we expose the engine and frame of our motorcycles. The result was spectacular: simple forms surrounded by a skeleton of galvanized steel, with the same attention to construction materials and craftsmanship that we give our motorcycles.

The museum building is anchored by four towers, honoring the four founders. All of the heating and ventilation and mechanicals are hidden in the three that frame the building, and the fourth is a big open tower of galvanized beams marking the entrance. We spent a lot of time trying to solve that fourth tower. We needed something that would identify the building, create an iconic entrance, and give a symbolic presence to that frame. Doodling in meetings, sketching, I had been drawing three-dimensional Bar & Shields, turning that icon of our brand into a four-sided sculpture. I brought one of those into one of our meetings, and that sparked a real eureka moment. Blown up to a monumental scale and internally lit, it accomplished everything we wanted. It sat up in that big open framework like a jewel, the way our engines fill our frames, and signaled "Harley-Davidson" for miles around.

I talked with my family about wanting to do something special, a gift of some sort from our family that would become part of the museum's identity. I was aware of the work of a sculptor named Jeff Decker, and we'd gotten to know him a bit. He's an incredible guy: an avid collector of special motorcycles; a historian of early motorcycle history, particularly racing; and a highly talented artist, able to capture the beauty and excitement of motorcycle competition in three dimensions, in bronze sculptures. We decided we'd commission a sculpture for the museum by Jeff.

When we went to visit Jeff at his studio in Colorado, we saw a wonderful piece he had done of a hillclimber on a DAH, captured just as the rider was losing control of the bike, about to go off the back. When I saw it I knew that was what we wanted for the museum, but we wanted to make it monumental. Jeff's sculptures are incredible: detailed and intricate, absolutely correct in capturing the motorcycles and the action. They're usually something like one-third scale. For the museum we wanted to make a big visual statement, and Jeff said he could do one-and-a-half times scale, so it would be towering and heroic, viewable from all over the museum grounds. And that's what we did. Jeff poured his soul into that thing, and it was incredible when we had the unveiling at the museum (before the official opening). It's in a special spot near the entrance, and it has done exactly what we hoped—become a sort of trademark of the museum, one of the most photographed pieces of the museum experience. Our family is proud to have made that happen, and Jeff views that, rightly, as his masterwork.

The museum opened in the summer of 2008, and since its opening we have received many architectural awards and feedback that our visitors are thrilled with their museum experience. The wealth of incredible artifacts that were presented so beautifully, and the way our proud history has been shown, has connected with visitors, both motorcycle enthusiasts and the general public. We had set out to create an experience that would appeal to everyone and managed to achieve it. It truly is a gem.

During the 105th Anniversary weekend a lot of my former colleagues visited—Vaughn Beals and his wife, and so many of the leaders who had helped bring our company back from the brink of disaster. It was wonderful to walk through the displays with them, seeing their reactions as they took in the way their accomplishments were portrayed. Lots of smiles and some tears. We'd worked hard to get to that moment of celebration, and it was great to enjoy it together.

I was down at the museum a lot over the next few years, and time was flying by. We had weekly bike nights, product launch events, an annual custom bike show—something going on all the time. I enjoyed talking with museum visitors the same way I enjoyed talking with riders at rallies, and a lot of pictures were taken. The museum displays were a great inspiration as our Styling team brainstormed new bikes, and it was a pleasure to watch as our senior Styling leads grew to become real leaders. Louie Netz had retired not long after the museum opened, which sped up some of the leadership transition with Ray taking on a bigger role.

Louie had been with me for thirty years, and I was coming up on fifty years in my position! That was hard to believe. I had reached the point in my career when the awards started to pile up. One I was particularly proud to receive came from the EyesOn Design institute in Detroit. Every year that group would meet in Detroit to evaluate designs of new prototype automobiles that were about to be introduced at the International Auto Show. I had been a juror for a number of years, which was an honor in itself. They also present one designer each year with a Lifetime Achievement award, considered the most prestigious honor in automotive design. In 2009 that group of the top designers in the industry gave me the award, the first time it was bestowed on a motorcycle designer. That was a real honor.

I always describe my relation to the Motor Company as a love affair, and that's really what it was, a fifty-year love affair with Nancy by my side. This had been our life. We still had a lot of life left, and it was getting time to think about how we would spend it.

On April 30, 2012, I announced my retirement.

I had no plans to fade into the background, and Harley-Davidson wasn't ready for me to do that either. In "retirement" I became Chief Styling Officer Emeritus and a brand ambassador. Nancy and I would remain a presence at rallies and events and contribute to a handful of projects. My colleagues had built me a nice office at the museum, and I'd be able to stay involved with all of the things I loved while having more time to paint and spend with my family. Increased time at the museum allowed me to bring surprise and excitement to many visitors when I was spotted on the grounds and stopped for autographs and pictures.

The event planning had been ramping up for the 110th Anniversary, which would again highlight the museum, and there was no letup in requests for my presence at events. With the global popularity of Harley-Davidson and H.O.G. chapters in every corner of the world, we'd been doing more international events, which both Nancy and I enjoyed. We visited Brazil in 2011 and saw firsthand the passion of our South American customers. I knew that Brazilians loved Harley-Davidson and was accustomed to our international customers embracing H.O.G. and our unique culture, but I was still surprised at the reception Nancy and I received in both São Paulo and Rio. The crowds greeting us were huge, with photographers pushing forward like paparazzi being held back by security. I did a lot of interviews, we signed a lot of autographs—as usual—and were able to spend some quality time with riders, looking at bikes and talking about the wonderful rides to be had in that huge country.

We had an escort to open a new dealership in São Paulo—expert riders proudly mounted on Harley-Davidson police specials—and in Rio we actually had some down time to shop and be tourists. Nancy and I visited the beach, ate in a great Brazilian steak house, and visited the famous *Christ the Redeemer* statue that towers over the city. What an incredible view and a beautiful trip.

With that adventure in the rearview mirror, we began preparing for another South American visit a few months after I announced my retirement. We attended dealership openings in Chile and Bolivia and visited with riders and dealers in Uruguay. Again, we were recognized and Harley enthusiasts lined up for autographs and pictures. I did interviews with local media wherever we stopped, and in Uruguay two thousand riders escorted us into the seaside resort city of Punta del Este. Our hosts made sure to introduce us to the local culture everywhere we went, and both Nancy and I enjoyed seeing the varied arts and crafts.

Preparations for our 110th Anniversary had begun well before I announced my retirement. Working with Ray on the anniversary bikes, he felt a special responsibility to come up with a great logo and design for the last anniversary we worked on together, and they really were something special. We had those designs locked in a couple months before that South American trip when I performed my first official 110th birthday duty, and it was something I would have never imagined: We flew to Rome with Bill where we met Pope Benedict XVI, presenting him with two Harley-Davidson gas tanks he had agreed to sign. I signed them, too, but for once we were having someone else sign our tanks. One of those went back to our museum, and the other was put back on the motorcycle it came off of and was auctioned to benefit the Good Samaritan Foundation. That trip was a media kickoff for a big anniversary event in Rome, to be held prior to our party in Milwaukee. The ceremony with the pope was one of a kind. Unforgettable.

We were back in Rome in June of 2013 for our European 110th Anniversary event. I've written a lot about our anniversary parties; each one had unique experiences—beautiful bikes, smiling faces, rides, parades, groups proudly showing off their H.O.G. vests and H-D loyalty. In Rome we had all kinds of music on the beach and a gigantic parade through the city, just like in Milwaukee but amid spectacular buildings and ancient ruins of Roman civilization. Pope Francis made an appearance for a bike blessing for thousands of riders, which gave it another unique Roman flavor. Harley-Davidson gave our family so many unique experiences beyond the joy of creating great motorcycles.

The bike blessing was a unique challenge for our marketing team to arrange and almost didn't happen. Many meetings with the Vatican and Pope Benedict's team had occurred to create this once-in-a-lifetime experience. All the arrangements were made, and the Vatican had approved our plans. A big announcement was made to our customers along with a lottery to select the lucky customers who would bring their bikes into St. Peter's Square for the blessing.

But then we were thrown a curveball. Just a few months before our event, in an extremely rare move, Pope Benedict stepped down and Pope Francis became the next pontiff. Nigel Villiers and Ken Ostermann from our marketing team scrambled to confirm the bike blessing would continue as planned. Pope Francis was drawing huge crowds, and customers were excited about him doing our bike blessing. Representatives from Pope Francis's team shared the news that for a variety of reasons, which we didn't fully understand, the bike blessing was canceled. We were stunned. Not wanting to disappoint our customers after we had already announced the bike blessing, our team went to work negotiating with the Vatican to see if we could change their minds. We reminded them of the funds that were being raised for charity and the positive publicity for the Vatican. We also worked to develop a good relationship with the Vatican police department who would have to manage the crowds. After all of that, our team got the green light, the blessing was back on, and our customers had an amazing experience.

Back in the US we had a big product launch a month before our 110th Anniversary bash in Milwaukee. We had been working for a few years on a major project to refresh our entire Touring lineup, everything from seating ergonomics to significant changes in cooling technology.

We did months of testing with customers to improve the riding experience, developed a sophisticated new infotainment system, added power—it was an exciting and long-awaited across-the-board update. Our team had worked hard to maintain the classic elements of our time-honored designs while meeting the needs of the present day, and the results made me proud of everything we'd accomplished going back to the first Electra Glide.

Back in the '60s, I'd developed the designs for the Batwing fairing and our classic saddlebags. Almost fifty years later, our designers had found a way to modernize that classic shape and use technology to improve the aerodynamics and function of the fairing. Brian Nelson, who worked on that design, referred to the batwing as a "Holy Grail" design, and great effort went into carefully evolving that recognizable form. A similar effort went into carefully evolving the form of the saddlebags while upgrading their functionality. Just making the latches work better on those bags while maintaining the profile and established look became very complicated, but engineering recognized the significance of the design and made it work.

It's not that I ever doubted it, but wandering through the new product tents at the museum during our anniversary party and watching our technicians demonstrate the new features to excited customers, I could see how my work as a designer would live on. Hanging out with Ray, Kirk, Frank, and all the designers during the celebration, I knew I was leaving the department in the hands of talented designers who were committed to being stewards of the brand.

Having spent fifty years designing the motorcycles that defined and redefined what a Harley-Davidson motorcycle looks and feels like, and how it makes the rider feel, I didn't have to be sitting at the PDC to influence future generations of designs. They would naturally build from the work I had done, the way my work built on the work of my father and grandfather. We were in good hands.

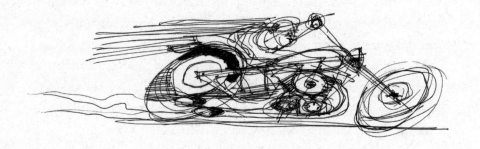

CHAPTER 17

FULL SPEED AHEAD

*W*hen I announced that I was retiring in April 2012, it should come as no surprise that it didn't end my nearly fifty-year relationship with the company that bears my name. I have stayed on as a brand ambassador and Chief Styling Officer Emeritus. I was fortunate to marry my passion for design with my love of the company that my grandfather, his brothers, and Bill Harley started in a shed in 1903. I carried on their vision for nearly a half century and was privileged to work with so many talented artists and stylists.

Even though I stepped away from day-to-day duties, I closely follow what's happening at Harley-Davidson and what our talented stylists are turning out. I read everything I can get my hands on about motorcycles, the auto and motorcycle industries, art, and the custom world. It's in my veins.

As an ambassador, I love attending company events and getting out to races. I loved the NHRA Pro Stock Motorcycle drag racing team and last summer went up to Road America for the Moto America King of the Baggers road race series. We had a great partner in Vance and Hines for our Pro Stock team, and watching them battle for wins and tear down the track was a thrill. Terry Vance became a good friend over the years.

The King of the Bagger series has brought tremendous excitement to our fans and a close connection to our touring motorcycles. The imagery of that great bike coming at you is stunning. Watching the bike moving, handling, and cornering—it's the epitome of look, sound, and feel. It really is. The sound they make is incredible. And of course, the riding skills of Harley-Davidson factory riders Kyle and Travis Wyman and their passionate team adds just the right ingredients. I was honored to design their race suits for the 2023 season. Projects like that are exciting for me and keep me close to the action. I'm proud of our riders and teams who are carrying on our great tradition on the tracks.

I've been an artist all my life, and in retirement I've been fortunate to follow my creative passions. I do occasional projects for our museum store, design graphics, work on T-shirt designs for our major events, and work on a handful of other special requests, so I'm active. Art, design, motorcycling, and family have defined my life, and they still do today. I might not get to ride as much as I once did, but my life is still full speed ahead. There's no use in slowing down now.

Over the years, I never lost my interest in painting. It's gone up and down at different points, but I love having so much more time to paint now. My office at the museum is really more of an art studio that includes one of my favorite antiques, a 1945 Knucklehead bobber, which is beautifully executed and sits on a rug next to a window overlooking the river. It is a beautiful spot to paint and be creative. For the past couple of years, I've done most of my painting in a studio at my house. It overlooks a pond and is the perfect spot for me. I enjoy coming into the studio, cranking up the music, and "wrecking some paper."

Having more time to focus on my painting lit my creative fire, and amazing things began to happen. I experimented with new colors and new techniques. I've been pushing myself, *seriously* pushing myself, as an artist, with new compositions, new subject matter, new ways of handling paint, new ideas of color, and new ideas of composition. After decades of still lifes and outdoor scenes, I started painting imagined cityscapes and wild abstracts. I'm constantly learning in my studio, always a student. I've done a fair amount of research and have read so many books about art. I'm learning all the time as if I'm climbing a mountain. I keep climbing and I'm never at the top. For me, painting is a passion, and I'm very interested in different techniques, so my paintings constantly change. They're all watercolors. I've always been a watercolor guy, going back to my time as a student at ArtCenter in Los Angeles. People ask me all the time why I don't paint in oils, but I've never been that interested. What I like most about watercolors is they're tricky, and I've got one shot at them. I can't change them much once I've started, and the white space has to be planned and preserved from day one.

About half of my paintings now are abstracts, while the others are traditional subjects like farms, cities, landscapes, old boats, cars, and trees. Abstracts allow me the freedom to play with shapes and colors. Over the years, I've had an interest in plein air painting, or working on location and outdoors. I've always loved Wisconsin's beautiful landscape and still enjoy going up to our lake house in the northern part of the state to paint. There are few things more peaceful to me than sitting on a boat on the lake.

While I have painted Harley-Davidson bikes, most of my watercolors are not motorcycle-driven symbolism. Really, it's anything interesting that catches my eye. There's great variety in my paintings, and that's something I work hard on.

During the COVID-19 lockdown, painting kept me from going nuts because everyone needs something to look forward to each day. I could step into my studio and become totally immersed in a painting. When that happens, you box yourself into the creativity in front of you. You lose track of time while it's happening because your mind is totally involved in that painting. That's part of the magic of art. When I'm in the studio, I play music pretty loud so I'm not distracted. I love it.

One unexpected thing happened during the lockdown—I became an avid basketball fan. I surprised a few people, including myself, with my interest in the sport. Our family has been lifelong Green Bay Packers fans and season ticket holders, but I never followed basketball. Watching Giannis Antetokounmpo and Brook Lopez, along with the rest of our hometown Milwaukee Bucks, reminds me of the great teamwork at Harley-Davidson: everyone playing their role, overcoming adversity, tackling the competition, and fighting for wins. So exciting, and I rarely miss watching a game. As a relatively new fan, I'm still trying to figure out some of the foul rules, but I don't think I'm alone in that!

Just like when I was designing motorcycles, when I'm painting, every blank sheet of paper is an inspiring new challenge. I can't wait to get my brushes wet. With each painting, I've got to figure out my contrast and white areas, negative and positive, and hard edges versus soft edges. Every time you stare at that white sheet of paper it's scary. It really is. It's problem-solving, and I enjoy the mental challenge. I have to develop some kind of a plan; I can't just attack it. I'll do a sketch first in my little sketchbook and then tape down a piece of paper before starting on the painting. I paint on special watercolor paper, and I'll just go to work. First, I'll rough in the main shapes and the lines. After that, I'll come back and fine-tune it. You have to *listen* to the painting; I'll walk into the room and see an area that is just asking for a color, shape, or line. To me, contrast is critical: light against dark, foreground, distance, how you use those colors, and how much pigment is mixed in with the water equals a very soft tint. If it's thicker, you'll get a stronger color. You can overlay colors and get color coming through, which produces beautiful washes depending on the amount of water and pigment in the composition. That's so exciting to me. For instance, if I'm painting a sky, I wash those in with very wet paper and kind of let the color wander around, which creates striking cloud shapes. When part of the paper is wet and part of it is dry, you can produce very beautiful contrasts. When it dries, you come back in with a small brush and add the important details.

When you think about designing a vehicle or a Harley-Davidson bike—its form, its color, its proportion—that's the same terminology you use when you're painting. One's two-dimensional and the other three-dimensional, but there are overlapping theories that apply to both.

Some of my really early artwork hung in my father's office on Juneau Avenue. One I gave to my dad when I joined the company in 1963 was of the original shack where the founders made their very first Harley-Davidson. I even tried to duplicate the type on the door, and my dad enjoyed having that. I guess that was one of the first times my artwork was on display. The first real showing of my watercolors was at the Harley-Davidson Museum in 2012 in an exhibit called "Watercolors by Willie G." Then in 2015, I was honored that the museum produced a special exhibit about me, "Willie G. Davidson: Artist, Designer, Leader, Legend." It featured dozens of drawings and paintings from different periods of my life along with bikes, cars, and other items from my personal collection.

In 2019 I had the great pleasure of doing a two-man show with my son Michael, "MKE Generations," at the University of Wisconsin–Milwaukee Union Art Gallery. Two years later, my artwork was on display at the Delafield History Center, not far from where I live. Those shows proved to me that I was doing well with my art because we had strong sales. It was neat to watch people walking around the gallery deciding which paintings were their favorites. Before long, people were putting stickers on them to let others know they were sold and headed for someone's living room. Urgency increased after that. It was fun to watch, and we're in the process of planning future shows now.

Michael has been one of my greatest influences as an artist. He received a bachelor of fine arts degree in both painting and ceramic sculpture from the University of Wisconsin–Milwaukee in 1985 and his master of fine arts at Purchase College–State University of New York. Michael taught painting and sculpture at the University of Wisconsin–Milwaukee and the Milwaukee Institute of Art and Design, where he also served as chair of fine arts. Along with being a wonderful art instructor, he is a very talented artist in his own right. His work has been on exhibit in New York and throughout the Midwest. When he was studying in New York, he worked with curators and artists installing art for the Guggenheim Museum, the International Center of Photography, the American Craft Museum, John Weber Gallery, Metro Pictures, and numerous other galleries and private collections.

There are few things I enjoy more than discussing my paintings with Michael. He appreciates my eye for art and my ability to recognize when something isn't right, or when it is exactly right. We apparently have a similar eye because we're often in agreement with what's working and what's not. Michael likes to joke that I never stop looking for things to be in balance. If I walk by a table in my house and notice that something is out of proportion, I can't help but move it, whether it's a book, plant, or candle. If we're out shopping or eating, I'll notice a beautiful sports car in the parking lot and won't leave for ten minutes. I'll stare at it and analyze its shapes, proportions, and lines. I never stop looking at what's around me. To appreciate beautiful design and art, you can't ignore your surroundings. Your eyes have to be wide open.

I'm very interested in Michael's feedback when I show him my new art. If he looks through my stacks of paintings and says, "Oh, they're all great, Dad," that's not enough. I want real criticism from someone who understands art the way he does. As Michael likes to say, any good creative, artist, or designer understands that one of the challenges is applying your vision but also getting outside of yourself. We are all limited in our perspective, and that is why the team at Harley-Davidson's Styling department was so critical. It takes different points of view to foster real creativity and get beyond yourself. I also love getting feedback from everyone who visits our house and sees my latest paintings, and many have shared it is a highlight of their visits.

While Michael and I have a shared interest in art, all three of my kids have a love for Harley-Davidson and the sport of motorcycling. It's in their DNA. Continuing the family connection to our sport and brand is important to all of us. We had a Harley-Davidson M-50, a two-stroke single cylinder model that I used to teach Michael, Bill, and Karen on one day when they were young. What a thrill to see them on two wheels.

Bill has been riding ever since that day when he was seven years old. After graduating from the University of Wisconsin–Milwaukee, he officially joined the company in 1984. Being a fourth-generation Davidson working at the Motor Company was a dream come true for him—and me. From the first time Bill rode, he was hooked on the history and tradition of Harley-Davidson and our family connection. He grew up riding dirt bikes and racing motocross, and he has ridden with customers and dealers all over the world.

Bill spent much of his career working in the company's marketing department. He is very good at connecting with riders, whether during rides or at rallies, and has been devoted to strengthening the company's relationship with them. Bill also spent time overseeing the early days of the Harley Owners Group and in product planning. In June 2010, he was named vice president of the Harley-Davidson Museum and factory tours and oversees the ongoing management and growth of the museum businesses. He loves walking visitors through the exhibits and sharing his unique family perspective on our history.

Karen has also had lead roles in the company. After her degree in apparel design and working in the apparel industry in New York and California, she joined the company and helped cofound our branded line of functional and casual apparel, MotorClothes. As a lifelong rider, Karen has a passion for leather and functional riding apparel and has been instrumental in setting new strategies for direction and growth for that business. She advanced the performance of functional riding gear and expanded casual apparel for both men and women into new categories. Her apparel designs for women contributed to the company's efforts to attract more women to the sport.

In recent years she spearheaded a new collection strategy for three distinct areas: heritage, contemporary design with multiple levels of performance, and retro-specific looks predominant in contemporary moto culture. We also worked together on the "Willie G" line of apparel. In 1991, Karen and the apparel start-up team accepted the Council of Fashion Designers of America industry award presented to Harley-Davidson for fashion influence. I am proud to say we are known worldwide for our iconic apparel and logos.

She believes that authentic H-D design and innovation must be original, and I'm proud to say she calls me her greatest inspiration for pushing newness and originality in design, making that left turn when everyone else goes right. As I did with our motorcycles, Karen is frequently out to the rallies and rides to assess inspiration and all the unique levels of rider customization. She encourages other women riders to get involved in motorcycling and become mentors for others getting involved in the sport. Karen and Nancy are women they could look up to.

Nancy and I have been proud parents when it comes to our children and the contributions they are making to our business, and it was a special opportunity for me to work together with Bill and Karen, just as I worked with my father, brother, and other relatives.

Of course, the biggest and hardest recent change in my life was losing Nancy after a long illness in July 2021. Nancy was the center of my world, my rock, and a beloved wife, mother, and grandmother. Her loss created a void that simply can't be filled. Nancy was never officially an employee of Harley-Davidson, but she was an integral part of the company in so many ways. She was the backbone and glue helping me make sure everything was running smoothly—at home and at the office. Behind the scenes, Nancy was the one in control, helping me and the kids and anyone else who needed it. She loved Harley-Davidson. She took a motorcycle rider's course, got her license, and rode a Harley-Davidson XL883 Sportster.

My fondest memories of our lives together were the many great trips Nancy and I took together. She was with me when we traveled to the Vatican and Rome, Italy, for Harley-Davidson's 110th Anniversary in June 2013. We rode together across Australia, Canada, and all over the United States. One year, Harley-Davidson's then chief executive officer, Jeff Bleustein, invited us to join him and his wife, Brenda, for a weeks-long trip through Europe. We started in England and went across the English Channel to France. We spent time in Paris before making our way to the French Riviera. It was such beautiful riding country and a wonderful trip. Those memories will stay with me forever.

Nancy was the parent who cooked most of the time, another of her many talents. Her maternal grandfather, Chas Nicoud, was a renowned French chef. There are family stories about him cooking for President Abraham Lincoln when he traveled to Milwaukee. Our home was the focal point for holiday parties and family reunions, which became rather large when Nancy's sisters had children and grandchildren of their own. She loved being around her family and friends more than anything. It made her so happy.

Nancy consumed her idle time with gardening, charity, and most of all, with Bill's daughter, Cara. Nancy and Cara had a special and close relationship. Cara became very involved in horses, and Nancy loved watching her ride in competitions. Cara recently graduated from the University of Kentucky, following in her dad's and aunt's footsteps with a degree in marketing and retail merchandising. She's already asking her dad about which ride we're going on for the 120th Anniversary.

Nancy was also involved in raising money for the Muscular Dystrophy Association and juvenile diabetes charities. She loved spending time with her friends in a women's club. Nancy was a great ambassador for Harley-Davidson. The enthusiasts called her the "first lady of motorcycling," and that's exactly what she was. She loved talking to women riders and answering their questions. In August 2010, Nancy was inducted into the Sturgis Motorcycle Museum Hall of Fame in South Dakota. At the time, she was one of just two women inducted. Nancy was also inducted into the AMA Motorcycle Hall of Fame in Pickerington, Ohio, in October 2021. The Biker Belles, who host a women's day ride at the Sturgis rally, present the Nancy Davidson Award each year to an "individual guiding and leading women in motorcycling and building the industry." Karen received the honor in 2021.

I miss Nancy dearly, and life without her hasn't been the same. She touched so many people over her life with her love, joy, and spirit. The chapel at her funeral was packed with people and it was covered with roses, her favorite flower. My children arranged a special tribute to Nancy by having roses placed around the base of the magnificent Hill Climber statue at the Harley-Davidson Museum. We had a wonderful life together, and there isn't anything I would change about the last seventy years. I can't wait to see her again.

CODA

I had an emotional rendezvous one morning in August 2022 a few miles from my home. I went to send off a large group that was riding out with Bill and Karen to Sturgis. There were eighteen or nineteen of them—family, friends, and colleagues, including our granddaughter, Cara, who was riding with Bill on her first motorcycle trip there. As I chatted with the riders like I have before so many rides, I could feel their excitement and anticipation. For a few, they were making their first trip to Sturgis. I have had so many great rides out to Sturgis, so many memories, so many adventures. I couldn't help but feel the pull to get on one of my bikes and join them.

Michael and I flew out to join them a few days later. There's a Sturgis Hall of Fame associated with the motorcycle museum out there, and Bill and Karen were being inducted as members of the Hall of Fame class of 2022. I had been in the initial pool of inductees when they started the Hall of Fame in 2001, along with the founders. Nancy was also given a "Lifetime Achievement" award in 2017. I was there to give the induction speech for Bill and Karen. Standing up there in that big hall filled with friends and colleagues I'd known for decades, I couldn't have been more proud to talk about Karen's and Bill's accomplishments, both in their roles at the Motor Company and in promoting the sport of motorcycling.

Watching the group ride off from Milwaukee on their Sturgis road trip without me, and then being in Sturgis to give the induction speech, drove a flood of emotions for me. The torch was being passed. I was proud and confident that the vision and direction I'd spent fifty years steering had been well established. With Bill and Karen in their roles, with all the great artists in Styling—all the great people throughout Harley-Davidson—I can see the amazing legacy that my grandfather and grand-uncles left us growing into the future.

As I look back, I have had the privilege of building on what the four founders started so many years ago and, along with my family, connecting with riders from across the globe. Very few 120-year-old businesses have our special family-founder connection. I've worked with incredibly talented individuals on products and witnessed the profound impact those products had on the lives of our customers. I've traveled the world, meeting customers and promoting our business and brand. We've had ups and downs, triumphs and hard times, and our relationship with our riders and dealers has provided the fuel for our ongoing success. Our family is one small part of this brand, part of the global community of Harley-Davidson that keeps the flame burning. I struggle to even put it all into words. Many days, it doesn't even seem like this adventure I have been on could have all been real.

I'm at home now, painting and doing occasional design consulting. Louie Netz and Ray Drea and some of my other colleagues visit regularly. We talk about the Motor Company some, but mostly about art, what's happening on the racing circuit, and interesting developments in the design world. Michael and I can talk about art all day, and we love to critique each other's work. Painting watercolors, I can finish about one painting a day, so there are many things to talk about. Bill, Karen, Cara, and the rest of the family are here all the time.

It's a family thing. It's always been a family thing. One hundred and twenty years and counting.

This book describes a love affair, an emotional bond, with one of the most important experiences of my life ... HARLEY-DAVIDSON! I feel very fortunate to have been a part of this great brand! May it live on forever!

Willie G. 2023

ACKNOWLEDGMENTS

I'd like to thank the people who helped me bring my story to life in this book.

My daughter, Karen, oversaw the overall project from concept to finished product.

Jim Fricke, former curatorial director at the Harley-Davidson Museum, guided me in shaping the many stories and content.

Ken Ostermann, former marketing leader at Harley-Davidson, led the editorial process and managed the image and watercolor assets we utilized.

And Karen and Ken, along with my son Bill, helped me select the photos and paintings, reviewed the many drafts, and assisted me with edits and feedback.

Additional thanks to Marc Oswald for shining the light on this opportunity, as well as our publisher Jonathan Merkh and his team, including Jennifer Gingerich, Billie Brownell, Phil Newman, and contributor Mark Schlabach.

A final thank-you to the Harley-Davidson Museum team and other individuals who reviewed my manuscript, provided valuable feedback, and assisted in making this book a reality.

We Ride With you !

ABOUT THE AUTHOR

*W*illiam G. Davidson serves as Chief Styling Officer Emeritus and Brand Ambassador at Harley-Davidson, Inc. Affectionately called "Willie G" by millions of motorcycle enthusiasts, his creations include the design of several of Harley-Davidson's most admired motorcycles. His artistic vision and passion for riding have made him a legend among throngs of enthusiasts worldwide that consider him the patriarch of motorcycling.

WILLIAM G. DAVIDSON
Chief Styling Officer Emeritus

Davidson is the son of former Harley-Davidson president William H. Davidson and the grandson of one of the original founders, William A. Davidson. For fifty years, he helped shape the look, sound, and feel that define Harley-Davidson motorcycles. During the 1980s and 1990s, he developed unique designs that kept Harley-Davidson motorcycles selling while the company completed technological and manufacturing improvements. Based in heritage and tradition, Davidson is responsible for the visual design of such classics as the FX Super Glide, FX Low Rider, Café Racer, Heritage Softail Classic, Softail Springer, Fat Boy, Road King, Softail Deuce, V-Rod, Cross Bones, and Street Glide.

A native of Wisconsin, Davidson attended the University of Wisconsin for three years before transferring to ArtCenter College of Design in Los Angeles. He joined Harley-Davidson in 1963, when he was invited to set up its motorcycle design department. In 1981, Davidson was one of thirteen executives who raised more than $75 million to purchase Harley-Davidson from AMF, Inc.

As an avid rider, Davidson has clocked thousands of miles on the open road each year. His family, including his wife, Nancy, made Harley-Davidson the center of their lives. Through his lifelong devotion to the Motor Company, Davidson has watched firsthand as Harley-Davidson has evolved into a true American icon.